Employment and the Family

Rates of employment amongst mothers of young children have risen rapidly in recent years. Attitudes to gender roles have changed, and both employers and governments have had to adjust to new realities. But some argue that recent changes in employment relations are making work more family 'unfriendly'. What are the real consequences of ... res the origins and background of ... rision of labour. Topics covered in ... nder roles and family life, the ge ... recent changes in employment rel ... fe articulation. A comparative an ... inland, the United States and Po ... assessment of the varying impact of state policies, and the changing domestic division of labour. Crompton draws on original research and situates her findings within contemporary theoretical and empirical debates.

ROSEMARY CROMPTON is Professor of Sociology at City University, London. Her previous publications include *Restructuring Gender Relations and Employment* (1999), *Class and Stratification* (1998), *Women and Work in Modern Britain* (1997) and *Gendered Jobs and Social Change* (1990). She is a past editor of *Work, Employment and Society*.

Employment and the Family

The Reconfiguration of Work and Family Life in Contemporary Societies

Rosemary Crompton

City University (London)

CAMBRIDGE UNIVERSITY PRESS

CAMBRIDGE UNIVERSITY PRESS
Cambridge, New York, Melbourne, Madrid, Cape Town, Singapore, São Paulo

Cambridge University Press
The Edinburgh Building, Cambridge CB2 2RU, UK

Published in the United States of America by Cambridge University Press, New York

www.cambridge.org
Information on this title: www.cambridge.org/9780521600750

First published 2006

Printed in the United Kingdom at the University Press, Cambridge

A catalogue record for this book is available from the British Library

ISBN-13 978-0-52184091-0 hardback
ISBN-10 0-521-84091-0 hardback
ISBN-13 978-0-521-60075-0 paperback
ISBN-10 0-521-60075-8 paperback

Contents

Preface   *page* vi

1 Understanding change in employment, family and
  gender relations   1

2 Caring and working   31

3 Women, men, organisations and careers   62

4 Work–life articulation, working hours and work–life policies   89

5 States, families and work–life articulation   115

6 Households, domestic work, market work and happiness   139

7 Class, family choices and women's employment   163

8 Conclusions   189

Appendix A Additional ISSP Family 2002 questions   219
Appendix B Joseph Rowntree Foundation (JRF) interviewees cited   223
Bibliography   226
Index   241

Preface

This book has been written with the aim of being accessible (and useful) to as wide an audience as possible – that is, undergraduate and post-graduate students, as well as academics and policy-makers interested in the diverse fields under study.

Thus concepts and issues are not introduced without definition and explanation, and efforts have been made to contextualise and provide a historical background to the debates and issues discussed. This means there will be parts of the text that may be rather familiar to experts in the field, who would be advised to skip these sections. Conversely, some students may prefer to gloss the sections where original empirical analyses are developed.

Each chapter has been designed to stand alone – that is, it may be read without necessarily being familiar with the previous chapter. This has inevitably involved some repetition, which has been kept to a minimum.

The empirical data reported in this book are the outcome of a series of research projects that included two projects funded under the Joseph Rowntree Foundation's Work and Family Life Programme ('Employers, Communities and Family-Friendly Employment Policies', and 'Organ-isations, Careers and Caring'). I worked with Sue Yeandle, Jane Dennett and Andrea Wigfield on the first project, and with Jane Dennett and Andrea Wigfield on the second. My thanks to them all. I would also like to acknowledge the contribution of all of those who agreed to be interviewed on the JRF projects, as well as the cooperation offered by 'Shopwell', 'Cellbank' and the two Local Authorities.

The book also draws on two projects funded by the ESRC: R000239727: 'Employment and the Family', and R000220106: 'Fam-ilies, Employment and Work-Life Integration'. Carolyn Vogler and Dick Wiggins were co-applicants on R000239727. Michaela Brockmann was a Research Officer on R000239727, and Clare Lyonette has been a Research Officer on both ESRC projects. Especial thanks go to Clare Lyonette, who has made invaluable suggestions relating to quantitative data analysis, carried out all of the regressions, and read the first drafts of several chapters.

The ESRC projects would not have been possible were it not for the help of a network of academics who provided advance copies of ISSP data sets, as well as agreeing to a small number of extra questions and participating in project-related workshops. So thanks to Gunn Birkelund, Al Simkus, Ligia Amancio, Karin Wall, Maria Cermakova, Hanna Haskova, Yannick Lemel, Clothilde Lemarchant, Anneli Annttonen, Jorma Sipila, Zsolt Speder and Zsuza Blasko. Thanks as always to Nicky Le Feuvre.

In large part, this book has a focus on aggregate trends. Recent changes have brought about increasing diversity in family arrangements, of which I am well aware. However, these are not addressed in any depth in this book.

It was something of a shock when I realised that I have been researching and/or writing this book for six years or more. Thanks to the Department of Sociology, City University, for two terms of study leave, as well as a small grant from the pump-priming fund. Many others, too numerous to mention, have contributed to the critique and development of my ideas as a consequence of the presentations I have made drawing upon the various projects. However, I would like to conclude with the usual disclaimer – many, many, thanks for all the help I have been given but any errors or omissions are entirely my responsibility.

1 Understanding change in employment, family and gender relations

All fixed, fast frozen relations, with their train of ancient and venerable prejudices and opinions, are swept away, all new-formed ones become antiquated before they can ossify. All that is solid melts into air ...

(Marx and Engels, *Manifesto of the Communist Party* 1848)

Man for the field and woman for the hearth
Man for the sword and for the needle she
Man with the head and woman with the heart
Man to command and woman to obey
All else confusion.

(Tennyson, 'The Princess' 1847)

Introduction

These well-known quotations serve to convey two themes that are central to this book: first, that rapid social change is endemic in modern societies, but nevertheless, that sexual differences, as expressed in gender relations, are characterised by both change *and* continuity. We do not lack attempts that seek to develop totalising accounts of global social change (for example, Castells' (1997) three-volume *Information Age*), but, in this book, we focus on a particular 'slice' of this totality, that is, the inter-relationships between men, women, families and employment. However, this 'slice' will be (and will always have been) crucially affected by wider normative, political and economic contexts and the manner of their development. In order to understand the present, we have first to understand the past.

The growth of capitalist industrialism from the end of the eighteenth century was accompanied by technical innovation, the development of the factory system, and the expansion of independent wage labour, which required individuals to be freed from traditional restraints on their mobility and employment opportunities. These social and technical developments led to a rapid increase in productivity and wealth (albeit distributed highly unequally) in capitalist societies. Changes in family arrangements accompanied changes in production arrangements, in that an increasing proportion of households were narrowed down to the conjugal unit of parents and children (Zaretsky 1976). Production for use within the household became less important as families were transformed into units of consumption rather than production. A capitalist market society is dominated by market relations: 'Instead of economy being embedded in social relations, social relations are embedded in the economic system' (Polanyi 1957: 57).

The ideological accompaniment of capitalist market development was political liberalism, with its insistence on the contractual rights of free and autonomous individuals holding property in their persons. These rights, however, did not extend to women who were in law subordinate to patriarchal domination. As Mary Astell asked in the eighteenth century: 'if *all Men are born free*, how is it that all Women are born Slaves?' (cited in Pateman 1988: 90). The long struggle for women's political and civil rights, however, was accompanied (in Europe and the US) by a major shift in thinking about women and the family. Women had always been regarded as 'naturally' inferior to men. However, as market relationships became increasingly individualised the bourgeois ideal of the family as a 'haven in a heartless world', in which women were the morally *superior* carers and nurturers, gained ascendance.

The ideology of 'separate spheres' – men being dominant in (and seen as more suited for) the public sphere of employment (and other aspects of civil society, such as politics), whereas women were responsible for the domestic or private sphere – was accompanied by the development of the 'male breadwinner' division of labour – men specialising in paid work, women in the unpaid labour of caring and domestic work. It is important to recognise, however, that even though women were no longer regarded as an inferior species in relation to men, both the prevailing ideology of separate spheres and its attendant division of labour were rooted in an essentialist model of the innate and natural character of differences between the sexes. The attributes specific to each gender were held to be of an intrinsic nature closely associated with physical, psychological and spiritual differences.

The male breadwinner model and its normative accompaniment, the ideology of domesticity, was buttressed by the institutional separation of women from both the political, and much of the economic, spheres of human activity. During the course of the twentieth century, the consolidation of the male breadwinner model was accompanied by institutional developments and arrangements that reflected its basic assumptions, from school hours to pensions and the delivery of health and welfare services (Esping-Andersen 1990; Sainsbury 1994). Men in full-time employment received a 'family wage' and related benefits, women gained benefits, often indirectly, as wives and mothers (Pateman 1989). This gender/welfare arrangement has been described by Crouch as part of the 'mid [twentieth] century social compromise' (1999: 53). This was in a broad sense a class 'compromise'. Governments of left and right supported social protections and increasing welfare, and left parties and their representatives did not seek to radically destabilise existing social arrangements. These arrangements may be described as characteristic of 'Fordism', a term that has been widely employed to describe the industrial and social order that emerged in many advanced capitalist societies after the Second World War. 'Fordism' was characterised by mass production, full employment (at least as far as men were concerned), the development of state welfare and rising standards of consumption.[1]

In the later decades of the twentieth century, Fordism began to unravel, as did the 'male breadwinner' model of the articulation of employment and family life. However, the gendered ideology that holds women responsible for the domestic sphere, together with its accompanying (implicit or explicit) gender essentialism, has proved to have deeper roots. Nevertheless, the major shift in gender relations and associated norms and attitudes that is currently in process raises a series of important issues that will be explored in this book. How is the work of caring to be accomplished given that it can no longer be automatically assumed that it will be undertaken (unpaid) within the family?[2] How may sets of institutions moulded to the contours of the 'male breadwinner' arrangement be reconstructed in order to accommodate to new realities? How do families adjust to these changing circumstances and what is to be done about the growing conflict between paid employment and the demands of family life? Will social and economic inequalities, between women and men as well as between different social classes, be ameliorated or intensified by these recent changes?

---

[1] The concept has been extensively contested, but nevertheless, as Thompson (2003: 362) has recently argued, 'we may have to learn to live with Fordism as the least worst term available to describe a set of social relations that manifest a degree of connectedness and coherence'.

[2] It may also be noted that social and demographic changes are also shifting the contours of requirements for care, although this will not be discussed in any detail in this book. Birth rates have declined, but childcare inputs have risen in the case of individual children. Increased life expectancy has brought with it care responsibilities for the ageing population, often at a point in the family life cycle when adults are also assuming care responsibilities for grandchildren. See Brannen, Moss and Mooney 2004.

Changes in employment, changes in women and the family

With considerable oversimplification, the characteristic workplaces of the Fordist era with which the 'male breadwinner' model of employment/family articulation was associated tended to be relatively large. Both production and administration were bureaucratically organised – that is, according to set routines, rules and regulations. In manufacturing (and here the motor industry was taken to be the exemplar), work tasks were broken down into sub-elements of the whole, and indeed, influential commentaries argued that such 'deskilling' was an inevitable accompaniment to capitalist development (Braverman 1974). Large bureaucratically organised workplaces offered stable (male) careers, particularly for administrative and managerial employees, and many employees spent their entire working lives with a single organisation. These features are no longer associated with much contemporary employment (Crompton et al. 1996). Technological change has removed many unskilled and semi-skilled jobs, particularly in manufacturing. Unskilled jobs in the burgeoning service sector tend to be found in smaller organisational units (fast food restaurants, care homes, supermarkets, etc.), unlikely locales for the generation of union membership and the development of workplace protections that were associated with Fordist organisations (Freedman 1984). Moreover, much lower-level employment in the service sector is highly flexible, dominated by women and young people, rather than the prime age males who predominated in semi-skilled manufacturing employment.

Flexible employment may be both numerical, which allows the number of workers or amount of labour time to be varied, and functional, where employees move from task to task (both strategies may be used simultaneously).[3] Strategies of numerical and pay flexibility are guided by neoliberal economic theory, which stresses the efficiency gains that come from making the costs of factors of production as flexibly responsive as possible (Crouch 1999: 79; see also Atkinson 1984, Smith 1997). 'Functional' flexibility, in contrast, has been regarded more positively and incorporates the kinds of innovations in production often associated with new management techniques and 'high-commitment' management – teamworking, upskilling and multiskilling, and so on. Advocates of functional flexibility see flexible specialisation as facilitating innovation in both production activities and institutional regulation,

---

[3] See O'Reilly 1992 as well as the example of 'Shopwell' discussed in the following chapters of this book.

allowing for the exercise of strategic choice and the positive development of productive resources (Hirst and Zeitlin 1997). Critics of neoliberal numerical flexibility, however, tend to regard flexibilisation as part of a package of measures that facilitate the superexploitation of the workforce (Pollert 1988).

Employment change has been under way in a global economic context in which the speed of transactions and information processing has been but one element in increased competitive pressures worldwide. Major economies – particularly the US and Britain – have also been profoundly affected by neoliberal economic and political ideas that have encouraged competition and promoted deregulation, particularly in the field of employment. These policies have found their echo in theories of management that have encouraged the 'lean organisation' (Womack et al. 1990), together with the removal of what are seen as obsolete and rule-bound organisational structures (Kanter 1990). Competitive 'de-layering' has been accompanied by layoffs and increasing employment insecurity for many employees, including managers, and thus the decline of stable career paths. Organisations have not only 'downsized', but have also sought to outsource much of their activities to other firms and consultants. For example, they increasingly buy in services such as catering and cleaning, as well as other elements central to the organisations' activities, such as essential components in manufacturing, and in banks key workers such as counter staff may be hired from an employment agency on a semi-permanent basis. In many countries (including Britain), public sector organisations have also been steered along neoliberal pathways. International companies in particular are no longer constrained by national boundaries, and can move production and services around the globe, taking advantage of lower wage rates and cheaper skills.

With the decline of the long-term single organisation bureaucratic career, individuals can no longer rely on structured progress through an organisational hierarchy in order to develop their careers, but rather, are supposed to self-develop their own career paths as they move from job to job, company to company. As Kanter (cited in McGovern et al. 1998) puts it: 'reliance on organisations to give shape to a career is being replaced by reliance on self'. Thus Sennett (1998: 27) has argued that the development of flexible capitalism has resulted in the 'corrosion of character ... particularly those qualities of character which bind human beings to one another and furnishes each with a sense of sustainable self'. That is, Sennett argues that the end of Fordism and the development of global, flexible capitalism has broken social bonds and undermined trust between individuals.

During the nineteenth and early twentieth centuries, the normative and material embedding of the 'male breadwinner' model of employment and family articulation and the increasing confinement of women to domesticity meant that as the modern occupational structure developed, women were systematically excluded from major professions such as medicine and the law, as well as from political life and higher-level administrative and managerial positions. Further down the occupational order, women were also kept out of the better-paid craft positions associated with the developing industrial economy – for example, in engineering, metalwork and printing. These exclusions were perfectly legal, but they did not mean that women were not employed – they were, for example as seamstresses, domestic servants, and in low-grade assembly and factory work – but their wages were considerably lower than those of men, even when working at the same tasks. This division of paid labour between the sexes was a significant aspect of women's subordination. As feminists argued, the *de jure* and *de facto* exclusion of women from better-paid and more prestigious occupations denied most women economic independence and increased their dependence, as wives, on men (Hartmann 1976; Walby 1986).

In the twentieth century, women in an increasing number of countries gradually acquired political and civil rights – although employment rights in relation to sex discrimination and equal pay were often not finally secured until after the Second World War. As a consequence of these and other changes including technological advances such as efficient contraception, as well as the changes in attitudes to gender roles and gender relations associated with second-wave feminism (organised feminist pressures were also key to the acquisition of civil rights for women), more and more women, including mothers, have entered and remained in employment at all levels. Changes in women's employment behaviour have been accompanied by changes in family formation and behaviour. Rates of marriage have declined, divorce rates have risen, and the numbers living in consensual unions have increased. The average age at marriage has risen – in England and Wales, the average age of first marriage was 28 for women and 31 for men in 2001, an increase of five years for both sexes as compared to 1961. These changes have been reflected in fertility rates, and in England and Wales the Total Fertility Rate (TFR) has fallen from 2.9 in 1964 to 1.7 in 2000. Births outside marriage have increased dramatically, from 7 per cent in 1964 to 40 per cent in 2000 in England and Wales (ONS data). These trends in women's employment, fertility and family behaviour are taking place in all 'Western' countries (for cross-nationally comparative empirical summaries of these developments, see Castells 1997: ch. 4, Crouch 2000: chs. 2, 7; see also Gonzalez-Lopez 2002; Drew 1998).

The increase in women's employment was paralleled by debates relating to employment flexibility (these first emerged in the 1980s). This is not surprising, given that women have always worked flexibly – in both the numerical and functional senses of the term. Castells has described 'new' social relationships of production as translating into 'a good fit between the "flexible woman" [forced to flexibility to cope with her multiple roles] and the network enterprise' (Castells 2000: 20). The growth of flexible capitalism has been regarded by some as making a contribution to the resolution of the tensions between employment and family 'work'. The non-flexible career bureaucrat was enabled to work in full-time, long-term employment because he could rely upon the unpaid work of a full-time homemaker. Flexible employment – part-time work, flexible scheduling, 'flexitime', etc. – might (indeed often does) enable an individual to combine both paid work and family work. Flexible working, therefore, is increasingly being presented as a possible 'win win' combination as far as employment and family life is concerned. With the rise in women's employment, both governments and employers have begun to turn their attention to the issue of work–life 'balance'. Work–life 'balance' has increasingly emerged as a major policy issue at the European level, as well as for national governments (COM 2001; Department of Trade and Industry (DTI) 2000, 2003). In all of these policy documents, flexible employment is seen as a key factor in achieving such a 'balance'.

Thus the more negative aspects of neoliberal numerical flexibility are being glossed as a positive contribution to the reconciliation of employment and family life, and employment and families might be viewed as changing in tandem with each other. However, as many authors have noted, flexible employment, which is concentrated amongst women, is not usually associated with individual success in the labour market, and flexible workers often tend to be in lower level positions. As Purcell et al. (1999) have argued, the 'uneasy reconciliation of work and family life in Britain has largely been achieved by means of a gender-segmented labour market and the part-time work of women'. Perrons' (1999) cross-national European study of flexible working in the retail industry demonstrated that in all of the countries studied (Britain, Sweden, France, Germany, Spain and Greece) it was women who worked flexibly, and took the major responsibility for caring work as well. As Lewis (2002) has argued, the fact that women continue, in aggregate, to be less advantaged in the labour market is the major reason why a 'modified male breadwinner' model of employment/family articulation persists empirically, despite the fact that in many states, official policy endorses an individualised 'adult worker' model in relation to legislation and welfare.

Developments in social theory – the inexorable rise of 'individualisation'

In the closing decades of the twentieth century, social and economic change was accompanied by wider political change – most notably, the collapse of the 'state socialist' societies of the Eastern bloc. These events contributed to an intensifying critique of encompassing, broadly materialist, theories such as Marxism. The 1980s and 1990s also witnessed a widespread 'turn to culture' in some sociological circles. This was accompanied by a renewed focus on the constitution of objects through discourse, that is, the *production* of meanings and dispositions. Thus meanings, symbols and representations became seen as more central to the study of social life, as compared to (indeed, rather than) concrete institutions. This intellectual shift was associated with theoretical commentaries that hailed the advent of 'postmodernism' (Featherstone 1991), as well as the influence of writers such as Foucault who emphasised the plurality and diversity of 'scientific' knowledge and the corresponding weaknesses of social science 'meta-narratives'. Many writers argued that 'culture' – meanings and symbolic practices – had become particularly significant in postmodernity and that indeed, that in contemporary social life, everything is 'cultural' (Baudrillard 1993).

Under the conditions of contemporary capitalism, these culturally oriented theorists argued that the distinctions between economy and culture have blurred and indeed, that 'cultural' considerations, broadly conceived, were driving economic activities. It was argued that 'cultural' rather than 'economic' issues had become more significant for our understanding of contemporary society. Indeed, many have suggested that the shift from 'economy' to 'culture' involves a larger societal shift, an epochal change towards 'postmodern' social conditions (Lash and Urry 1994; Crook et al. 1992). With globalisation and the speeding up of social and cultural change, it was argued that the nature of the world, and how people operate within it, have changed irrevocably.

Alongside the emphasis on culture there developed a growing emphasis on the significance of 'identity', particularly in respect of politics. The class-based politics of the Fordist era were seen to be increasingly irrelevant, and were being replaced with issue-based and identity politics, concerned with such matters as environmental issues and the rights of self-identified minorities such as, for example, gays, and sub-national and ethnic identities. The consequences of the apparent abandonment of a 'politics of redistribution' in favour of a 'politics of identity' have been extensively rehearsed (Fraser 2000; Frank 2000) and O'Neill (1999: 85), for example, has argued that there has been something of a 'convergence of a postmodern leftism with neoliberal defences of the market'. An emphasis on the reflexive individual and a focus on individual identities rather than collective actions and outcomes has many resonances with neoliberalism, and the promotion of individual rights and recognition meshes well with the arguments of those on the right who have criticised the way in which collective provision has 'disempowered' individuals.

Thus in 'reflexive modernity', the overwhelming importance of 'choice' is emphasised by left and right alike: 'The contemporary individual ... is characterised by choice, where previous generations had no such choices ... he or she must choose fast as in a reflex' (Lash 2002: ix). Here we find echoes of a much older theoretical debate concerning the utility of 'action-oriented' as opposed to 'structural' explanations of social behaviour. In the 1960s, the economist Duesenberry is reputed to have quipped that 'Economics is all about how people make choices, Sociology is all about how people don't have any choices to make.' Duesenberry was drawing a contrast between the self-maximising 'rational economic actor' of neoclassical economic theory and the excessively institutionalised, normatively regulated 'actor' of Parsonian sociology (Wrong 1964). However, in 'reflexive modernity' (Beck *et al.* 1994) individuals, it is argued, 'make themselves'; as Giddens (1991: 75) puts it: 'We are, not what we are, but what we make of ourselves ... what the individual becomes is dependent on the reconstructive endeavours in which he or she engages.' Thus neither fixed family obligations, nor rigid labour market and/or organisational practices, serve to determine individual social positioning. In this process, it is argued, the positioning of individuals via class and status mechanisms is replaced by a focus on the construction of individual identities.

It is true that the emphasis on materialist (Marxist) explanations in the 1960s and 1970s sometimes resulted in a 'vulgar materialism', in which the totality of human behaviour might be explained by the workings of 'the system' and its associated institutions. However, it is equally the case that the 'cultural turn' has also sometimes resulted in a 'vulgar culturalism', in which economic inequalities are seen largely as expressions of cultural hierarchies, and thus the revaluation of unjustly devalued identities 'is simultaneously to attack ... deep sources of economic inequality' (Fraser 2000: 111). The position taken in this book is relatively sceptical as to the extent to which individual 'agency' and capacities for 'self-construction' have 'replaced' structural constraints (of all kinds).[4] Rather, a guiding theme of this book will be that material (economic) institutions are embedded in cultural practices and vice versa (Granovetter and Swedberg 1992), and it is often problematic to attempt to disentangle the 'material' from the 'cultural' – although both have to be taken into account in social explanations. Important changes have indeed occurred, but a similarly sceptical stance will be taken regarding whether an 'epochal break' in the social order has taken place, requiring radically new concepts and approaches to social analysis (as authors such as Beck have argued). Rather, changes in material conditions, norms and cultures mean that institutions such as employment, class and the family are being reconfigured, but this does not mean that these institutions are redundant, or have been completely replaced.

Despite the claims of theorists of 'individuation', embedded normative and material patterns, even in 'reflexive modernity', still persist and have continuing power. As far as women are concerned, one of the most significant elements of embedded traditionalism is the persistence of the ideology of domesticity, in which the work of caring and nurturing is normatively assigned to women. As we shall see, women continue to carry out most of this work. This is yet another reason why it is essential to retain a simultaneous focus on both the material *and* the cultural in our attempt to understand the rearticulation of employment and the family. It will be argued that this approach not only will generate a better understanding of social change, but hopefully will also indicate positive strategies and responses to change. Taking this broad theoretical perspective, in the next sections of this chapter, a series of topics relating to the family, employment and their contemporary rearticulation will be critically examined.

Understanding family and employment behaviour: individual 'choice' versus social structure

Family life encompasses some of the most intimate aspects of human behaviour, and for most people it is their primary source of socialisation.

---

[4] Nevertheless, the discourse of individualism has been influential – and, as has been suggested above, it has many resonances with neoliberal thinking. Margaret Thatcher once famously remarked that 'there is no such thing as society, just individuals and families'.

As we have seen, many social theorists have argued that contemporary societies are characterised by an increase in levels of 'individuation', as, in the growing absence of 'traditional' normative prescriptions and roles, people are faced with the necessity of 'working on' their own biographies in order to construct their 'reflexive selves' (Giddens 1991; Beck 1992). Indeed, the contemporary transformations of sexual behaviour and family life (including the increasing instability of marriage and partnership) have been held up as examples of this 'individualisation' in process (Giddens 1992; Beck and Beck-Gernsheim 2002). As Giddens asserts, for example:

Individualisation has been the driving force for change in late modern societies. Men and women gain not only the freedom to choose their own values and lifestyle, they are also obliged to make their own choices, because there are no universal certainties and no fixed models of the good life. (Giddens in Hakim 2000)

Indeed, Hakim (2000) has argued that contemporary changes in women's employment reflect this relatively recently found capacity of women to exercise their 'choices'. Women's employment patterns, she argues, are different from those of men because of the choices made by different types (or 'preference groupings') of women. She identifies three categories of women: home/family centred, work centred and adaptives/ drifters. Home centred women give priority to their families, work centred women give priority to their employment careers, and adaptive women shift their priorities between family and career over their life cycles. Because the proportion of home centred and work centred individuals is higher amongst women than men, women's employment patterns are different.[5] A greater proportion of women 'choose' part-time work, and/or sideline their employment careers in favour of their families, thus levels of part-time work are higher amongst women than men, and in aggregate, women are less successful in the employment sphere.

Hakim is emphatic that contemporary women's employment patterns are a consequence of their individual choices, rather than any constraints arising from the nature of employment or other structural factors (such as, for example, the availability of alternative caring resources): 'self-classification as a primary earner or as a secondary earner is determined by chosen identities rather than imposed by external circumstance or

---

[5] The main explanation that Hakim offers for these male/female differences is biological – i.e., different testosterone levels between men and women (see Hakim 2000: 258ff.).

particular jobs' (2000: 275).[6] Hakim's arguments have, not surprisingly, found favour in conservative/neoliberal political circles.[7] Women *do* make choices in respect of both their employment and their family lives. However, a crucial question is the *basis* upon which people make these choices, as 'choices' will be shaped (or constrained) by the context within which choice is being exercised.

In Britain, the government has recently implemented policies designed to raise the frequency with which an employment option is 'chosen' amongst groups perceived to be socially excluded, including lone parents (mothers) and families on benefit. These policies are premised on the argument that individuals with caring responsibilities who are currently on state income support will be materially (and socially) better off if they take up paid employment. It assumes that individuals will behave as 'rational economic persons', who will choose the course of action that is demonstrated to be in their best (economic) interests. However, this change in the policy context has been criticised by Duncan *et al.* (2003; see also Duncan and Edwards 1999; Barlow *et al.* 2002) as evidence of what they describe as a 'rationality mistake'. They argue that individuals with caring responsibilities (such as lone parents) take decisions relating to care and employment 'with reference to moral and socially negotiated (not individual) views about what behaviour is right and proper' (Duncan *et al.* 2003: 310), rather than with a view to individual (self) maximisation. Thus some female lone parents identify themselves as 'primarily' mothers, and will not respond to economic incentives or pressures, seeing their primary responsibility as that of caring for their child(ren).

With its emphasis on 'choice', Duncan *et al.*'s argument has some superficial similarities with that of Hakim, but is in fact rather different. Most importantly, Duncan *et al.* argue that in respect of the 'balance' between employment and caring, people do not behave as individuals (as in Hakim's classification of different 'types' of women), but rather, in negotiation with others within a relatively fluid moral framework. This broad perspective is also to be found in Finch and Mason's (1993) study of family responsibilities. They argue that family responsibilities do not operate on the basis of fixed rules, enshrined as 'rights'

---

[6] Notwithstanding this direct quotation, it should be pointed out that Hakim's arguments tend to be inconsistent and at other points she appears to acknowledge the significance of structural factors.

[7] For example, her ideas were enthusiastically adopted (2002–3) by the Australian Conservative government. See the *Sydney Morning Herald*, 7 February and 3 March 2003: www.smh.com.au.

or 'obligations'. Rather, they are developed and created over time, interweaving material and moral dimensions. In developing family responsibilities, people also develop their own identities – as a mother, sister, father or whatever. Thus the creation of these norms and understandings has been placed at the centre of contemporary family sociology (Silva and Smart 1999). Whilst this book will give an equivalent emphasis to the institutional and national contexts of choice making, it will not be disputed that individuals make 'choices' both in relation to others as well as being guided by normative (moral) frameworks, rather than on the basis of individually rational calculation alone.

Both Finch and Mason and Duncan *et al.* emphasise that particular kinds of negotiated moral frameworks, as well as ideas about family responsibilities and parental employment, cut across class boundaries.[8] Duncan *et al.* argue that women who define themselves as 'primarily mothers' are located at all points on the social spectrum. Nevertheless, as we shall see in Chapters 2 and 7, a question that still needs to be raised is *why* particular 'moral rationalities' are to be found more frequently within some class groupings than others.

Thus although it is indeed important to take normative and moral frameworks, as well as individual preferences, into account in our analysis of the reconfigurations relating to employment and the family, we should be careful not to take up an uncritical stance in respect of either. As Nussbaum (2000: 114) has argued, 'preferences' are not (as in the utilitarian perspective), necessarily the best guide for policy-making. She argues that we also need to 'conduct a critical scrutiny of preference and desire that would reveal the many ways in which habit, fear, low expectations and unjust background conditions deform people's choices and even their wishes for their own lives'.

Regime change, gender and state policies: the centrality of caring work

At the most general level, Crouch (1999) has described recent changes in economic and labour market policies as a move in the direction of 'extreme capitalism'. Others, as we have seen, have used the language

---

[8] Silva and Smart (1999: 7) argue that: 'Personal scripts are written in the context of the different social and economic locations of families, as well as individuals, within wider social structures. But there is now more than one normative guideline to provide the context for these choices. Moreover, social class, gender, sexuality, age and ethnicity no longer operate as inevitable or one-dimensional pre-determining aspects of these normative guidelines.' Parsons notwithstanding, it is unlikely that the 'normative guidelines' provided (by social class in particular) were ever as rigid as suggested by this argument.

of 'regime change' – from 'modernity' to 'postmodernity', from highly regulated and structured employment and production regimes (Fordism) towards an increasingly marketised, deregulated, neoliberal set of institutions (post-Fordism or neo-Fordism). Such general frameworks have also addressed the question of changes in women's employment. For example, Castells (1997) sees the erosion of patriarchalism, together with the increasing availability of women's cheap, flexible labour, as a central element contributing to the growth of the 'network society', and Crouch identifies changes in the family, together with women's changing relationship to employment, as making a significant contribution to the growth of individualism and the fracturing of the 'mid-20th century social compromise'.

Thus the question of gender has been central in discussions relating to the nature and possibilities of contemporary regime change(s) and their outcomes. Indeed, some authors have placed the notion of a shift in the 'gender contract' at the centre of their analyses (e.g. Gottfried 2000). For example, Drew et al. (1998: 3) have argued that: 'Cross-national variation in the labour force participation of women can be generally explained in terms of "gender contracts" ... These concepts refer to a composite of national characteristics including state policy on taxation, childcare provision and services and gender equality in employment. The formation of these gender contracts has been brought about by a series of historical, religious and cultural factors.' This kind of work has emphasised the grounding of Fordist regimes in the 'male breadwinner/female housewife' gender contract (Hirdman 1998), and its subsequent erosion. The 'housewife contract', it is argued, is in the process of transformation into a (conditional) 'equality contract', or 'citizen-worker' model, that is, one which derives from an individual's participation in paid employment, rather than their role within the family.

The concept of a 'gender contract' is a useful tool, but it is not sufficient by itself to grasp the implications of contemporary change in employment and the family. Hirdman's original formulation constituted a crucial initial insight into the ongoing shift in gender relations taking place during the later decades of the twentieth century. Nevertheless, the changes we discuss cannot be viewed through the prism of 'gender' alone. Although the question of gender, and changes in gender relations, is central to our analysis, these developments must be examined in parallel with other aspects of change, particularly in relation to class and the structuring of inequality.

As O'Connor et al. (1999: 10) have argued: 'gender relations cannot be understood apart from the state, politics and policy; states influence gender relations, and are in turn influenced by gender relations'. Here the question of the welfare state – the systems of social insurances and protections that were developed as part of the 'mid century social compromise' – is crucial.[9] A considerable feminist literature has addressed the issue of women in relation to the state (e.g., Showstack Sassoon 1987; Walby 1990) – which is not surprising given that, even when 'separate sphere' ideologies have been dominant, women have taken a major role in initiating social reforms (e.g., Skocpol 1992). During the 1980s, a number of feminist writers were critical of the role of the state in relation to women, arguing that state policies served to reinforce patriarchy and the 'breadwinner model' – for example, by channelling benefits to women as wives and mothers, rather than as citizens in their own right (Land 1986; Pateman 1989). These arguments were themselves challenged, particularly by Scandinavian authors, who argued that a 'woman-friendly' state might – and could – take action to remedy women's inequalities in relation to men (Hernes 1987). Feminist literature on the state initially developed in parallel with 'mainstream' welfare state analysis, which had tended to privilege issues related to class and politics in developing its explanations of welfare state development. However, as O'Connor et al. observe (1999: 15; see also Bussemaker and Kersbergen 1999), although 'mainstream' and gender-sensitive literatures on the welfare state developed separately throughout the 1970s and 1980s, there was considerable convergence during the 1990s.

In particular, Esping-Andersen's influential categorisation of welfare 'regimes' generated an international critique and debate that has considerably enhanced our understandings of the manner in which state and labour market policies are embedded in gendered assumptions relating to the division of labour. Esping-Andersen (1990) described how different regimes were linked to the development of women's paid employment. The development of universalist Social Democratic (Scandinavian) welfare regimes tended to increase the level of women's employment, particularly in the large and expanding sector of state-provided welfare (education, health, social services, etc.). 'Corporatist' employment insurance-based welfare regimes (such as in Germany) tended to hold down the level of women's employment as benefits were

---

[9] It is not our purpose here to enter into an extended discussion relating to the definition of the 'welfare state'. However, the approach here is very similar to that of O'Connor et al. (1999: 12) in that it assumes a broad meaning of the term: 'not just income maintenance programs, but also the state regulatory apparatus (for example, as deployed around reproduction or workplace equality) and public services (for example day care)'.

linked to a breadwinner wage and the way in which they are distributed assumes that welfare will be physically provided within the family. 'Liberal' (such as the United States) welfare regimes only provide a safety net for the most disadvantaged, and all individuals are expected to provide for their own welfare through employment. Liberal regimes, therefore, also tend to increase the level of women's employment, particularly in low-level, marketised, service provision.

Esping-Andersen's framework was widely criticised for its lack of attention to unpaid family labour (or caring) – as Lewis (1992: 14) put it: 'women can only enter Esping-Andersen's analysis when they enter the paid labour market'. Subsequently, Esping-Andersen (1999) has acknowledged the significance of the family and women's employment in his analysis of the welfare state. However, he is 'not interested in women *per se*' (2000: 759), and focuses on women as employees rather than on changes in the pattern of gender relations themselves. Thus he is primarily interested in the *economic* significance of women's behaviour, and, it may be argued, Esping-Andersen does not give adequate attention to the *social* dimension of changes in gender relations.[10]

With considerable oversimplification of the detail of the debates, feminist and mainstream welfare state analyses came somewhat closer together during the 1990s. Increasingly, feminist analyses took on an important comparative dimension (e.g., Sainsbury 1994; O'Connor *et al.* 1999), and we may identify two major themes that have emerged from this fruitful convergence. First, comparative research has demonstrated the importance of national variations in institutional arrangements as well as in gender relations (or contracts), as we shall see in Chapters 5, 6 and 7. Second, in part as a consequence of these debates, a number of vital feminist insights have been incorporated into the arguments. First, 'the family' and conventional gender roles have been 'denaturalised', and the public/private dichotomy rejected. As feminists have argued, neither 'the family', nor women's (and men's) work within it exists 'by nature', rather, they are economic, legal and social constructions, and the distinction between 'families' and 'markets' has been similarly generated (Olsen 1983). Second, the issue of unpaid caregiving has become central to the debate. Neither unpaid nor paid 'work' is necessarily exclusively associated with either sex. However, women's propensity to love and care is often treated as existing 'by nature', rather

---

[10] Indeed, Esping-Andersen agrees with Hakim that the underlying distribution of different attitudes amongst women may be seen as a relative constant, and thus the impact of normative shifts in attitude and aspiration need not be taken into account. This topic is discussed further in Chapter 5 of this book.

than 'recognising the role of custom, law, and institutions in shaping the emotions' (Nussbaum 2000: 252; Cheal 1991).

In contrast, feminists have emphasised that care is necessary work – as Glucksmann (1995: 70) has put it: 'The *economic* bottom line is that if babies are not looked after they will die; if food preparation ceased people would eventually starve' (emphasis in original). Feminists have also emphasised the *interconnectedness* of the varying elements of 'work'. Thus the feminist approach is essentially relational, 'starting from how activities connect to each other and would not "work" without each other' (*ibid.*). Glucksmann (1995: 67) has described this as the 'total social organisation of labour' (TSOL), that is 'the manner by which all the labour in a particular society is divided up between and allocated to different structures, institutions, and activities'. From this perspective, care work provides an indispensable contribution to human flourishing, and is central, not peripheral, to human survival. As Sevenhuijsen (2002: 131) has argued: 'individuals can exist only because they are members of various networks of care and responsibility, for good or bad'. Thus: 'Care should not be conceptualised as a safety net in times of misfortune and transition but rather as an ongoing social process that demands our attention daily and thus should figure prominently in any scenario for future social policy' (*ibid.*: 138). Therefore as Lewis (2002) has argued: 'The gendered division of care work ... is crucial to understanding the gendered nature of welfare state change.'

Caring is universal, caring is work. Caring work has been identified as a peculiarly 'feminine' attribute, but this is not the case. Centuries of ideological renditions of 'the feminine', to say nothing of gender socialisation and normative expectations, render it extremely likely that in any given population, women will carry out more care work than men. As Williams (1991) has argued, the ideology of domesticity carries with it a powerful set of normative beliefs that imply that the abandonment of the home by women might undermine the fabric of society itself. Nevertheless, men can care as well as women, and it is important to recognise that caring is gender *coded*, but not 'gendered' in any essentialist sense (Fraser 1994). Indeed, as Fraser argues, gender equity is only likely to be achieved if the gendered division of labour is 'deconstructed' – that is, if men become more 'like women', combining the work of both employment *and* caregiving in their day-to-day lives.

The question of class

The assertion that 'class' is no longer a concept relevant to the analysis of 'late modern' societies has been made so often as to be almost banal.

As we have seen, one frequent argument is that in 'reflexive modern' societies, the individual has become the author of his or her own biography (e.g., Beck 1992, 2002; Pakulski and Waters 1996). That is, rather than simply being able to 'follow the rules' as laid down by the established collectivities of class, status and gender, the individual is now 'forced to choose'. As Bauman (2002) puts it: 'Modernity replaces the determination of social standing [*i.e., of 'class'*] with compulsive and obligatory self-determination.' However, it will be argued that although there has indeed been considerable and extensive social change, and individuals may indeed appear to have more 'choices' to make than in the recent historical past, the concept of class is by no means redundant. In developing a critique of the 'individualisation' thesis in relation to class, it will be necessary briefly to review past theoretical debates relating to the nature of the concept of 'class', as well as their associated traditions of empirical investigation.[11]

The modern concept of class is inextricably associated with the development of capitalist industrialism (or 'industrial society'). The development of capitalism was accompanied by the emergence of the 'two great classes' identified by Marx: the bourgeoisie (the owners and controllers of capital or the means of production), and the industrial working class or proletariat (those without capital or access to productive resources who were forced to sell their labour in order to survive). This does not mean that industrial capitalism was ever a 'two-class' society, as many other groupings, distinguished by a variety of relationships to both production and the market, have always existed in capitalist societies (Crompton 1998). Thus the classic theorists defined 'class' in largely material terms. However, social and cultural factors have always accompanied material distinctions (Bourdieu 1973). Indeed, in today's everyday discourse, the idea of 'class' is probably even more closely associated with the social and cultural differentiation of hierarchy than with material factors.[12]

A key issue relating to class (deriving largely, but not entirely, from the work of Marx) is that of class identity or consciousness. This is the assertion that as different classes had different (indeed conflicting) interests, deriving from their positioning in relation to production and markets, these interests would be articulated in some way or other (indeed, Marx saw class conflict as the major driving force of social change). In fact, from the nineteenth century different class interests

---

[11] This discussion will necessarily be brief. These topics are extensively explored in Crompton 1998.

[12] See, for example, the popular television programme 'Keeping up Appearances'.

were represented by a range of different bodies including the political parties of left and right, as well as trade unions and employers' organisations. Thus, there were reasons to argue that the interest groupings representing different 'classes' could be broadly mapped (albeit in by no means an exact or unproblematic fashion) onto the material groupings identified by the classic theorists of class – owners and non-owners of the means of different elements of production as well as broad occupational groupings.[13] By the late nineteenth and early twentieth centuries (albeit to varying degrees), the greater majority of the population in industrial capitalist societies came to rely on paid employment of some kind. Official statisticians (as well as social investigators) sought to 'classify' these populations in some kind of meaningful fashion. Increasingly, the occupational order began to emerge as a useful axis of classification that gave a summary indication of standard of life as well as 'life chances' (Szreter 1984). The convention developed of describing the different occupational groupings created by the application of a range of classificatory schemes as social 'classes'. This has been described as the 'employment aggregate' approach to class analysis (Crompton 1998). Within the 'employment aggregate' approach, in the second half of the twentieth century there developed a sophisticated body of quantitative empirical research that investigated the relative 'life chances' of different occupational 'classes', largely focusing on the topic of social mobility (Blau and Duncan 1967; Goldthorpe 1987; Wright 1997).[14]

However, in parallel with the development of the employment aggregate approach, transformations in the occupational structure (its empirical foundation) generated a series of difficulties that seemed to challenge many of its basic assumptions. One important problem was the increase in women's employment (Acker 1973). Early studies of social mobility, initiated during the high-water mark of the 'male breadwinner' era, had drawn on 'men only' samples, allocating the class

---

[13] There were and are considerable variations between different capitalist societies and different nation states in the nature and extent of 'class' representation, particularly in respect of religious factors.

[14] Savage (2000) has argued that this approach to 'class analysis' was a particularly British concern. However, the tradition of quantitative 'class analysis' is well established in international academe, for example via the work of Research Committee 28 of the International Sociological Association. It may be noted that one feature of this tradition of empirical class analysis, to be found in the work of Goldthorpe in particular, has been to emphasise the stability of class processes, particularly in relation to rates of relative social mobility. This assertion of 'no real change' (once change has been controlled for) has led to a further criticism of this approach – i.e., its apparent failure to analyse or take account of the very real transformations of the occupational structure.

position of women to that of her most proximate male 'head of household'. Although this procedure might be justified if women were not in paid employment, could the 'class position' of the employed, partnered, woman be so described? This issue was further complicated by the fact that the class outcomes of the same occupation appeared to be different for men and women. For example, lower-level clerical work, which for men was associated with good promotion prospects and therefore 'life chances' (Stewart et al. 1980), was, for the majority of female clerks, a final destination (Crompton and Jones 1984). Another major occupational shift taking place in the final decades of the twentieth century was the decline in traditional male 'working-class' occupations as a consequence of deindustrialisation. If the traditional working class was in retreat, how could it realistically be considered as a potential force for social change? Another significant strand contributing to the 'death of class' arguments was the apparent failure of coherent class identities or consciousness to develop during the second half of the twentieth century (see Savage 2000: ch. 2). The political successes of neoliberalism, together with the collapse of 'state socialism' in Eastern Europe, seemed to further confirm the redundancy of the concept of class as an appropriate analytical tool for the social sciences.

The intention here is not to return to, or attempt to resolve, these older debates relating to gender, employment aggregate 'class analysis' and the changing occupational structure. Rather, the aim is to illustrate some dimensions of the burgeoning set of arguments to the effect that 'class analysis' was not only fatally flawed, but no longer relevant to the analysis of 'late modern' societies. The aggregates generated via the application of sociological class schemes had never corresponded, in any direct or unmediated fashion, to the cultural or consciousness categories identified by the classic theorists. Indeed, within broad occupational class groupings, it was possible to identify a wide range of different cultures and class identities (Lockwood 1966). With the coming of the 'cultural turn' within sociology and other related disciplines, arguments were developed to the effect that cultural issues, particularly those associated with consumption, had become more significant than material (or class) factors in determining attitudes and associated behaviours (Bauman 2002; Crook et al. 1992).

However, the approach that will be developed in this book will be to argue that class processes have both economic and cultural dimensions. 'Class' is a structured type of economic inequality resulting from the operation of market mechanisms (that sort people into occupations) together with the distribution of inherited wealth. As Sayer (2002: 4) has put it: 'People are born into an economic class or have it thrust upon them through operations of market mechanisms which are largely indifferent to their moral qualities or identity.' Nevertheless, class processes also have a significant cultural dimension. For example, as studies of class cultures have demonstrated (Skeggs 1997; Reay 1998), class inequalities are themselves associated with systematic degradations of identity that can contribute to the formation of 'preferences' that have the effect of perpetuating material class inequalities. That is, constructions of social difference shape both material inequalities and inequalities of recognition (Bottero and Irwin 2003: 465). Individuals do make choices, but they do so within sets of material circumstances and normative frameworks that serve to reproduce social hierarchies and thus 'classes'.

Individualism, women, class and careers

As has already been noted, a major consequence of increasing individualisation of the employment relationship has been the decline of the bureaucratic or organisational career and the growth of the 'portfolio career' (Handy 1994). It is argued that individuals no longer rely on steady progress through an organisational hierarchy for career development, but make their own career paths as they move from job to job, company to company. The supposed development of the 'portfolio career' is a consequence not simply of the growth of individualistic discourses, but also a result of deindustrialisation and organisational 'delayering' and 'downsizing', as companies strive to make themselves competitive by adopting the practices of the 'lean organisation' (Womack et al. 1990).

Bureaucratic careers were typical of Fordism. In larger organisations and enterprises – such as the railways, civil service, major banks and insurance companies as well as major manufacturing organisations – individuals (usually men) were enabled to work their way up through the bureaucratic hierarchy via a combination of long service (thus gaining organisational knowledge or 'assets', see Savage et al. 1992), acquiring the relevant qualifications where required, as well as general good behaviour. Indeed, the availability of an organisational career ladder was widely argued to be the key factor that distinguished 'working-class' from 'middle-class' occupations (Abercrombie and Urry 1983; Erikson and Goldthorpe 1992). However, although the actual extent of 'portfolio' career development has been disputed (see Wajcman and Martin 2001), there can be little doubt that within organisations that are broadly shaped by neoliberal approaches to management, contemporary career development has been 'individualised'.

Until the second half of the twentieth century, women did not have employment careers and were formally and informally excluded from managerial and professional occupations. Major professions, such as medicine and the law, refused women entry to training and qualification. Large bureaucracies (such as banking, and the civil service) similarly excluded women through formal rules such as the marriage bar (whereupon a woman was required to resign on getting married), as well as informal (masculinist) exclusionary practices (Crompton and Sanderson 1990; Cockburn 1991).[15] Not surprisingly, therefore, much of the discussion of 'women and careers' had a focus upon the obstacles faced by women *per se* in their attempts to gain entry into higher-level occupations and make progress through organisational hierarchies (e.g., Kanter 1977). During the 1990s, these discussions crystallised around the idea of a 'glass ceiling' (Davidson and Cooper 1992) keeping women out of the topmost level of management. Linked to these kinds of arguments we find an increasing emphasis on the significance of cultural processes, particularly in relation to gender and sexuality, in shaping women's organisational fates (Acker 1990).

Cultural degradations (of race and age as well as gender) are indeed significant in positioning and locating individuals in organisations and labour markets. However, it may be suggested that the 'cultural turn' in research and writing on women's employment and careers has tended to deflect attention away from the role of the sexual division of labour (in its broadest sense) in perpetuating gender inequalities. The significance of family responsibilities in shaping and limiting women's career progression has, of course, been widely recognised, even if it has not been a major focus of contemporary sociological research on gender and organisations. Evidence from empirical research in the 1970s and 1980s showed that women suffered occupational downgrading as they re-entered the labour force after a childrearing break (Dex 1987). Recent studies of women in managerial positions have emphasised the difficulties they face in combining a managerial career with family responsibilities, and indeed there is evidence that these difficulties lead many women managers to limit their families or even forgo childbearing altogether (Halford *et al.* 1997; Wajcman 1996; Crompton 2001). In respect of the unequal positioning of women within contemporary employing organisations, therefore, 'workplace injustices'

---

[15] Many higher-level jobs were effectively 'two person careers', in which the career bureaucrat or professional was assumed to have the support of a non-working wife (see Finch 1983).

do not only (or even primarily) derive from the politics of identity, but largely from the persistence of male breadwinner assumptions in a non-male-breadwinner era.

Data and methods

This book will draw on both qualitative and quantitative data. The qualitative materials include 126 work–life interviews carried out during 2001–02 for a project funded by the Joseph Rowntree Foundation (the 'JRF project'): 'Organisations, Careers and Caring'.[16] The project built on case studies of employment in three service sectors, retail banking ('Cellbank'), supermarket retail ('Shopwell'), and local government, in two localities in Britain, Sheffield and East Kent (as two local authorities were involved, the case studies incorporated four employers). Where relevant, these organisations will be described in more detail as the evidence is presented in subsequent chapters. In general, however, they encompass a wide range of service employment, from unambiguously 'managerial' to unskilled service sector occupations. Interviews were carried out with men and women at all organisational levels up to middle management. We will be using these interviews, together with other secondary materials, in order to paint a picture of contemporary service work, and service careers, and their articulation with family life. The interviews used in this book have been listed in Appendix B. Each interviewee has been given a pseudonym, and in some cases details have been altered in order to protect anonymity. When these qualitative interviews are drawn on in our discussions, they will be described as deriving from the 'JRF research'.

The quantitative data draws upon the British Social Attitudes (BSA) and International Social Survey (ISSP) programmes (Davis and Jowell 1989; Jowell et al. 1993). The BSA has been running since 1983. Each year, the ISSP fields a particular module relating to a specific topic, and the same questions are asked in all participating countries (the questions may vary from module to module in different years, but a core set of questions are repeated). In Britain, an ISSP module on family and gender roles has been fielded as part of the BSA survey in 1989, 1994 and 2002. These three surveys are used in this book to describe changes over time in Britain in attitudes to gender roles, and work–family behaviour. In addition, as part of an Economic and Social

---

[16] See Crompton et al. 2003. Many thanks to the JRF for its support of this work. Dr Andrea Wigfield and Ms Jane Dennett also carried out interviews on this project.

Research Council (ESRC) project, a set of questions that focused on careers and organisational experiences was added to the Family 2002 module in Britain (Appendix A). The number of respondents was also enhanced.[17] Colleagues in France, Norway, Finland and Portugal provided copies of the ISSP Family 2002 data sets (in these countries, a limited number of additional questions were also asked, see Appendix A). A copy of the US ISSP data set was also obtained.[18] In the text, we will refer to the 'BSA survey' when data for Britain only are being presented, and to the 'ISSP surveys' in our comparative analysis. In the following chapters, quantitative analyses have been presented largely in tabular form, and regression analyses have been placed as appendices at the end of the relevant chapters.

In the social sciences, comparative research is widely employed both to test theories as well as to generate theoretical explanations of particular phenomena. With considerable oversimplification, two broad strategies of cross-national comparative research may be identified: 'variable oriented' and 'case oriented' (Ragin 1991). In variable-oriented cross-national research, the 'ultimate aim should be to replace the proper names of nations ... with the names of variables' (Goldthorpe 1994: 2). Thus social science explanation and investigation is not being directed at national peculiarities (or 'cultures') as such, but rather, at particular factors (variables) that can be measured in the same manner in all of the societies under investigation (this has also been described as the 'indicators' approach, see Glover 1992). For example, rates of heart disease (the dependent variable) may be measured against 'per capita consumption of saturated fat' (the independent variable) in different nation states; UN 'Human Development Indexes' compared with 'GNP per capita' and so on. When comparisons reveal similar associations between variables across a range of nation states, this is held to be confirmative of a universal social structural tendency (or 'law'). Thus cross-national comparisons are employed to test or confirm social theories – as in, for example, Kohn's (1987) explorations of the association between social structure and personality.

[17] This research was supported by two grants from the ESRC: R000239727: 'Employment and the Family', and R000220106: 'Families, Employment and Work–Life Integration'. ESRC support is gratefully acknowledged. The National Centre for Social Research (NatCen) carried out the surveys.
[18] Thanks to Tom Smith (NORC) for providing an advance copy. ISSP data sets were also available for Hungary and the Czech Republic. However, in the event, these countries were not incorporated into the comparative analysis as a number of important measures proved not to be reliable for these countries.

Variable-oriented comparative research, therefore, has a tendency to be focused on the identification of *similarities* in different national contexts. Generalising theoretical statements will be supported or reinforced to the extent that these similarities can be demonstrated across a range of different national contexts, thus the researcher has an interest in ensuring that N (the number of national 'cases') is as large as possible. The specificities of national cultures are not a primary concern of this strategy of inquiry. In variable-oriented comparative research, one major problem is that of ensuring that the same phenomenon is, in fact, being measured in the different countries in the study – that is, that the variables employed are commensurable with each other. This requirement is problematic, not least because many social science variables are socially constructed. For example, occupational (class) classifications vary cross-nationally, and the same occupation may be located in a different 'class' in different national schemes (Goldthorpe 1985). This problem can be addressed by standardising the measurement of variables; for example, comparisons using agreed class schemes (see Erikson and Goldthorpe 1992; Wright 1997), or, as in the International Social Survey Programme, agreeing questions and engaging in extensive back translation (see Jowell 1998).

Nevertheless, it is impossible to completely overcome problems of commensurability or equivalance. To continue with the example of occupation, variations in national education and production systems can generate occupations that are simply not found in other national contexts (see Maurice *et al.* 1986). Indeed, Maurice and his colleagues come close to suggesting that, as nation states *are* so different, then meaningful comparisons are not really possible (Rose 1985). However, persisting national differences do not destroy the case for comparative work. Indeed, and in some contrast to the variable-oriented comparative approach, case-oriented comparative work has focused on national *difference* in order to generate theoretical explanations of particular phenomena. Through a close examination of the factors contributing to variation in the phenomena under investigation (in the case of the comparative analysis in this book, a range of variables relating to modes of employment/family articulation), the relative significance of different factors (variables) may be identified and theoretical explanations generated (Ragin 1987). Thus case-oriented comparative work also depends on the identification and use of variables, and problems of commensurability remain. Nevertheless, a number of contrasts may be drawn between 'case' and 'variable'-oriented comparative strategies.

One contrast lies in the significance attached to national specificities. In the variable-oriented approach, national specificities may be called upon to explain departures from the regularities that are the primary focus of variable-oriented research. The case-oriented approach, in contrast, looks for difference rather than focusing primarily on similarity (but does not assume that every national society is somehow intrinsically unique and therefore non-comparable). In contrast to the variable-oriented approach, the case-oriented approach does not seek to limit the number of variables under investigation, but rather, begins from the premise that each case constitutes a whole. Thus a range of variables will be likely to contribute to any final explanation, and some factors (variables) will be more important in some societies than others. In summary: variable-oriented approaches to comparative cross-national research tend to start with a focus on similarity, to work with a limited range of variables thus abstracting from the national context, and to call upon national specificities only to explain 'deviations'. Case-oriented approaches begin with a focus on difference (as well as similarity), and treat societies as wholes rather than as abstractions, and tend to incorporate a wider range of variables.

Given that the processes contributing to a particular 'gender system' (or 'gender order') are highly complex, much of the comparative analysis in this book will be case, rather than variable-oriented (Crompton 2001). As we shall see, national specificities have been of considerable significance in structuring different modes of family/employment articulation, although these specificities are cross-cut both by more 'universal' capitalist processes (in particular, rising levels of work intensification), as well as normative assumptions relating to gender roles and gendered behaviour and the persisting differences between men and women that derive from these assumptions.

Chapters 2, 3 and 4 below will focus largely on the British case. This emphasis is in part shaped by the availability of empirical materials, but it may also be argued that a number of other factors render Britain a 'critical case' in discussions relating to employment and the family. Britain was the 'first industrial nation', and the 'modern family', with its associated gender division of labour and patterning of gender roles, emerged first of all in the British context. However, this is not to suggest that all other countries have simply followed the 'British' path. As we shall see, both state and employer policies have also played an important part in shaping family behaviour, and these policies have varied from country to country. The British case, however, is also of interest in that historically the state has not sought to 'interfere' in domestic and household arrangements. For example, responsibilities for kin (beyond the conjugal family) have not been precisely specified in Britain, as they have, for example, in Germany and Portugal. The British state has also adopted a relatively hands-off approach to employers, and the regulation of employment relations, as has the USA.

Some have argued that the relative lack of family and employment regulation in Britain makes this country a 'natural experiment' via which the expression of unrestricted 'preferences' may be investigated (Hakim 2004). This position will not be taken here. However, the contrast between Britain, the US and other European countries makes for a particularly fruitful comparative analysis. As we shall see, other countries, particularly in Scandinavia, offer considerably more by way of support for working parents. In the Nordic countries, the state has to a considerable extent assumed the responsibility for the organisation of non-parental daycare for children. In the second part of this book, therefore, through comparative analysis we will explore the impact of different policy regimes on the articulation of employment and family life and the division of domestic work.

Summary of chapters

Chapter 2 examines the emergence of the modern family, together with associated patterns of employment and gender roles. It is emphasised that the 'golden age' of the male breadwinner form of the nuclear family was a relatively short and unusual era in family history. The question of class differences in both gender roles and the division of labour within families, is examined. It is demonstrated that changes in women's (particularly mothers') employment since the 1980s have been accompanied by a considerable shift in gender role attitudes and attitudes to employed mothers, and that these attitudinal shifts are taking place amongst older, as well as younger, people. There would seem little likelihood, therefore, of a return to a dominant 'breadwinner' model of employment and family life, as some conservative authors would prefer. Nevertheless, some have argued that 'preferences' for such a family model (in which women reduce their levels of employment, or leave employment altogether) remain strong amongst a substantial minority. We therefore investigate the patterning and distribution of couples' work arrangements, as well as attitudes to gender roles, women's paid work and the family. This shows substantial variation by occupational class with routine and manual employees being the most conventionally 'familial', and routine and manual women the most likely to reduce their level of employment when they have children. The question is raised as to whether the class distribution of apparent preferences is in fact more of a rationalisation of the constraints of class-related inequalities.

In Chapter 3, we focus on organisational change, particularly in respect of careers. Women's lack of career opportunity has been a major campaigning focus for 'second-wave' feminism. Although a formal equality of women and men in the sphere of employment has been established by the mid 1970s, research in the 1970s and 1980s demonstrated that there was systematic discrimination against women in respect of organisational career advancement (Crompton and Jones 1984). Increasingly, the 1990s saw the end of the traditional, bureaucratic career path, in which long-service employees (usually men) were 'rewarded' with promotion. Careers in contemporary organisations have become more flexible and 'individualised', in that the onus is on the individual to make their own way through the career structure, rather than relying on organisational sponsorship. Individualised career paths are themselves an element of 'high-commitment' management practices, in which employers seek to encourage employee self-direction and 'commitment' to the organisation. Our case study evidence demonstrates that even at the lower levels of the job ladder, managers and supervisors were expected to show their 'commitment' by working long hours, and that these positions were therefore not attractive to people with caring responsibilities – in practice, women with children. An analysis of the BSA survey identified two groups amongst those seeking promotion – professional and managerial women and routine and manual men – who reported above-average levels of stress in combining employment with family responsibilities. It is argued that the pressures of the changing workplace are particularly difficult for these groups (and managerial and professional women are likely to have lower levels of domestic support than similar men).

Our examination of changes in employment, and in the employment relationship, continues in Chapter 4. Employees in Britain work the longest hours in Europe, although the prevalence of the 'one and a half' breadwinner model in Britain means that the total hours worked by households may be lower than in countries where the most frequently occurring combination is two full-time workers. Evidence from the JRF research indicated that most of those interviewed thought that working hours had increased, and that pressures to increase work intensity, as well as other managerial innovations such as target setting, were largely responsible. Similarly, a majority of the BSA respondents also thought that working hours had increased, and those respondents working longer hours (particularly households where both partners worked full time) found it particularly difficult to meet their family responsibilities. It would seem, therefore, that contemporary changes in work organisation associated with organisational 'delayering' and 'reengineering', as well as 'high-commitment' management practices, are increasing work–life pressures. However, employers are also being encouraged to introduce positive 'work–life' or 'family-friendly' policies, particularly in countries such as Britain and the US, where statutory supports are weak. These policies, however, may be undermined by other dimensions of managerial strategies that serve to increase work intensity.

In Chapter 5, the analysis moves up a level and begins to explore, via cross-national comparisons, the impact of statutory policies and provisions on the articulation of employment and family. Contrasting national production and welfare regimes are examined. The major focus of this chapter is on different national welfare regimes and their impact on inequalities of class and gender, as well as on work–life articulation. The impact of variations in national policies in respect of dual-earner families, employment and family life is visible in the cross-national comparisons, in that the Scandinavian countries report lower levels of work–life conflict even when a range of other factors are controlled for. Levels of work–life conflict are highest in Britain and the US, where working hours are long and family supports are marketised. However, the case of France proved to be something of a puzzle, in that even though relatively generous general family and dual-earner supports are provided in this country, the reported level of work–life conflict is relatively high.

Employment and family rearticulation, however, is affected not just by the changes employers might introduce into the employment relationship, as well as the presence or absence of state policies, but also by what happens within the household – in particular, the division of domestic work between women and men. In Chapter 6 the comparative analysis is extended into an exploration of the division of domestic labour and its impact (particularly on work–life conflict). Women still carry out most of the domestic work in all of the six countries in the ISSP sample. Of interest was the fact that men in Britain and the US carried out almost as much domestic work as men in the Nordic countries, and it was France and Portugal that reported the most gender traditional domestic division of labour. Indeed, in the case of France, the puzzle referred to above was in part explained by the finding that gender traditionalism in respect of domestic work contributes significantly to work–life conflict. Gender conservatives (who also tend to be gender essentialists) have argued that women (and men) will be happier if gender traditionalism prevails in the domestic sphere. However, in all countries, it was found that those women who reported the most 'liberal' combination (of gender role attitudes and division of domestic work) also reported the highest level of personal and family happiness.

Nevertheless, it remains the case that women are often divided amongst themselves, particularly in relation to matters such as childcare and whether or not mothers should take personal responsibility for it. In Chapter 7, we return full circle to the question of 'choice' and the extent to which women and families are more 'individualised' in 'reflexive modernity'. We find, via an analysis of the ISSP data, that couple working arrangements are significantly shaped by institutional constraints, particularly national working time and labour market regimes, but that attitudinal factors also play an important role. Attitudes are themselves shaped by circumstances, and attitudes to the employment of mothers were found to be related to occupational class, and employment, partnership and family status, as well as national variations. Individuals of lower occupational status were found to be generally more 'traditional' in respect of family and domestic arrangements, and indeed, women in the lower occupational categories are less likely to be in employment when their children are young. This class-associated pattern of women's employment behaviour will serve to deepen class inequalities.

In the final chapter, the empirical evidence and theoretical arguments developed in this book are brought together in order both to develop an extended critique of theories of 'choice' and individualisation, as well as to discuss the policy implications of our findings.

2 Caring and working

'Families' and 'employment' are inter-related, socially constructed, phenomena via which the division of labour between men and women is organised, and social production and reproduction thereby achieved. In this chapter, a brief historical description of the emergence of the 'modern' family in Britain, together with associated patterns of moralities and normative beliefs relating to 'the family', will be given. We will also examine recent transformations in these arrangements, as well as their state of contemporary flux, focusing on the changing pattern of men's and women's employment within couple households. We will also look more closely at changing attitudes to the family, gender roles and women's employment. In particular, recent debates addressing the question of whether mothers in Britain have 'chosen' to take up paid work or not will be examined in some detail.

'Modern' family theory

The functionalist theory of the 'modern' (or 'standard') family was a key element of the 'orthodox consensus' (Giddens 1982; Cheal 1991) that emerged in sociology after the Second World War and persisted until the 1970s and even the 1980s. This model (as developed by e.g., Parsons 1949; Goode 1964) viewed the family as an institution that fulfilled universal prerequisites for the survival of human societies. The smooth functioning of societies, it was argued, depended on the proper articulation of the interdependent parts. Therefore as societies change, so will families change to meet new needs. In particular, it was argued, the major change in family life that followed upon the transition to industrialism was the emergence of the 'conjugal' or 'nuclear' family, consisting of parents and children, and lacking in particularly close ties to extended kin. It was argued that this modern or 'standard' family does not conflict with the requirements of an industrial economy as it is small enough to be highly mobile. Its major functions are the socialisation of children and personality stabilisation or 'tension management' – previous

family functions such as children's education, as well as directly productive activities, having been reallocated to the state and employing
organisations. Within the nuclear family, the husband/father was described as the 'instrumental leader' and market provider, whilst the
wife/mother was the 'expressive leader' and carer and nurturer (Parsons
1949).

Debates within the framework of this particular paradigm tended to
focus on issues such as the extent to which the 'extended' family had in
fact been replaced by the 'nuclear' family (Young and Willmott 1962;
Laslett 1965), the extent to which the 'modern' family had indeed lost
its functions, and so on. However, as Cheal (1991) has argued, from the
1970s standard family theory was 'blown apart' by numerous criticisms.
The universality of the 'modern' family and its functions was challenged
by the recognition of the diversity of actual family forms, as well as
non-'family' (or kin) institutions (such as neighbourhood and friendship
groupings) that met 'family'-type functions (Morgan 1985; Gittins
1993: ch. 3). As we have seen in Chapter 1, the assumption that the
family existed 'by nature' (implicit in structural functionalist theorising) was also challenged. Many of these criticisms came from feminists,
who pointed to the extent of conflict and tensions within the family,
as well as the crucial role played by family obligations and the conventional gender division of labour with which they were associated in
perpetuating women's subordinate position in society (Barrett and
Mackintosh 1991).

There would be few (if any) contemporary defenders of structural
functionalist theories of the 'modern' family. Nevertheless, standard
family theory had a number of foci that remain important to our arguments. First, its emphasis on the 'fit' between the family and the prevailing economic order may have made unreasonable assumptions as to
the actual 'goodness of fit' that in fact prevailed, but its key insight –
that family and economy are inevitably inter-connected and mutually
developing – was correct. Second, the theory did have the gender division of labour at its core, even though it made unwarranted assumptions as to the 'naturalness' of this division of labour. In short, the
'standard theory' of the family may be roundly and rightly criticised for
the answers it gave to the questions it raised, but not for the nature of
the questions themselves.

Industrialisation, employment and the family

Patriarchy, or the rule of the father, has characterised most known
societies for most of human recorded history. Men and women have

always worked to generate the resources needed in order to sustain and reproduce themselves. With considerable overgeneralisation, productive activities in pre-industrial (largely agricultural) societies had three characteristics relevant to the arguments being developed here: (i) there was a relative lack of separation between the household and most productive activity; (ii) there was a degree of segregation between men's and women's productive tasks, closely linked to women's domestic responsibilities; and (iii) men retained ownership and overall control. Thus patriarchy was a major organising societal principle.

With the development of industry in Britain from the mid-eighteenth century, manufacturing, trade and commerce began to take precedence over agricultural production. These changes were accompanied by massive social transformations in both employment and family life. The rapidly expanding population increasingly moved into urban centres, new occupations and specialisms emerged, and new class locations were forged as the ownership and control of productive capital began to equal and supersede the ownership and control of land as the key to power and wealth. In the early stages of the development of industrialism, women, married and unmarried, still took an active role in money-making activities. As a tract of 1743 addressed to unmarried servant girls put it: 'You cannot expect to marry in such a manner as neither of you shall have occasion to work, and none but a fool will take a wife whose bread must be earned solely by his labour and who will contribute nothing towards it herself' (cited in Pinchbeck 1981: 1–2).

Amongst the emerging middle classes, in the eighteenth and the first part of the nineteenth centuries, women as wives made an essential contribution to business activities. They brought in capital (via marriage and kin connections) for the development of enterprises, as well as working within the business itself (Davidoff and Hall 1987). However, upon marriage a woman's property became that of her husband, and, until the married women's property acts of 1870 and 1882, women had no legal rights to their earnings within marriage, or any property they brought to the marriage or acquired whilst married. Increasing prosperity amongst the middle classes, therefore, was a largely male affair. In any case (and of equal importance to our argument), throughout the nineteenth century there were profound cultural changes under way relating to both the division of labour between men and women and the manner in which it was justified.

The middle-class ideology of 'separate spheres' for men and women developed and was, increasingly, put into practice. As described by Davidoff and Hall:

Their [the middle classes'] rejection of landed wealth as the source of honour and insistence on the primacy of the inner spirit brought with it a preoccupation with the domestic as a necessary basis for a good Christian life. Evangelical categorizations of the proper spheres of men and women provided the basis for many subsequent formulations and shaped the common sense of the nineteenth century social world. Men were to be active in the world as citizens and entrepreneurs, women were to be dependent, as wives and mothers. (1987: 450)

Thus by the mid nineteenth century, 'whenever family finances would permit, the energy, organisational skill and sense of commitment which middle-class women had put into economic activity were deflected into domestic affairs' (1987: 313).

The ideology of domesticity as the 'proper' sphere of activity for women went beyond the gendered division of labour as such, as it also had a significant moral dimension. Williams (1991) has argued that 'domesticity' was the other side of the coin that acted as a counterweight to the growth of possessive individualism. Early liberalism had embodied a number of moral prescriptions relating to civic responsibilities, but by the nineteenth century such moral prescriptions had become less important and the individualistic pursuit of self-interest was increasingly celebrated. Virtue, selflessness and morality increasingly became the preserve of women, or rather, of the wives and mothers confined to the domestic sphere: 'only by giving up all self-interest and "living for others" could women achieve the purity that allowed them to establish moral reference points for their families and for society at large' (Williams 1991: 71).

The 'luxury' of domestic morality and the stay-at-home wife was initially established within the middle classes. Amongst the emerging proletariat or working poor, the first half of the nineteenth century was characterised by a 'family wage economy' in which wives and children participated in paid employment that was essential to the survival of the family unit. Among the industrial classes, whole families were employed (in, for example, mining and the cotton industry) and the earnings of wives and children were often included in the sum paid to the head of the family. With some notable exceptions (such as the cotton industry) large-scale factory production was not the norm and much industrial production was carried out as domestic production (i.e., outworking), and in small workshops. In these circumstances, children were seen as an economic resource, and birth rates were high – as were rates of infant and child mortality.

In these conditions of superexploitation, labour power was, as Seccombe (1993: 73) puts it, 'extensively' consumed and reproduced as the poor were literally 'used up'. The 'bottom half of urban working class ... were overworked and underprovisioned to such an extent that they were unable to maintain the vitality of their labour power over the course of several generations ... Growing up in conditions of residential squalor, people were put to work by the age of eight or ten and used up by forty ... No matter, they could be replaced by young rural recruits.' For example, an 1843 report of the Factory Commissioners on the notoriously long hours and bad working conditions of dressmakers and milliners in London indicated that their working life was estimated at not more than three or four years, and that only a 'constant accession of fresh hands from the country' enabled the business to be carried on (Pinchbeck 1981: 309).

The second industrial revolution from the 1870s onwards brought with it a massive increase in the development of steam power together with improvements in transport and urban amenities such as piped water and sewers (the conditions of the urban poor, as well as the health of urban residents more generally, had long been a focus of reforming concern). The shift of production into larger, more technically advanced factory units, together with the decline of subcontracting and domestic industries, increased the number of relatively skilled jobs for men and reduced the demand for female and child labour. With these changes, Seccombe argues that there was a shift from an 'extensive' to an 'intensive' mode of consuming and reproducing labour power. Working hours were legislated in 1847 (the Ten Hours Act), but the pace of work itself was intensified. The Elementary Education Acts of the 1870s and the extension of schooling decreased the economic benefits of children whilst raising their costs.

Against the background of these changes, the working-class male-breadwinner wage norm began to emerge, and was finally consolidated, during the second half of the nineteenth century: 'The male-breadwinner ideal is the notion that the wage earned by a husband ought to be sufficient to support his family without his wife and young children having to work for pay' (Seccombe 1993: 111ff.). Although the breadwinner ideal was a relatively new one (at least as far as the labouring poor were concerned), it nevertheless reinforced established patriarchal principles in confirming the position of the man as the 'head of household'. As we have seen, the middle-class ideology of 'separate spheres' had been established by the middle of the nineteenth century. The driving forces of this ideological development were primarily cultural and religious. However, although cultural and religious factors were no doubt of importance in establishing the breadwinner ideal amongst working-class people, there were also significant economic arguments for instituting the breadwinner norm.

The labouring family in the eighteenth and early nineteenth centuries had been a unit of coproducers to which all who were able made their contribution. The 'second industrial revolution' and its consequences led to a decline in family subcontracting and opportunities to produce at home. Increasingly, job opportunities were individualised and moved outside the family unit. Patriarchal convention made women a potential source of cheap labour (compulsory education having removed young children, the other source). Thus Seccombe (1993: 113) argues that the consolidation of the male breadwinner norm was 'the outcome of a protracted struggle in which the mainstream of the union movement reacted in a narrow exclusionist fashion to the very real threat which the mass employment of women as cheap labour represented to the job security and wage levels of skilled tradesmen' (see also Humphries 1982). Women were not excluded from factory work – indeed, as Pinchbeck (1981: 314) demonstrates, factory women were well paid in comparison to needleworkers, domestic servants, agricultural workers and homeworkers (the other main occupational categories for women). However, male unionists and employers excluded women from the better-paid craft positions and factory jobs. That is, increasingly, occupational segregation by sex was used as a mechanism to ensure that women did not compete for employment directly with men.

In claiming the right to a 'family wage', trade unions and their members were engaging in a discourse that resonated with the middle-class ideology of separate spheres – if middle-class women required protection from the vulgarities and moral pitfalls of the 'public sphere', then why not working-class wives and daughters?[1] Indeed, much of the debate relating to women's employment took a distinctly moral tone in relation to the dangers of mixing the sexes in the absence of proper patriarchal supervision (Humphries 1984). Economic necessity also cut across the breadwinner ideal. Even though to have a working wife was widely considered to be shameful amongst the superior working class, many wives worked by necessity because of their husband's low wages. Thus the issue of the family wage was cross-cut by class and gender: 'While poor men defended their wives' employment rights, the wives of artisans endorsed attempts to limit female access to their husbands' trades' (Seccombe 1993: 118).

---

[1] These attitudes persisted well into the twentieth century. An interview with a female bank employee (born 1946, interviewed 1996) described her career decision-making process in the following terms: 'I knew my father (a skilled machine maintenance fitter) didn't want me to go and work in a factory office – that was the only thing he said – 'cos of his experience of going in and out of factories – which can be quite rough – even the office premises can be fairly horrendous – he didn't want me to go into factory premises.'

The question of women's employment, however, went beyond that of wives alone. It should be remembered that right up until the end of the nineteenth century, families were in constant danger of being broken by the death of a spouse. Indeed, when the impact of death is taken into account, the proportion of 'broken' families and lone parent children in the nineteenth century was similar to that of today (Anderson 1985). Even those who supported the 'family wage' and the exclusion of women recognised – albeit to a limited extent – that all women did not have a male provider and that some would be constrained to work to support themselves and their dependants. The pursuit of a 'family wage', therefore, may have raised the general level of working men's earnings, but its impact was negative for women as a whole. Women's lack of economic independence was felt at all levels of society. Nineteenth-century fiction is replete with examples of the dire fates of middle-class women lacking sufficient economic support in an effective male provider, forced into governessing or genteel penury. Indeed, 'superfluous women' were identified as a social problem amongst the middle classes, and schemes developed to ship them to the colonies as potential wives.

The breadwinner norm also had an impact on family life. Men's identification as sole breadwinners was accompanied by an increasing emphasis on the household as a woman's sphere – indeed, it was widely seen as improper for men to undertake domestic work. A man's contribution to the family was seen as having been fulfilled once a sufficient portion of his income had been handed over to his wife. Women had always taken the major responsibility for domestic work, but with the consolidation of the breadwinner ideal, the division of labour between men (market work) and women (caring and domestic work) became increasingly rigid. Living standards amongst the working classes improved in the second half of the nineteenth century, but these improvements tended to increase, rather than decrease, the amount of domestic labour required of women. Domestic labour would also be increased by the presence of numerous children. However, from 1890 to 1920 there was a sharp decline in marital fertility, and the number of children borne per married woman was halved in two generations (Seccombe 1993: 157; Irwin 2003: 572).

Deliberate family limitation was originally a middle-class phenomenon (Banks 1954) and had a noticeable class and occupational dimension. The skilled working class were early family limiters, followed by semi and unskilled workers.[2] Any explanation of fertility decline will be

---

[2] Seccombe (1993) argues that this occupational variation is a reflection of the relative value of children's earning power to the family unit, as low-income families would

multidimensional, incorporating both economic and cultural factors. Children had become considerably more expensive. Whilst, in the recent past, children had from a young age contributed to the family economy, the advent of mass schooling meant that parents had to support dependent children, and for a longer period (Irwin 2003: 573). Mortality rates were in decline, and children came to be seen as less of an economic asset in the present, and more of an investment for the future. As Irwin (2003: 575) argues, these changes fed into new norms regarding morally appropriate family behaviour, and working-class 'respectability' became linked to modest family size.

Medical interventions emphasised the dangers of repeated child-bearing for women's health, and there is ample evidence that many women were anxious to limit their families even before fertility decline. Seccombe (1993) argues that a decisive factor in family limitation lay in the changing nature of the conjugal relationship, given that effective 'stopping' of further births would depend crucially on male cooperation (before the widespread introduction of barrier methods, coitus inter-ruptus and abstinence were the main methods of contraception). Thus fertility decline was not simply a matter of external circumstances and constraints, but also an outcome of pressures, by women, from within 'the family' itself.

In summary, this brief historical sketch has argued that:

- In contrast to the arguments of universalist 'standard' family theorists, the 'male breadwinner' nuclear family was not a normal or natural functional adaptation to the development of industrialism, but emerged out of a conjunction of specific historical circumstances.
- Changes in family organisation are outcomes of both 'economic' and 'cultural' developments. The bourgeois ideology of 'separate spheres' for men and women, that emphasised female purity and selflessness and included the withdrawal of women from economic activity and public life, meshed positively with both increasingly individualised wage systems and struggles to obtain decent wages for working-class men. As individuals, women lost out in economic terms.
- Family change is a consequence of pressures from within the family itself – especially from women – as well as economic and cultural developments in the wider society.

benefit from the earnings of teenage children. Note that Seccombe's account has been critiqued by Szreter, who argues that fertility decline was not linear by class, but mediated by diverse local cultural and occupational contexts. For a discussion see Irwin (2003: 574).

Into the twentieth century

By the early decades of the twentieth century, official statistics in Britain recorded the rate of married women's employment at under 10 per cent. This figure is likely to be an underestimate of the actual amount of paid labour undertaken by married women. Less-well-off women have always sought to generate money for their families by a variety of means including seasonal agricultural work, homeworking, taking in lodgers or laundry, informal (paid) childcare, and so on (Glucksmann 2000). In some areas of Britain, such as parts of Lancashire and the East Midlands, a greater proportion of married women remained in employment. Nevertheless, the male breadwinner principle was normatively established and widely accepted. For example, during both world wars women were drafted, with the agreement of the trade unions, into occupations (such as engineering) that had previously been reserved for men, but on condition that they left these jobs at the end of hostilities (Walby 1986). During the economic recession and high unemployment of the 1930s, marriage bars for women were commonplace in many occupations, not least because of the assumption that the jobs that did exist should be reserved for men.

In other respects, the position of women improved. The campaigns of 'first-wave' feminism had focused largely (although by no means entirely) on women's lack of civil rights.[3] Married women were given voting rights after the First World War, and universal franchise was achieved by the 1920s. Although the decline in the birth rate was sustained throughout the 1930s, there were few pressures to increase employment amongst married women – not least because, as noted above, rates of unemployment amongst men were high (although married women's employment did rise slightly during this period). Divorce was difficult and expensive, and from the outside at least, the conjugal male breadwinner family appeared as a stable and 'natural' phenomenon.

The end of the Second World War was followed by the election of a reformist Labour government with a commitment to 'one nation' policies (Hudson and Williams 1995). These included full employment as well as the expansion of education and state welfare services such

---

[3] First-wave feminism was not concerned only with the vote but also with social reform (e.g., Eleanor Rathbone and the campaign for family allowances, Florence Nightingale's work for public health, Beatrice Webb and Sylvia Pankhurst on women's low wages), as well as with legislation that discriminated against women. For example, Josephine Butler's campaign against the Contagious Diseases Act (Walkowitz 1980).

as health and housing. The state was also committed to economic regulation ('Keynesianism'), to be achieved via the control of demand via fiscal measures as well as the direct control of production as a result of nationalisation of basic industries and services (mining, railways, gas, electricity, water). Other state provision, of services such as health and education, was extended.[4] The trade union movement and employers' organisations were brought into the arena of political decision-making, most notably in attempts to hold down the level of wage increases via successive incomes policies. These measures constituted the 'mid-century social compromise' (Crouch 1999) described in Chapter 1. Birth rates increased, and married women employed during the Second World War withdrew from the labour market into domestic life. Much of the social policy implemented during this period was explicitly built around the male breadwinner model. For example, the Beveridge Report (1942), that laid the foundations for postwar social policy, commented that 'The attitude of the housewife to gainful employment outside the home is not and should not be the same as that of the single woman. She has other duties ... In the next thirty years housewives as mothers have vital work to do in ensuring the adequate continuance of the British Race and of British Ideals in the world' (cited in Wilson 1977: 151–2). In 1951, only about a third of all women of working age or more were economically active. This was the period during which the 'standard theory' of the 'modern' family was formulated. By the mid-1980s, Anderson (1985) was describing the 'modern family life cycle' as characterised by early marriage, early childbearing and family limitation.

'One nation' policies, lasting approximately from 1944 to 1975, did serve to reduce inequalities in Britain, even though they were premised on the inequality of the sexes. Women were in large part the formal equals of men in the civil sphere, but, nevertheless, in the sphere of employment, substantial inequalities persisted. A number of these were formally constituted. Skilled trades such as printing, for example, were barred to women (Cockburn 1983), and medical schools had 'gender quotas' that rationed places for women (Witz 1992). Organisations such as the clearing banks (amongst the most prestigious of the financial institutions) had, until the 1960s, maintained 'women only' grades (lacking in promotion opportunities) into which women were required

---

[4] This might be described as Fordism but the definition is a loose one; as many have argued, there are problems in describing the British case as Fordist (Hudson and Williams 1995).

to move on marriage. It was legal to pay women at a lower rate than men, even when they carried out the same job. All of these practices were built around the assumption that a woman would be provided for by her husband, and would leave employment at the birth of her first child. These assumptions were also built into state welfare policies. For example, married women were enabled to 'opt out' of state pension contributions, and benefits were denied to divorced and separated women – even if they had responsibility for children – if it could be demonstrated that the woman was cohabiting with another man (Pateman 1989).

By the 1960s, the pattern of early marriage followed by a period of compressed childbearing and rearing meant that many women began returning to paid employment by their late 20s and early 30s. A characteristic 'M'-shaped pattern of women's economic activity was established, that is, high levels of participation in the youngest age groups, followed by a sharp dip during the childbearing years, followed by a substantial rise as women returned to the labour force (Hakim 1979). Married women who returned to the labour force in the 1960s and 1970s not only faced both formal and informal exclusionary practices, as described above, but were also relatively underqualified in comparison to men. This was in part a consequence of barriers in respect of initial job training and access, compounded by the fact that many women (and the parents responsible for their support) considered it 'not worth' investing in education and training for girls and young women. Thus even though Equal Pay and Sex Discrimination legislation was implemented by 1975, women's pay and labour market situation continued to be vastly inferior to that of men.

If 'first wave' feminism was largely concerned with civil equalities, 'second wave' feminism was largely concerned with economic equality, and the struggle for sex equality in the world of paid work was a major theme. Women faced discrimination as individuals, and it was (and is) also the case that 'women's' occupations (for example, nursing, secretarial work) were low paid compared to 'men's' occupations such as skilled craft jobs. Even when in employment, most women did not earn sufficient to maintain an independent household. As divorce rates continued to rise (in part as a consequence of the Divorce Reform Act of 1969), increasing numbers of women (and children) found themselves in poverty. Rising divorce rates were themselves an expression of the rapid change in sexual and social mores that took place from the 1960s onwards, an era viewed by many as representing the first stage in the 'decline' of the modern family and family values (Dench 1999; Kristol 1998).

These changes in family life and the position of women were being played out against a backdrop of political developments that put a decisive end to 'one nation' political strategies. Up until the 1960s, even 1970s, Conservative and Labour governments had shared a commitment to policies of state intervention in the economy and the attempt to raise living standards. This convergence between the major political parties was summed up in the label of 'Butskellism' that was given to this era, an amalgam of the surnames of Labour (Gaitskell) and Conservative (Butler) politicians. However, in 1979, with the election of the Conservative Thatcher government, a decisive political shift took place. The government was elected on a reforming platform that included curbs on trade union power and influence, and a greater role for market forces – that is, the implementation of neoliberal economic and social policies. Conservative strategies included privatisation and the removal of controls and protections, such as the Wages Councils, that had set wage rates for workers in poorly paid low-unionised industries, and the removal of rights conferred by the Employment Protection Act of 1975, together with cuts in taxation that had their most beneficial impact at the top of the income range. In short, economic neoliberalism had well and truly arrived on the British political scene.

Deindustrialisation and deregulation from 1979 led to a massive increase in inequalities of income and wealth (Joseph Rowntree Foundation 1995; Hills 2004). During the period of 'one nation' politics (particularly the 1960s and early years of the 1970s), income inequalities had declined, but there was a sharp increase in income inequality from the end of the 1970s. By 1992, wages for the lowest-paid workers were lower in real terms than in 1975, median wages had grown by 35 per cent, but high wages had grown by 50 per cent (Joseph Rowntree Foundation 1995: 20). Between 1979 and 1986, out of £8.1 billion in tax cuts, nearly half went to the richest 10 per cent and almost two-thirds to the richest 20 per cent, and social security payments accounted for a fifth of all income in 1992 and 1993 (Goodman et al. 1997). The sharp increase in women's employment during the 1980s no doubt kept many households in conditions of relative comfort, but will have contributed to widening inequalities between 'one-earner' and 'two-earner' households.

The women who entered (or re-entered) the labour force in the 1980s and subsequently would have been rather different, in aggregate, from women entering (or re-entering) the labour force in the 1960s. Qualification levels have risen rapidly among both men and women, but faster among women. By the beginning of the twenty-first century (2001), in the 25–34 age group there is practically no difference in qualification levels between men and women, and 20 per cent of women, and 22 per cent of men, have a university degree (Dench *et al.* 2002). Women today are less likely to have taken extended periods out of employment or, increasingly, to have left employment at all. Women's aspirations have risen, and, at least in a formal sense, policy and organisational contexts are now supportive of these aspirations. We have come quite a long way since Beveridge.

Changing attitudes to the family, gender roles and mother's employment behaviour

It has been argued that the nature of the transformations in the gendered articulation of paid employment with family and caring work has reflected historical change in both economic and political circumstances, as well as normative and ideological change within the household (particularly amongst women) and the wider national context. Above we have briefly described recent economic and political changes, and their impact on women's employment and family life. To what extent have these changes been reflected in the way people think about women's employment and the family? In fact, attitudes to gender roles and women's employment have changed considerably in the last two decades. Here we will draw on evidence for 1989, 1994 and 2002 from the British Social Attitudes surveys (see Data and Methods: ch. 1, p. 23). Table 2.1 shows that there has been a steady decline, among both men and women, in the proportion of respondents who support the once-conventional view that 'a man's job is to earn money, a woman's is to look after the home and family'. Whereas around a third of men took this view in 1989, this is now down to a fifth. The equivalent change among women has been from a quarter to one in seven.

There has been a corresponding change in attitudes to women's employment, particularly that of mothers. In 1989, over two thirds of those interviewed thought that a woman should 'stay at home' when

Table 2.1. *'A man's job is to earn money; a woman's job is to look after the home and family'*, *BSA surveys, 1989–2002*

% who agree	1989	Base	1994	Base	2002	Base
Men	32	587	26	448	20	852
Women	26	720	21	536	15	1108
All	28	1307	24	984	17	1960

Table 2.2. *'Women should stay at home when there is a child under school age', BSA surveys, 1989–2002*

% who think women should stay at home	1989	Base	1994	Base	2002	Base
Men	67	*587*	60	*448*	51	*852*
Women	61	*720*	51	*536*	46	*1108*
All	64	*1307*	55	*984*	48	*1960*

she had a child under school age, by 2002 the proportion of people holding this view had declined to under a half (Table 2.2). Another feature of Tables 2.1 and 2.2 is that men tend to hold more 'conventional' gender role attitudes than women; that is, both men and women have become more gender 'liberal', but the attitudinal difference between the sexes persists.

It may also be noted that the extent of attitudinal change in a more 'liberal' direction was greater between 1989 and 1994 than in the 1994 to 2002 period, although the trend still continues in the latter period. In fact, women's employment rose most rapidly during the 1980s, and levelled off somewhat during the 1990s (although employment rates amongst mothers of young children continued to rise; see Dench *et al.* 2002). This suggests that rates of attitudinal change have in fact followed quite closely on actual changes in women's employment behaviour.[5]

These changes in people's views appear likely to be permanent. A comparison, over the three surveys, of people born in the same year suggests that in the older age 'cohorts' men and women are uniformly becoming more liberal in their attitudes. For example, whereas in 1989 74 per cent of women born between 1933 and 1945 agreed that a woman should stay at home with her children when they were under school age, by 1994 the percentage holding this view amongst this birth cohort had declined to 63 per cent, and by 2002, to 58 per cent. Older people are still more gender conservative than younger people, but age differences in gender role conservatism have narrowed since 1989, and there is little evidence of increasing gender conservatism with age (Crompton *et al.* 2003).

---

[5] This pattern of attitudinal change – i.e., extensive attitudinal change in the 1980s followed by a slowing down in the 1990s – was also found amongst women interviewed successively in 1980, 1993 and 1999. See McRae (2003: 326); see also Crompton *et al.* (2003).

Changes in behaviour, as well as attitudes, are reflected in the three surveys. In 1989, 62 per cent of the mothers interviewed reported that they had stayed at home with a child under school age, but by 1994 this had declined to 52 per cent, and by 2002, the percentage of mothers reporting 'staying at home' had declined even further to 48 per cent. Changes in mothers' employment behaviour have been recent and rapid. The majority of mothers of children born in the 1960s and 1970s simply did not 'go out to work', as reflected in qualitative evidence from the JRF research. In part this was because of normative pressures – as Irene puts it, 'It was just what you did':

IRENE (born 1950, basic grade supermarket worker, two children): Then it was just what you did. They didn't seem to work a lot like they do now … When I had mine it wasn't the thing. You left work and that was it … Once they were at school I had more time so it was a case of going back to work, but then the holidays … though I did manage to get them in somewhere. What I earned didn't cover that but I kept the job and it kept me out of the house.

Important though these normative pressures were in the shaping of behaviour, it is essential to remember that before legislation relating to sex discrimination, many women were simply required to leave employment when they had children:

RACHEL (born 1943, bank worker, two children): There was no such thing as maternity leave. You *had* to leave when you were six months pregnant. You couldn't stay longer than that. You certainly couldn't go back.

NERYS (born 1949, bank worker, two children): I didn't go to work (when children were young), it was as simple as that. I went back to work when the youngest was 7. I only worked for eight hours a week for quite a while … Things were different 27 years ago. For instance, your job wasn't held open for you as it is now.

As we have already noted, the last decade has seen a substantial increase in the employment of mothers with young children, and indeed the rate of increase has been much greater amongst mothers than amongst women in aggregate. However, there are substantial class variations in mothers' employment. As Table 2.3 demonstrates, amongst the mothers interviewed in the 2002 BSA survey, there is over a 20 per cent difference in the proportions of managerial and professional, as compared to routine and manual, mothers reporting that they had stayed at home when they had a child under school age.[6]

---

[6] There are a number of social class schemes currently available. In the analysis of the BSA survey, the three-category version of the NS-SEC classification (see *The National Statistics Socio-Economic Classification User Manual*, Office for National Statistics, April 2002,

Table 2.3. *Employment of mothers when a child was under school age, by occupational class, BSA/ISSP 2002*

	Managerial and professional	Intermediate	Routine and manual	Total
% reporting in employment[a]	62**	50	40	50
% reporting staying at home[b]	38	50	60**	50
N	255	173	319	747

**p < .01.

[a]managerial and professionals significantly more likely to be in employment than routine/manuals.

[b]routine/manuals significantly more likely to stay at home than managerial and professionals.

The increase in employment amongst mothers of young children has been a relatively recent phenomenon. However, as suggested by Table 2.3, rates of increase have not been evenly distributed throughout the occupational structure. As Rake *et al.* (2000: ch. 3) have demonstrated, low- and mid-skilled mothers are more likely to reduce their employment than mothers with higher skills, thus the cost of motherhood (in forgone earnings) is greater amongst these women. These trends are also demonstrated in the BSA data. In the 2002 survey, amongst mothers with a child under 5, 44 per cent of routine and manual mothers were 'looking after the home' as compared to 28 per cent of professional and managerial mothers, and whereas 41 per cent of managerial and professional mothers were in full-time employment, only 15 per cent of routine and manual mothers were working full time.

Not surprisingly, therefore, there are variations by class in the combinations of employment statuses within households, particularly as to whether or not the woman is working full time (Table 2.4; here we use the

also Rose and Pevalin 2002) is employed. Our analyses using this scheme sometimes do not include the 'Intermediate' category. This is because the NS-SEC classification places the majority of self-employed men in the 'Intermediate' group. As the ESRC/ISSP questions were asked of employees only, women are considerably overrepresented in the 'Intermediate' group (in any case, women are overrepresented in the 'Intermediate' grouping as it includes lower-level clerical workers, the largest single occupational category for women). The BHPS data uses the five-category version of the Registrar General's Social Class classification, which has been superseded by the NS-SEC. Nevertheless, the 'Managerial and Professional' category largely corresponds to the 'Managerial and Professional' category of the NS-SEC. 'Skilled Non-manual' and 'Skilled Manual' categories mesh broadly with NS-SEC 'Intermediates', and the three 'Manual' categories with the 'Routine and Manual' NS-SEC.

Table 2.4. *Household employment status by occupational class,*[a] *couple households only, BHPS (British Household Panel Survey) 2001*

| | Registrar General Social Class (5 categories) | | | | | |
	Prof./ managerial	Skilled non-manual	Skilled manual	Partly skilled occupations	Unskilled	Total
Both ft	52	45	41	35	23	45
Man ft, woman pt	26	36	35	38	43	33
Man ft, woman no job	13	8	19	15	15	14
Woman ft, man pt/no job	5	5	2	4	3	4
Pt/no job only	3	6	3	9	15	5
Total	100	100	100	100	100	100
	2,673	1,505	1,418	942	295	6,833

[a] See p. 45 note.

British Household Panel Study, as the number of respondents is considerably greater than in the BSA survey. The BSA data reveal the same pattern).

These variations by class in the distribution of market work between couples reflect the increasing polarisation between those who are 'cash-rich, time-poor' and those with fewer material resources but (supposedly) more resources of time available. From the perspective of work/family articulation, it may be suggested that individuals and households with more resources of time available might experience fewer stresses in managing their employment and family lives. As we shall see in Chapter 3, individuals in the 'routine and manual' occupational class do report shorter working hours, and lower levels of work–family conflict, than individuals in professional and managerial occupations. However, it is vital to remember that although levels of work–family conflict might be lower amongst routine and manual workers, this is achieved at some economic cost as far as individuals and families are concerned. In the 2002 BSA survey, 61 per cent of employees in managerial and professional occupations reported an annual household income of £32,000 and above, compared with only 22 per cent of those in routine and manual occupations. Carolynne, a basic grade supermarket employee aged 27, describes the (2002) finances of a household consisting of two (early) retired parents (one working part time), herself, her sister and her sister's baby:

I earn £4.47 an hour – £630 a month. My sister (who works at the same supermarket) gets about the same for part time because she gets working family tax credit. Mum gets £30 a week pension plus about £60 a month dinner lady. Don't know what dad (an ex-warehouse employee) gets – he's got a private pension and that's all until he's 65.

The annual income of the three women is just over £17,000 (before tax and deductions). The father's pension is unlikely to take the total household income beyond £20,000. As Blossfeld and Drobnic (2001: 381) have argued, 'the decrease in gender inequality in terms of labour-force participation is accompanied by an increase in social class inequal-ities'. However, Carolynne's example suggests that even when working-class women are in employment, family finances are still likely to be somewhat constrained. For Carolynne, a 'good job' would pay £5.50 an hour, but she remains in supermarket retail because the flexible hours enable her to share the care of her nephew.

Furthermore, as Warren (2003) has argued, even though working-class households may be in employment for fewer hours in total than middle-class households, their 'time poverty' is of a different order. Working hours organised around caring responsibilities, particularly for children, may result in few hours spent together as a family and thus low 'time quality' (Perrons 1999). Warren's (2003: 742) analysis of the BHPS demonstrates that 50 per cent of dual manual couples with children worked split schedules (i.e., partners reporting that they worked at different times during the day), as compared to 24 per cent of middle-class couples. Fathers in split schedule families made a significant con-tribution to childcare. However, qualitative research suggests that 'time quality' in such families is at a premium. James (aged 39, children aged 8 and 10) was a craft grade supermarket employee who was very family-oriented and shared the care of his children: 'I always thought that I'd get married and have children, I just thought that would happen. We lived together for a few years and wanted to start a family and got married so we could do it. Children are your lives, your own lives go on the back burner.' He describes his childcare arrangements as follows:

We work shifts. I was on nights and she worked days and now it has changed. I work Monday to Saturday early mornings and she works Friday, Saturday and Sunday. It's been a nightmare really ... Childcare is very expensive, there should be places to take your kids. We share childcare, but we both work so we have to work out our hours. We have a rota here and so I try and work the rota around her hours. This place doesn't pay well enough for two people not to work.

As the BHPS evidence analysed by Warren demonstrates, 'shift parenting' (see also La Valle et al. 2002) has a marked class dimension.

In the absence of two 'middle-class' incomes, split scheduling may still be required, as the example of Joyce (a female 'main breadwinner') demonstrates:

JOYCE (aged 41, council employee (managerial), 2 children 13 and 4, partner supermarket employee): He works nights. I don't get home from work until half four, quarter to five, so we all sit down to a meal together. So he cooks meals during the week. At weekends I tend to do more with the younger one because I haven't seen so much of her during the week. Sundays we try and make a family day. He works Sunday nights. I also do evening meetings so then my dad picks her [i.e., the younger child] up from school, I go back there to have tea and see her for a bit, and then I go back to work and mum and dad put her to bed, keep her overnight, and take her to school in the morning.

Class, mothers' employment patterns and attitudes to family life

Both age and occupational class have an impact on whether or not a woman is likely to be employed with under school age children. Older women are three times as likely to have stayed at home when their children were under school age as younger women, and routine and manual women are twice as likely to have stayed at home as professional and managerial women.[7] As we discussed in Chapter 1, some authors have argued that women's employment patterns, particularly when their children are young, are a reflection of their 'choices' (Hakim 2000) and/or 'moral rationalities' (Duncan and Edwards 1999). How does our attitudinal data relate to these arguments?

How children are cared for is a highly contentious, not to say emotive, issue. The ideology of 'separate spheres' located women, particularly mothers, within the home (as indeed did 'standard' sociological family theory), and mothers are widely considered to be the most appropriate carers for young children. Indeed, an absence of maternal care has been argued to be psychologically damaging. In the 1950s and 1960s, an influential text suggested that children lacking in maternal care were likely to suffer mental health problems as adults (Bowlby 1965). In Britain, this was widely interpreted to mean that one-to-one maternal care was essential, and such arguments contributed to the running down of the network of state-sponsored nursery provision that had been established during the Second World War (Riley 1983). Much of the debate surrounding the increase in mothers' employment, therefore,

---

[7] Logistic regression odds ratios, ISSP 2002 survey. Both associations were highly significant.

has tended to focus on the question of whether non-maternal care is 'bad' for children. Another closely related topic relates to the motivations of mothers themselves. To what extent do mothers (or fathers, for that matter) of young children 'choose' to specialise in childcare rather than employment (or vice versa), and to what extent should these 'preferences' be taken into account in making policy recommendations?

In Chapter 1, we discussed the supposed trend towards increasing 'individualisation' in 'reflexive modernity' (Beck and Beck-Gernsheim 2002; Giddens 1991). Hakim has drawn upon these arguments in developing her arguments as to the primary significance of women's 'choices' in determining individual employment and family 'careers'. Indeed, Hakim argues that 'preferences' should be the major guide to policy-making. As we have seen, she identifies three categories of women: home/family centred, work centred and adaptives/drifters. Home-centred women give priority to their families, work-centred women give priority to their employment careers, and adaptive women shift their priorities between family and career over their life cycles. Thus: 'policy-making becomes more complex ... as policy-makers need to make allowance for at least three distinct household work strategies' (Hakim 2000: 277). However, as Nussbaum (2000: ch. 1) has argued, 'preferences' are not necessarily the best guide to policy-making, not least because 'preferences' do not exist in thin air, and are shaped by (amongst other things) habit, low expectations and unjust background conditions. It is, therefore, vital to explore the context within which 'choices' are made and 'preferences' developed.

Duncan and his colleagues have emphasised the significance of 'moral rationalities' in shaping mothers' employment decisions. Duncan *et al.*'s intensive research design draws on qualitative interviews with partnered mothers of varying ethnicities, sexualities and class situations (Duncan *et al.* 2003; Duncan and Edwards 1999; 2003; Barlow *et al.* 2002). The research identified three broad categories of 'gendered moral rationalities' amongst the groups studied: 'primarily mother', 'primarily worker' and 'mother/worker integral'. Afro-Caribbean mothers were more likely to be in full-time employment, and tended to take a 'mother/worker integral' perspective. That is, they saw their employment as providing a positive role model for their children, and saw paid work as being part of 'good' mothering. In contrast, white mothers tended to be ranged along a 'primarily mother'–'primarily worker' continuum, clustering mainly within the 'primarily mother' category. As we have seen in Chapter 1, Duncan and his colleagues argue that these 'gendered moral rationalities' are major determinants of mothers' employment behaviour. Thus although government policies may be developed on the premise of an 'adult worker' model (i.e., the assumption that all adults, including mothers, will benefit from paid work), these policies commit a 'rationality mistake' in that women who define themselves as 'primarily mothers' will not take up employment even if it is in their (economic) interest to do so (Barlow *et al.* 2002; see also Duncan and Edwards 1999).

Self-definitions of motherhood and maternal responsibilities will, obviously, have an impact on employment decision-making, particularly when children are young. However, in Duncan *et al.*'s study, the distribution of 'mothering identities' varied by race, class and locality. Amongst white women, middle-class 'suburban wives' had similar 'primarily mother' identities to marginal working-class women, even though they were well educated and well qualified and would have been able to earn reasonable salaries had they chosen to be employed. Other middle-class women, described as 'gentrifying improvers' sought to combine 'the less gendered role of independent worker with that of partnered mother' (Duncan 2003: 19) and resembled skilled working-class/intermediate mothers in tending more towards the 'worker' end of the continuum. However, although it may indeed be the case that specific 'gendered moral rationalities' in respect of childcare and mothering (and, following from this, individual decisions relating to combinations of childcare and employment) are distributed across the range of occupational class groupings, the question still remains as to why, in aggregate, these attitudinal and identity variations appear to be distributed unevenly across the class structure, as would seem to be suggested by the variations in women's employment by occupational class described in Tables 2.3 and 2.4 above.

Our critique and analysis will begin from the premise that ideas about 'the right thing to do', as well as 'preferences' relating to particular combinations of employment and caring, *will* shape individual employment and family decision-making. However, to what extent can discrete (and stable) 'preference' categories be identified amongst women, as Hakim has argued? As we have seen, Duncan *et al.* suggest that 'moral rationalities' are distributed along a continuum rather than existing as sharply defined 'preferences'. Similarly, McRae's longitudinal analysis of women's sex role attitudes and work histories over an eleven-year period demonstrates a '*continuum of views* rather than sharp breaks between women with different work histories' (McRae 2003: 327, emphasis in original). Qualitative research has demonstrated that women's attitudes (and related behaviour) to employment and family responsibilities vary according to both context and stage in the family life cycle (Crompton and Harris 1998; Procter and Padfield 1998). That is, it is difficult to conclusively establish the presence of concrete and stable 'orientations to work' amongst women (or men, for that matter).[8]

---

[8] See a previous debate relating to work orientations amongst male manual workers (Goldthorpe 1972; Daniel 1969, 1971).

In practice, as Glover (2002) has argued, most women (and an increasing number of men) seek to achieve some kind of balance between paid work and caring work. How this balance is achieved will depend in part on individual preferences, but in addition, as Glover argues, on a range of other factors including particular occupational and geographical constraints (see Crompton and Harris 1998b), the social policy context, as well as broader cultural and normative prescriptions as to 'acceptable' family and employment behaviours (Pfau-Effinger 1999). As McRae (2003: 329) argues, both normative *and* structural constraints shape women's decisions relating to the 'balance' achieved by individual women in respect of market and caring work. Structural constraints will include immediate practicalities such as the availability (and acceptability) of childcare, the demands of a particular job and so on. However, as McRae (2003: 329–30) has suggested (and as will be argued at greater length here), there is a body of evidence that suggests that underlying *class* processes also significantly shape the attitudes and employment behaviour of women. As we have seen, it is an established fact that less well-educated women, in the lower levels of the occupational structure, are more likely to withdraw from or limit their employment when their children are young. As we will demonstrate, there are also significant attitudinal differences to family and gender roles between women in different class/income groupings (see also McRae 2003: 330).

Before we explore this topic further, we will briefly (re)examine the question as to the extent to which attitudes or 'preferences' actually determine behaviour. Hakim is emphatic that clear preference categories determine behaviour: 'The decision to do paid work or not is personal ... there are several family models that European couples can choose from ...' (Hakim 2003a: 27); 'Affluent and liberal modern societies provide opportunities for diverse lifestyle preferences to be fully realised ...' (Hakim 2000: 273). Duncan and his colleagues also seem to suggest that the major factors determining mothers' employment decisions are particular 'moral rationalities'. The question as to whether attitudes determine behaviour, or vice versa, is one of those 'chicken and egg' social science topics that are incapable of unambiguous resolution (although it should be noted that there is no such thing as an individual 'attitude' that is not socially constructed). However, Himmelweit's analysis of the British Household Panel Survey (BHPS) suggests that in respect of mothers' employment, attitudinal change is more likely to follow upon behavioural change, rather than the other way round.

The BHPS regularly includes an attitude statement relating to the impact of mother's employment on children: 'a pre-school child is likely to suffer if his or her mother works' (this statement is also included in the

BSA survey). Over time, Himmelweit (Himmelweit and Sigala 2003) compared (for mothers of pre-school children) responses to this statement with the employment status of the mothers interviewed. Her analysis showed that mothers who were in the contradictory position of being in paid work but believing that pre-school children suffered as a result of their mother's employment were more likely to change their attitude than their behaviour; 46 per cent of such mothers had changed their attitude within two years, a proportion greater than the 29 per cent who gave up employment. As Himmelweit argues, neither identities nor behaviours are fixed, but adapt to each other in a process of positive feedback (Himmelweit and Sigala 2003: 23). As has already been argued, Tables 2.1 and 2.2 suggest, in Britain, an aggregate pattern of attitude change following closely on aggregate changes in women's employment behaviour.[9]

However, even though identities and behaviours might be variable at an individual level, the BSA data indicate consistent variations by social class in respect of both. Our discussion above (see Tables 2.3 and 2.4) has demonstrated that working-class women reduce their levels of employment to a greater extent than professional and managerial women when their children are young. Table 2.5 demonstrates that across a range of attitudinal variables, routine and manual respondents profess more gender stereotypical and 'familial' attitudes than professional and managerial respondents.

Although consistent (and statistically significant) class variations are demonstrated in Table 2.5, the response rates are also shaped by sex and age. Older people are in general more 'conservative' than younger people on all topics. Only 31 per cent of professional and managerial respondents are aged over 55, as compared to 50 per cent of routine and manual respondents (however, class differences are still significant when controls for age are introduced). Women's attitudes to gender roles are less conservative than those of men. For example 15 per cent of women agreed with question (a), 12 per cent with question (b), and 22 per cent with question (c). However, women were more likely than

---

[9] It has been suggested that a distinction should be drawn between responses to polling questions relating to 'attitudes' and the personal values etc. that shape behaviour. For example, a woman might support abortion rights but not be prepared to have an abortion herself (Hakim 2003b). This is a valid distinction to make, but it does not follow that the value of attitudes as indicators of likely behaviour is therefore removed. For example, in the BSA/ISSP data there was a highly significant association between whether or not women worked (full or part time) when their children were under school age and their views as to whether pre-school children suffered if their mother worked.

Table 2.5. *Attitudes to gender roles, women's paid work and the family, by social class (BSA/ISSP 2002), percentage agreeing*[a]

	Professional and managerial	Routine and manual	Total (including Intermediate)
(a) 'a man's job is to earn money, a woman's job is to look after the home and family'	10	27**	18
(b) 'it is not good if the man stays at home and cares for the children and the woman goes out to work'	11	20**	14
(c) 'a job is all right, but what most women really want is a home and children'	16	35**	24
(d) 'watching children grow up is life's greatest joy'	76	86**	81
(e) 'if a person cannot manage their family responsibilities, they should stop trying to hold down a paid job'	25	42**	33
Base[b]	692	759	1844

**p < .01.
[a]details of 'Intermediate' responses are not given in this table, see p. 45 note.
[b]indicative figures, actual base numbers vary by response rates to different questions.

men to agree with questions (d) and (e) (83 per cent question (d), 39 per cent question (e)).[10]

There are systematic class differences, therefore, in both attitudes and behaviour in respect of the patterning of employment and family life. One response would be to interpret these findings as demonstrating that there is, indeed, a greater level of 'familialism' amongst working-class people, and that this is reflected in the employment behaviour of working-class women. However, this begs the question as to *why* people in routine and manual occupations might place a greater degree of emphasis on their family lives and obligations. One fairly obvious answer would be that professional and managerial jobs are more rewarding than routine and manual jobs, not only in a material sense, but also in respect of social recognition and self-esteem. Classic texts such as Sennett and Cobb, *The Hidden Injuries of Class* (1973) describe how manual workers suffering from 'injured dignity' turn to their families as

[10] It may be noted that these kinds of complexities suggest that the 'minimalist' approach of relying on a limited number of diagnostic questions (Hakim 2003a) might be fraught with difficulties (see Table 3.2).

a way of recovering lost pride. It should be emphasised that this pattern is not peculiar to manual employees, as middle-class men who feel unsuccessful in their careers may also seek solace in their family lives (Crompton 2001). It is not being argued here that a tendency to place a greater emphasis on the family is class-specific, but rather, that the characteristics of working-class jobs are more likely, in aggregate, to result in people in such jobs putting a greater emphasis on their families than people in more rewarding jobs.

In the case of working-class women, case study evidence has documented the manner in which many are socialised into caring careers. Skeggs interviewed over 80 women who enrolled on courses in community care in the early 1980s. As she emphasises, it would be difficult to represent the decision to enrol on such a course as a positive 'choice':

The women are not just positioned by ... historical legacies ... but also by the range of opportunities available to them. Their own inheritance (and lack) of forms of capital mean that their access to certain routes such as higher education and the primary labour market is already restricted. Their understanding of their possibilities is one of the motivations to pursue caring. To put it bluntly, there is very little else for them to do but go to college. (Skeggs 1997: 57)

Once on the course, the students were presented with a model of family practice based on a model of full-time care: 'It is never assumed that carers themselves may have needs, nor that they may have other responsibilities outside of caring, such as paid full-time employment ... The courses contribute to the development of an individualised caring conscience in which the women come to take responsibility for all the problems in their family ...' (Skeggs 1997: 64, 67). When the women were re-interviewed (after a gap of six to eight years), they were overwhelmingly cynical about the content of their courses, 'but what remained was a firm subjective construction as carer' (*ibid.*: 71). Thus Skeggs concludes that 'The desire to be valued and to demonstrate respectability and responsibility predisposes the women to voluntary and unpaid caring' (*ibid.*: 72). Particular familial orientations, therefore, may be seen to arise not only from a relative absence of fulfilment and opportunity in employment, but also out of the manner in which jobs for working-class women are constructed.[11]

Similarly, a qualitative study (including interviews with a mixed class sample of ninety-six women with young children) found that those women who were most consistently 'pro' direct maternal care for young

[11] Jobs in community care are populated almost entirely by working-class women, and may be seen as the modern functional equivalent of the domestic servant class.

children were white, working class and relatively constrained in respect of their employment opportunities (Irwin 2003b). They believed that mothers' exclusive care and commitment should extend throughout children's primary school years. Here there was a contrast with the more highly qualified and advantaged middle-class women who were interviewed. Even if these women considered maternal care to be best for young children, they nevertheless held (realistic) aspirations for themselves as workers and careerists. In contrast, as Irwin argues, 'a more limited scope for strategic employment decisions (amongst poorly qualified working-class women) is consistent with holding moral commitments which lie for much longer with the exclusive care of children' (Irwin 2003b: 17). In short, these women's perceptions of 'good mothering' were closely related to their social location.

A considerable literature has demonstrated that jobs have long been 'gendered' in a manner that calls upon stereotypical constructions of 'masculinity' and 'femininity' – although these stereotypes are themselves fluid and subject to change (Acker 1990; Adkins 2002; Bradley 1989; Crompton and Sanderson 1990; Gottfried 2003; Reskin and Roos 1990). Many 'women's' jobs – as in the case of the community care trainees interviewed by Skeggs – call upon supposedly 'natural' female propensities to care. Nursing would be another obvious example here. Other jobs reproduce patriarchal relationships within the workplace. Kanter (1977), for example, has described the boss–secretary relationship as a 'patrimonial relic' within contemporary organisations. Up until the 1960s and 1970s, these assumptions were built into the education and training of girls, even those who were academically 'successful' (see Crompton and Sanderson 1986). To take an example from a JRF interview:

ALISON (bank worker, born 1947, two children, grammar school, 'A' levels):
The school I went to, you either did the shorthand and typing commercial side of it, or the pre-nursing side. It was only in the later period that they came to push girls for university, but then it was nursing or office work.

Occupational 'choice', therefore, has a gendered dimension that has, until relatively recently been systematically built into education and job training, and still persists today (Cockburn 1991).

There were class variations in levels of job satisfaction amongst the BSA respondents: 35 per cent of professional and managerial employees described themselves as being 'completely' or 'very' satisfied with their jobs, as compared to 29 per cent of routine and manual employees; 29 per cent of routine and manual employees described themselves as indifferent to or dissatisfied with their jobs, as compared to 18 per cent of managerial and professional employees. Interestingly, there were no class variations in responses to other general 'satisfaction' questions relating to general happiness and family life. However, class variations in job satisfaction did not find their echo in levels of work commitment. 'Work commitment' has frequently been measured by asking 'If without having to work, you had what you would regard as a reasonable living income, do you think you would still prefer to have a paid job or wouldn't you bother?' The lack of response variation, by sex and occupational class, to this question was somewhat surprising:[12] 63 per cent of managerial and professional men, and 69 per cent of routine and manual men, indicated that they would continue in paid work even if they could 'live comfortably', as did 64 per cent of managerial and professional, and 68 per cent of routine and manual, women.

Job satisfaction, therefore, but not, apparently, levels of work commitment, varies by occupational class. Both conventional gender roles, and the emphasis placed on family life, appeared to be more powerful amongst routine and manual respondents. A 'familial' emphasis was relatively marked amongst routine and manual women. For example, whereas fewer than one in ten of young professional and managerial women (aged between 18 and 34) thought that 'what a woman really wanted was a home and children', a quarter of routine and manual women in the same age group held this view. It has been argued that such 'preferences' are as much the outcome of class-associated restrictions of circumstance and differential socialisation as they are of unrestricted 'choice' and 'preference' but, leaving this question to one side for the moment, to what extent are these class-differentiated 'preferences' realised?

In order to explore this topic further, a further analysis was carried out on the attitude statement 'watching children grow up is life's greatest joy'; 79 per cent of managerial and professional women, and 89 per cent of routine and manual, 'agreed' with this statement. Amongst managerial and professional women, 60 per cent of those who 'agreed' with the statement had worked when their child(ren) were under school age, as compared to 74 per cent of those who were 'neutral' or 'disagreed'. This suggests that 'preferences' are having some kind of impact on whether managerial and professional women take up employment when they have young children. Amongst routine and manual women, however, 'agreeing' or being neutral/disagreeing made

---

[12] Hakim has argued that this single question can be relied upon to divide a population into 'committed' and 'uncommitted' workers (2003b). This assumption is not being made here.

no difference at all to whether or not a woman worked when her child was under school age (just over 40 per cent of women in both attitudinal categories worked). It would seem, therefore, that middle-class women are in a better position to realise their 'preferences'.[13] As James (a JRF respondent) said of his wife: 'She didn't want to go back to work. But then financially she had to so she got another job ... Most women don't want to come back after maternity leave but they have to come back for the money.'

Conclusion

In this chapter, we have focused on the changing ways in which families in Britain have combined market work and domestic caring over the last two centuries. It has been emphasised that the family and employment mechanisms via which these objectives have been realised should not be seen as somehow 'natural' but, rather, are permeated by normative assumptions – particularly in relation to women – as well as being structured by societal and economic circumstances and constraints.

The status of women has been transformed over the last century. In Britain, women achieved most civic equalities before the Second World War. However, systematic inequalities in the 'public sphere' of politics and employment persisted. Perhaps because of the evident subordination of women, as individuals, within employment, much of the debate initiated by 'second-wave' feminism from the 1960s onwards was largely concerned with the disadvantages experienced by women in this regard. Indeed, *systematic* discrimination against women in employment was not formally removed until the 1970s; women still earn relatively less than men (i.e., there is a persistent wage gap), and are underrepresented in higher level positions in the occupational structure (see Chapter 3). Our dual focus on employment and the family, however, has led us to examine not simply the employment of women *per se* but also the distribution of employment within families and households. That is, we have addressed the question of the 'total social organisation of labour' (Glucksmann 1995), and how it has changed and developed over time.

---

[13] Hakim (2003b) does to some extent recognise the effect of constraint on choice via her identification of 'contrary' groups whose behaviour is not in accordance with their 'preferences' – in particular, women who espouse a 'role segregation' family model but are nevertheless in employment. This is explained by the presence of a mortgage, and/or the partner's insecure employment. The class implications of these findings are not explored.

It has been shown that (not surprisingly) there have always been systematic class differences in the 'total social organisation of labour', or employment/family articulation. In the early years of 'extreme capitalism' all members of labouring families, including children, worked when they were able. The emergence of the 'male breadwinner' ideal from the second half of the nineteenth century onwards was seen by many – men and women alike – as part and parcel of the attempt to modify the 'extensive' (Seccombe 1993) exploitation of labour that occurred during early industrialisation. The 'mid 20th century social compromise' (Crouch 1999) may be seen as the culmination of these attempts to modify the exploitation of labour, but at the cost of the perpetuation of a 'semi-feudal' (Beck 1992) regulation of women. That is, although most men were expected to actively participate in the capitalist marketplace for most of their adult lives, most women were consigned to caring and domestic work.

As we have seen, in Britain the mid twentieth-century social compromise was rudely interrupted with the election of the Conservative government in 1979. Deindustrialisation and deregulation led to a massive loss of (male) working-class jobs. Inequalities increased, and relative wages declined at the lower levels of the occupational hierarchy. The impact of neoliberal economic policies might be seen as a resurgence of 'extreme' capitalism (Crouch 1999), which has some parallels with the 'extensive' exploitation of labour in the first part of the nineteenth century, during which all members of labouring households who were able to work were expected to do so. Carolynne's family, adequately (if not luxuriously) supported by the income of three adult women, all of whom also contributed to childcare, might be cited as an example of this trend. Thea (a supermarket worker) describes other examples of 'multiple carer' families:

People seem to work it around the grandparent now. One girl who works here, her mum works in the morning and she works in the afternoon and they share the childcare like that. One other lady, she had a baby and got a job on the checkout and her mum takes over when she comes to work. There are quite a few mothers and daughters who work here.

From this perspective, women and other carers might be seen as having been 'forced' into employment as a consequence of the relative decline of working-class incomes. However, the increase in employment amongst middle-class women, who are more likely to be able to depend on the income of their partners, would not be amenable to this explanation.

The resurgence of political and economic neoliberalism from the 1970s ran in parallel with second-wave feminism, and the consolidation of some of its gains, particularly in relation to employment. In line with these changes, we have demonstrated that attitudes to gender roles, and women's and mothers' employment, have been transformed across the social spectrum. Nevertheless, there are persisting class differences at the household level in women's economic activity, as well as in individual attitudes to the family and gender roles. We have drawn upon these class variations in developing a critique of those authors who have emphasised the primary (and causal) significance of individual 'choice' in explaining mothers' employment behaviour. As we have noted, an emphasis on the primacy of 'choice' resonates well with neoliberalism, and the current class pattern of 'choices' in relation to employment and caring will serve to perpetuate and deepen material inequalities.[14]

Nevertheless, even though an overemphasis on the significance of 'choice' in social science explanation may be criticised, it is important to remember that even though we may be entering a new era of 'extreme capitalism' (in which the privileging of 'choice' becomes one way of rationalising increasing inequalities), history is not simply repeating itself. In particular, in parallel with legislation against sexual inequalities, normative and moral frameworks relating to women and gender roles have been transformed during the twentieth century. This transformation has been largely achieved by women themselves, both via formal mechanisms such as the women's movement, as well as by more subtle pressures from within the household. By the middle of the twentieth century, many women were unhappy with their 'semi-feudal' state (Friedan 1965), and as we have seen, even Irene (p. 45), who did not for one moment question her primary responsibility for childcare and domestic life, wanted to 'get out of the house'. Thus as Irwin and Bottero (2000) have argued, there has been a shift in the 'moral economy' and women's claims to economic participation on equal terms with men have been recognised. However, if the tension between the demands of capitalist employment and the requirements for care

---

[14] Similar arguments have been developed in relation to the question of supposed parental 'choice' in relation to secondary education (Reay and Lucey 2003: 138): 'The prevalent focus on "choice" within educational theorizing as a form of agency often masks the fact that "choice" is a marker of economic privilege. The more distant subjects are from economic necessity, the more "choice" becomes a possibility ... In contrast, the majority of children in our ... study had no "choice" ... They were forced to accept the least bad option.'

can no longer be resolved via the domestication of women, then contemporary societies will have to seek new solutions. Nevertheless, as we shall see in subsequent chapters, the persistence of the ideology of domesticity means that most women, even when in employment, still retain the major responsibility for domestic work and caring, which can give rise to further difficulties in the spheres of both employment and the household. These tensions, and their possible solutions, will be explored in the following chapters.

3   Women, men, organisations and careers

Changes in employment

In this chapter, our main focus will be on the changes in the world of work (as employment) that have already been briefly introduced in Chapter 1. As we have seen, the stereotypical organisation of the Fordist era was large in scale and bureaucratic in its organisation, male dominated in its employees, uniform in its products and 'deskilled' in its work organisation. In manufacturing, the motor industry was seen as the exemplar of these trends (Beynon 1973; Blauner 1964; Braverman 1974). However, from the 1970s onwards, the pace of technological change, together with new forms of work organisation, generated an increasing flow of commentaries suggesting that the nature of employment was changing irrevocably. In *The Future of Work* (1984), Handy described a future in which large organisations became increasingly flexible as, following the Japanese model, they subcontracted and outsourced an increasing number of operations, manufacturing jobs were lost as a consequence of technological change, and low-level service (rather than manufacturing) work proliferated. He was writing at a time of rising unemployment, that (at the time) was thought by many as likely to become a more or less permanent state of affairs. Ten years later, Handy (1994) was describing the advent of the 'portfolio' career that would become the norm in the newly emerging, flexible, labour market. Individuals, he argued, would no longer depend on a single organisation in order to develop a career, but would move from job to job as they 'self-developed' their career trajectories.

As Nolan (2003: 477) has recently argued, many of the predictions formulated in the late 1980s and first part of the 1990s have proved to be somewhat wide of the mark: 'In the United Kingdom and United States ... employment levels have been rising fast and permanent employment accounts for roughly four in every five employees. Job tenure rates ... have remained almost constant over the past 20 years. Approximately one third of the employed workforce has been with the same employer for more than ten years ... Contrary to predictions there has been no growth in self-employment over the past ten years ...' Nevertheless, as we shall see, these broad continuities do not mean that employment, and employment relations, have not changed. Employment has become increasingly flexible, jobs in manufacturing have continued to decline, and service employment has grown. Employees on full-time, permanent contracts may be subject to a variety of flexible working practices including variable shift working and compulsory overtime. Labour supply contract employment has been increasing, and as such work will be by its very nature variable, as Purcell *et al.* (1999: 6) have argued, the proliferation of non-standard contractual and working arrangements means that these developments are impossible to monitor in national employment statistics.

Management practices have changed and developed. 'High-commitment' (or 'high-performance') human resource practices, which seek to obtain a greater discretionary effort from employees, have been widely introduced in many contemporary organisations. These include teamworking and quality circles, individual appraisals and training, and performance-related pay. Indeed, it has been argued that: 'we do not have "hands" in today's organisations. The popular view is that organisations are opting, by choice or necessity, to engage with hearts and minds instead' (Thompson and Warhurst 1998: 1). Individualised career development is also central to high-commitment management practices. Rather than (as in the past) being sponsored through a fixed and stable bureaucratic hierarchy, individuals are encouraged to self-develop through what is often a fluid and changing organisational structure. Thus, increasingly, employees are being 'worked on' in order that they may develop an 'entrepreneurial self' (Rose 1989).

The emphasis on employee 'performance' in high-commitment management has led some authors to argue that the nature of work as employment is in the process of being transformed. 'Work', it is argued, is becoming increasingly 'cultural' rather than 'material'. Service work in particular depends for its successful accomplishment on the 'performance' of service employees (Du Gay 1996). Thus Du Gay argues that the boundaries between production and consumption are increasingly blurred. This, it is argued, will have consequences for women's employment as, increasingly, qualities once considered to be essentially 'feminine' (for example, nurturing and empathy) are required in an increasing number of occupations (Hochschild 1983). In the next section, therefore, we will explore the implications of these developments for our understanding of the contemporary employment situation of women. In particular, we will focus on the question of careers.

Women, organisations and careers

Traditional bureaucratic careers were overwhelmingly male. Women who did have 'careers' (in the sense of upwardly mobile, long-term employment with a single organisation) were rarely married (in any case a marriage bar operated in major bureaucratic organisations such as the civil service, financial institutions and many major employing organisations until after the Second World War), and most unlikely to have children. Weber's original formulation of the bureaucratic ideal-type characterises office-holding as a 'vocation', demanding the 'entire capacity for work for a long period of time' (Weber in Gerth and Mills 1958: 198–9). Under the circumstances of the 'male breadwinner' model, male bureaucrats could fulfil these conditions. Indeed, managerial wives were widely expected to supply the kinds of domestic supports (entertaining, well-behaved children, clean shirts etc.) that would help a man in his organisational career. They were, indeed, 'career wives' (Finch 1983).

Within debates on social class, the presence (or absence) of a career has been widely employed as an indicator that distinguishes 'middle-class' from 'working-class' occupations (Abercrombie and Urry 1983; Erikson and Goldthorpe 1992; Lockwood 1958). In the past, working-class careers have been characteristically short range, to foreman/supervisor level only. Indeed, this was a major reason for the fact that, whereas middle-class incomes increased with age, working-class incomes tended to flatten beyond the peak earning age groups of the 20s to mid-30s (Westergaard and Resler 1975: 80ff.). Savage (1992) and his colleagues (following Wright) have described service with, and knowledge of, a particular organisation as 'organisational assets', 'possessed' by managers and contributing to their superior class situation. As individuals, women were, until relatively recently, unable to acquire these 'assets'. This was in part because of normative and cultural assumptions as well as masculine exclusionary practices within organisations. Most women took employment breaks for childrearing, and/or switched to part-time working, or less demanding jobs (Dex 1987). It might be argued, however, that one of the more positive aspects of the demise of the bureaucratic career, organisational 'delayering' and the development of the 'portfolio career' might be to reduce women's disadvantage in this respect, as modern 'careers' no longer require long-term, unbroken dedication to a single organisation. We will return to this topic shortly, but, for the moment, we will briefly review some of the substantial literature that has focused on the lack of women's progression within organisational contexts.

As has been described in previous chapters, much of the emphasis in 'second wave' feminist writing on women and employment-focused on the barriers faced by women in the male-dominated employment sphere (Walby 1986; Cockburn 1991). Before the advent of legislation against sexual discrimination, these barriers were explicit and overt. Women were barred from particular occupations and excluded from access to training and qualifications, as well as being subject to direct exclusionary practices within organisations, as described in the example of careers in banking discussed below. The women who, increasingly, returned to paid employment in the 1960s and 1970s, besides having 'broken' employment careers, were not, on the whole, particularly well qualified either in respect of school leaving qualifications or employment-related credentials and training. Nevertheless, many expressed considerable frustration at the very real and considerable barriers they faced within the world of employment (Crompton and Jones 1984). The upsurge of qualification levels amongst women from the 1970s led to suggestions that, once women had acquired levels of 'human capital' (i.e., qualifications and work experience) equivalent to that of men, they might use the 'qualifications lever' in order to gain higher-level positions (Crompton and Sanderson 1990).

In most Western employing organisations, explicitly 'gendered' barriers against women's progression have been largely removed (although in some male-dominated occupations, such as engineering, they are still very much an issue, see Bagilhole et al. 2000). More women have moved into management and the professions (Hakim 1992), but nevertheless, women are still underrepresented at the topmost levels. In explaining and understanding the persisting differences in women's and men's occupational locations, a number of overlapping strands of argument may be identified. First, those that focus on the characteristics of women as individuals, second, those that emphasise the characteristics of the organisations themselves, and the qualities they require, and third, arguments relating to the wider context of employment and care.

In common with prevailing approaches within social science in the 1960s and into the 1970s, early discussion of 'women in organisations' treated bureaucratic organisation as if it were gender neutral. Kanter (1977) argued that bureaucratic organisations were structures of power from which women were excluded. The key, therefore, was to enable women to acquire powerful positions. Male 'homosociability' (the preference of men for working with people like themselves) would have to be overcome, but getting women into positions of power and authority meant equipping them for these jobs via training in assertiveness, getting the right credentials, and ensuring that recruitment to promoted positions was a scrupulously fair process. Thus the focus was on women as individuals, their characteristics, and how the 'right' characteristics might be gained in order that they might progress though the hierarchy (an emphasis on the importance of training and qualifications for women was central to this kind of approach, see Crompton and Sanderson 1990). However, others argued that far from being gender neutral, organisations are 'gendered'; in particular, that bureaucratic hierarchies are inherently masculine, embodying male qualities of dominance, hierarchy, abstract rationality and so on (Ferguson 1984). Thus 'feminine' qualities were not seen as relevant to career success. This essentialist approach counterposed 'feminine' modes of organising, based upon cooperation and friendship, to 'masculine' bureaucratic hierarchies (Marshall 1984).

It might be suggested that it is not particularly appropriate to regard 'organisations' *per se* as either gender neutral, masculine or feminine. Nevertheless, it is important to recognise that organisations are 'socially situated practices' in which gender is constructed, and that they have a 'gendered substructure' (Halford *et al.* 1997: 16; Acker 1990). Gender is, so to speak, 'played out' in organisations, particularly in respect of overtly sexual aspects of masculinities and femininities:

> Bureaucratic organisations validate and permit forms of male embodiment and invalidate or render impermissible forms of female embodiment ... For women, the discursive construct of the reproductive body assumes particular importance in *disqualifying* them from authority positions ... The sexualised body represents another discursive construction of female embodiment whereby women have been included, *qualifying* them for certain front-stage and subordinate organisational functions. (Gottfried 2003: 260–1)

Increasingly, such 'cultural' assumptions about women were cited as evidence of the 'glass ceiling' that existed between women and the topmost organisational positions (Davidson and Cooper 1992). The 'cultural turn' in the study of work and organisations led to a considerable emphasis being placed on the construction of sexualities within organisations. For example, McDowell's (1997) study of City (of London) finance workers emphasised how appearance was central to workplace performance for men and women, and how both men and women drew upon particular masculinities and femininities in their work. Similarly, Halford *et al.* (1997: 79) document the shift in retail banking from the old-style, paternalist male manager towards a culture of 'competitive masculinity' in which decisive action and risk-taking predominate.

Thus Adkins (2002) argues that (masculine and feminine) 'identities' have assumed increasing importance in contemporary workplaces and that 'The politics of identity are ... not only at the heart of workplace politics but also of the labour process and the organisation of production ... the significance of issues of identity at work means that a politics of deconstruction (for example, of the hetero/homo binary) is now best suited to the task of addressing workplace struggles' (Adkins 2002: 36). The purpose here is not to reject this kind of culturalist theorising. However, it may be suggested that its contribution to our understanding of the persisting dominance of men in higher-level positions is somewhat inadequate. Indeed, it will be argued that, notwithstanding the insights that may be gained from the study of the 'embeddedness' of gender in organisational cultures and structures, the major explanation for the continuing underrepresentation of women in managerial positions lies in the third strand of argument identified above – that is, the wider context of employment and care, or the gender division of labour as a whole. The persistence of the ideology of domesticity means that family responsibilities, particularly for childcare, are allocated to women. This means that most women do not actively pursue a managerial career, even when relatively well qualified. We will explore this argument via recent case studies (deriving from the JRF research) of two large service sector organisations, both of which relied heavily upon the 'performance' of their employees in order to achieve their objectives, and both of which had made considerable efforts, via 'high-commitment' management practices, to build organisational cultures supportive of these ends.

'Cellbank' and 'Shopwell'

'Cellbank' is an international bank, and 'Shopwell' a major supermarket chain. Both organisations are market leaders in their (highly competitive) fields. Both organisations had experienced recent reorganisation that had reduced the number of lower levels in the job hierarchy. In the case of Cellbank, this had involved job losses. Compulsory redundancies had been avoided, but many employees had taken redundancy packages when their jobs had disappeared with reorganisation and business 'reengineering'. Both organisations were characterised by high-commitment personnel policies. These included the building of a strong and positive organisational culture aimed at transforming employee behaviour (the 'Shopwell way of working', Cellbank's 'big behaviours'), as well as teamworking, target setting and the development of individualised career paths. Both organisations also made a point of presenting themselves as 'friends and family friendly', and offered a range of benefits including flexible employment options, extended maternity and paternity leaves, and paid carers' leave.

In other respects, particularly as regards the nature of their employees, the organisations were rather different from each other. Employment in banking has traditionally been regarded as a 'career' job, and in the past banks relied upon the recruitment of well-qualified school leavers (Crompton and Jones 1984). Despite recent upheavals and reorganisations, the majority of Cellbank employees had spent most of their working lives with Cellbank, and only 16 per cent had less than five years' service with the bank.[1] Although few Cellbank employees had university degrees, all Cellbank employees had reasonable school leaving qualifications clustering at the GCSE/O/A level. In contrast, Shopwell is characterised by high labour turnover (67 per cent of employees had less than five years' service), and its labour force is largely unqualified (70 per cent had either no school leaving qualifications or GCSEs only). At the lower levels, Shopwell employees were not well paid – as we saw in Chapter 2, Carolynne earned £4.47 an hour in 2002 – and although employment is extremely flexible, if workers take time off for family reasons this will usually be unpaid. Cellbank employees are better paid, and none of the Cellbank employees interviewed reported an annual household income of less than £15,000.

These broad class differences between banking and supermarket employees were reflected in the nature of managerial 'commitment' and 'performance' practices. First names were universal at Shopwell, at Cellbank surnames were included on name badges. Cellbank workers had team meetings, Shopwell employees had 'huddles'. Targets at Cellbank were set individually, as well as for teams, whereas Shopwell employees received (or did not receive) a share of a store profits bonus.[2] 'Class' differences were also perceptible in the nature of the individualised promotion schemes in the two organisations. Shopwell employees completed 'So You Want To Be a Manager' modules, Cellbank employees enrolled at 'Cellbank University'.

Banking was once the locus of the classic bureaucratic career (Lockwood 1958). Relatively well-qualified young men were carefully

---

[1] These figures are taken from a survey of employees in the three organisations carried out in 2001. See Yeandle *et al.* 2002.

[2] Nevertheless, individually targeted 'shaming' was a feature of management policy. Stores were scored by mystery shoppers who identified underperforming individuals (for example, failing to smile, not offering to pack) by name. Mystery shopper reports, naming the individuals concerned, were then posted around the staff area – for example, on the inside of lavatory doors.

guided through the grade levels of a 'job for life'.[3] Banks held to a 'no poaching' policy (that is, they did not recruit employees from other banks), and promotion track positions were not advertised, either externally or internally. Rather, they were offered to individuals who had demonstrated good behaviour and commitment to the bank (Crompton and Jones 1984; Halford *et al.* 1997: 161). This usually involved getting the professional qualification supported by the banking industry (the Chartered Institute of Banking, CIB). Until the 1980s, career paths for men were preserved by the recruitment of young female school leavers, usually at lower levels of qualification than young men, who could be relied upon (or were required) to leave the bank at the birth of their first child (Crompton 1989; see also Rachel: ch. 2, p. 45). However, banks have now abandoned discriminatory recruitment and promotion practices and, indeed, many are now at the cutting edge of equal opportunity employment. External recruitment is now practised (although, as we have seen, the tradition of long service in circumstances of overall job reduction means that the extent of new recruitment is at a relatively low level), and all jobs are advertised internally on a weekly basis. The CIB examinations are no longer considered relevant, rather, employees prepare themselves for job progression by taking modules provided by 'Cellbank University'. Job advertisements specify the characteristics (modules completed plus work experience) required, and employees are responsible for putting themselves forward for promotion. Cellbank has recently reduced the number of job grades from fourteen to seven. Managerial grades begin at G4, so a short hierarchy remains before management level. However, in the retail division, in which the JRF research was carried out, only 10 per cent of employees were management grade (G4) or above.

Shopwell also had an individualised promotion structure that was open to all – although very few will actually achieve promotion, as only 6 per cent of store employees are managers (this includes departmental managers), and supervisor positions (once paid fractionally more than

---

[3] Extract from interview with bank manager carried out in 1980: 'Every new entrant comes in on a four-month probationary period. After two months we do an interim report. Depending on their qualifications on entry, and how well they perform during their probationary period, it may be that we will decide to mark them potentially for accelerated promotion ... Assuming that they join at 18: they've taken their A levels and they come in shortly before they get their results. They are going to be in grade 1 for say 12–15 months. They are probably going to stay in grade 2 then for another 18 months to two years ... They may be in for as little as 9–10 months in grade 2. I would think that three years through the grades is probably normal ... In the first year, regardless of whether it's accelerated training or not, they are not assessed and advised of their position. They are assessed, but it's just on our records at that stage.'

basic grade employees) had been recently downgraded.[4] Supervisors had been replaced by 'key workers', but were not paid any more than other employees. They were, however, likely to earn more in total as those wishing to be promoted to the first rung of management were expected to work long hours. Carolynne was a 'key worker', and described the next steps on the ladder as follows:

You don't get paid as supervisors, and you're not classed as one. But if anything goes wrong, it comes to me first. We are just there to make sure everything is being followed properly, all the complaints are being done ... we all get paid the same. [So when do you start getting paid extra?] When you go onto 'So You Want To Be a Manager', and you go through the modules. You go to an assessment centre and you are given three tasks in a group to see if you've got the capability and confidence, I suppose. Once you've passed that, you go on to a store of learning. We are a store of learning here. And for four weeks it would be solid training in modules. You can't fail: you can just be re-referred to a few more weeks. And then you're given a position.

Both organisations, therefore, were flexible, 'family friendly' and characterised by 'high-commitment' management practices emphasising egalitarianism, openness and fair-mindedness. In both organisations, the majority of employees were women, but there were few women in senior positions. Just over 3 per cent of Shopwell store managers were women, and 7 per cent of women in Cellbank retail were G4 or above (these percentages include part-time employees; if only full-time employees were included, the proportion of women managers would be higher).

It is not being suggested here that either organisation was characterised by direct discriminatory practices in respect of sex. Rather, it will be argued that recent changes in the way in which employees are managed and the kind of work they do, has resulted in promotion to a managerial position bringing with it the requirement for long hours working, even at relatively low levels of the organisational hierarchy. This makes promoted positions unattractive to individuals with domestic responsibilities, however well qualified they might be in other respects. It will be suggested that changes in the organisation of work, including 'high-commitment' managerial techniques, have actually increased the pressures on individuals who wish to be promoted.

In Cellbank, the perception was widespread that promotion opportunities had, relatively, declined (as we have seen, the number of grade

---

[4] These figures for Cellbank and Shopwell include part-time employees. The proportion on managerial grades amongst full-time employees will be higher. All managers were full-time employees.

levels had been reduced). Peggy (aged 45, G4) describes the rapid pace of recent change:

So much has changed in the bank. There are still more men in top roles but women have moved up. As the branch manager I can't make decisions, like branch managers could before. There's not a prestige attached to this job like there was before. The branch managers are now all women, the job has been deskilled, we have little discretion now. My immediate boss is a man.

Although many bank employees were unhappy with recent changes, others saw them as necessary for survival:

ADAM: About three or four years ago it was realised that if it [the bank] didn't change it was not going to be around. So it's changing the culture, but the people don't want to let go ... they are still coming across the resistance from staff. 'We didn't use to have targets ten years ago.' That's great, but we may not be around in years to come if we don't do something about it.

This change to a culture of targets and selling meant that although Cellbank had excellent work–life policies, 'high-performance' management practices meant that they were often not used:

PHILIP: In the sort of environment we're working in, which is very much target-driven, if you are on carer's leave, that's a day you've lost that you don't get back, you're not there to do anything towards achieving your targets. You're playing catch-up all the time.

As has been noted above, most banks would be considered to be at the leading edge of equal opportunity policies. Women are now offered extended maternity leave, opportunities to return to part-time work, opportunities for job sharing, etc. However, despite these opportunities, they were not seen as being compatible with managerial employment. Flora was a relatively senior manager who had returned to a job share after the birth of her two children. However, she had just taken voluntary redundancy as the last wave of reorganisation would have meant a move to a full-time job: 'There were ten of us, and with the reorganisation three of us had to go. Realistically, to do the whole [new] job on 28 hours a week [her current hours] would be just an absolute nightmare ... I would have to have done it full time. They hadn't said that, but I know how big my job is now. And with twice the patch, twice the size, I just couldn't have done it and I wasn't prepared to go full time.' Flora continues:

As much as the bank encourages job share and the home/work life balance, realistically it doesn't work. The higher up you go, the responsibility you've got ... the higher up in the bank you go, it just gets harder for the bank to be family friendly. They've still got the same policies there and I can still take advantage of the same policies that everyone else has, but it's harder for me to do that ... So there is a cut-off point where it becomes more difficult to be family friendly.

Flora's dilemma was widely recognised within the bank. As Hannah put it: 'I like my job and I want to work. I couldn't sit at home but I wouldn't let it affect my family life to be a manager. The higher up women go, they tend not to have kids.' And Abigail, who was working 20 hours a week with two young children, said: 'I admit I could have gone further, but I'm high up here anyway [she was G3]. But it's because I can't come back full time. If I came back full-time then I could go a lot further, but I haven't got the childcare facilities to do that.' That women face tensions between family life and building a management career is, of course, hardly a new or dramatic finding. None of the women managers interviewed in Halford *et al.*'s study had children, and all thought it would be impossible to be a manager and have children (1997: 202). Similarly, Wajcman's (1998) research on higher-level managers showed that whereas most of the men had children, most of the women did not – 'It is impossible for women to compete and still be mothers.' These studies were carried out more than ten years ago, and it is depressing to have to note how little seems to have changed.

As we have seen, Shopwell had an open, individualised, system of promotion. A very large proportion of Shopwell employees worked part time. Part-time employees were predominantly mothers with young children or students – indeed, student recruitment during school holidays and university vacations meant that mothers could be offered 'term-time only' contracts, one aspect of Shopwell's high-profile 'friends and family' employment policies. Indeed, Shopwell policies were extremely flexible in this regard. Employees were encouraged to 'shift-swap' in order to fit their employment around family responsibilities, and the company offered extended maternity, paternity and grandparental leave as well as flexible part-time hours. This was because at the basic employee level, workers were highly substitutable: 'If you work on groceries, although it's different in terms of products you're selling you could put them on to home and leisure ... It would take ten minutes to show them the differences but other than that they can get on with it' (HR manager, Shopwell). However, more relevant to our argument is that one of the major tasks of Shopwell in-store managers was to cover for absent employees, as described by Grace, a first-level manager:

I have to do their shifts, work out the rotas, sickness, their reviews, how they're doing, their training. There is a lot involved in it, especially at the moment. I've got five off. I'm running around! ... Managers do a 45-hour week and we are supposed to spend only 12 ½ hours of that time on the shop floor ... But all the time I've been at Shopwell, I've never known any manager only to do that ... I'm 45 contracted, but can do 50, 55, 60 depending on how bad your department is. Because, as a manager, you are responsible for your department. So if there is a lot of sick, like there is at the moment, you won't get your two days off.

Shopwell employees were well aware of the long hours worked by managers. One of the major advantages of working at Shopwell, for many employees, was the flexibility of hours on offer, as Alice put it: 'The reason I'm here is not the money, believe me. It's the flexibility that I get here that makes it worth staying for' (she had four children). Thus when Alice was asked about whether she wanted promotion:

The kids are too young for me to put myself forward like that ... You can go all the way to store manager and higher. They don't hold you back at all. You can go as far as you want to go. They will develop you ... At the moment I can't physically do any more hours than I'm doing now ... they don't have part time supervisors. You have to work full time ... we are a 24-hour store, 7 days a week. And it's not fair to have a manager working 25 hours.

Not only were even first-level managers expected to work full time, but 'putting in the hours' (in the sense of being able to work extra shifts when asked to) was also seen as necessary in order to demonstrate 'promotability'. Megan: 'I want to go further in the company and become a manager. It's quite easy to be a manager but I won't do it straight away. The children are too young, you need to work long hours at work. In two or three years I will want to do it.' All of the Shopwell managers interviewed worked long hours (as we have seen in the example of Grace above), and higher-level managers were explicit that a serious Shopwell career was incompatible with family life:

CRAIG: It's supposed to be family-friendly but the hours are impossible ... part of the reason my marriage broke down ... I'm contracted 45 hours, I actually work 60 ... you have to, for the needs of the business ... there are good career prospects ... Definitely, yes. As long as you are prepared to sacrifice other things such as family to move up.

Our case study evidence, therefore, reveals both continuity and change. Career paths in contemporary organisations appear to be very different from those that prevailed in conventional bureaucratic organisations. Long service as such is not essential to an organisational career, and career paths are open and competitive. Service breaks with a particular organisation, and/or temporary withdrawal from the labour market, will not necessarily inhibit the building of a successful organisational career (for example, Craig had been unemployed for several years in the 1990s). However, individuals seeking managerial career development will have to work full time, and they will also have to be prepared to work long hours. As women still take the major responsibility for domestic work and caring, many women find it simply impossible to find the hours necessary to build a career, and as we have seen, some men also face these problems.

Full-time employed mothers

We have to have quite a strict structure. I leave the house at 7.30 to take our son to the nursery ... my husband picks him up at night, so I can work later and make up time ... my husband makes tea, I feed and get Tom ready for bed ... we split time at weekends, so we can both work ... the thought of trying to work with two children fills me with cold horror ... the logistics of trying to do it are very very hard ... and it physically wears you out. (Banker, aged 37, interviewed 1996)

This career banker, interviewed in the 1990s, managed to hold down a demanding full-time job with considerable help from her husband, together with paid help with housework and ironing, and nursery care for her son. How much, if anything, has changed? Men are beginning to take more responsibility for domestic work and childcare – although there is evidence that the pace of change has slowed in recent years, and women still carry the major responsibility for domestic work and childcare (Crompton *et al.* 2003; see also Chapter 6). This may not necessarily be because men are 'shirking' their domestic responsibilities. If men's jobs have become more demanding, they will have less time for domestic work. Many of the women interviewed in the JRF research made a direct reference to their partners' hours of work in response to a direct question about the sharing of childcare:

NERYS: Probably not very much [involvement in childcare] because he was working full time as an electrical engineer, so he always had quite a demanding job. I felt that because he was working full time – he was always very interested in the children, but I wouldn't say he was ... and why should he when I was there all the time?

DONNA: He's not bad now. He has recently stopped working away. Before he worked away and it was all me. Now he's stopped and he stops work at 4.30 and he does all the running around, picking them up and taking them places. He does a 40-hour week now, before it was 70.

JEAN: Not with the first two, more with the last one. At one stage he was made redundant, he used to work for [name of company]. He was also a bingo caller and he was also trying to set up his own business, so he had three jobs at one stage. He was working all hours so he didn't really ... not with the first two.

In Britain, most women with young children do not work full time (two-thirds of women with children aged under 5 years work part time, and this proportion decreases as the age of the youngest child increases. See Dench *et al.* 2002: 45). Women in part-time employment tend to take on a considerably larger share of domestic and caring responsibilities than women in full-time employment. However, as we have seen, working part time is not seen to be compatible with career development, and managers are expected to both work full time and 'put in the hours' when required.

However, the numbers of women in full-time employment are rising. Does this mean that more mothers will, increasingly, seek to develop their careers? In order to explore the issue further, a separate analysis was carried out of seventeen interviews with mothers with a child under 16 who worked more than 35 hours a week at Shopwell and Cellbank.[5] Interestingly, although this was a qualitative study with no pretensions to random sampling, the number of mothers of young children working full time at Cellbank (9) was nearly twice that of full-time Shopwell mothers (5), reflecting the class variations in women's employment discussed in Chapter 2. Some, but not all, of the full-time mothers were career oriented, and three of the bankers were in managerial positions. All of these women would have liked to go further in Cellbank but felt that the demands on family life would simply be too much:

KERRY (Cellbank): If you are the sort of person that doesn't mind picking up your roots and moving every couple of years to heighten your career development, then there are the opportunities to do that. But if you want to build a family life and your children are at school so you can't heave them up all the time and move them around the country, then it's quite limited what's available to you.

Other full-time women not in managerial jobs (like Megan, quoted above), were 'holding back' career development until they were able to 'put in the hours'. One feature of interest about these mothers in full-time employment, however, was that a majority (eleven out of the seventeen) had past or present work/life circumstances that made economic independence important. Four were 'main breadwinners' in that their husbands were in low-paying jobs or not working through sickness (three of these husbands took major responsibilities for childcare). Four had experienced divorce and/or lone parenthood, and three had

---

[5] The JRF study included interviews with local authority employees, and three full-time mothers working for local authorities have been included in this analysis of seventeen mothers in all.

partners who had been made redundant in the past. Given that family life is becoming more risk-prone, we may anticipate that the proportion of women seeking economic independence is likely to rise in the future.

However, this micro-analysis suggests that even women who work full time find career development somewhat problematic. In the next section of this chapter, therefore, we will broaden our discussion to examine how men and women in different occupational classes are affected by the often conflicting demands of employment, career development and family life.

Class, gender, careers and 'work–life balance'

The discussion above has emphasised the difficulties, particularly those associated with the need to work long hours, that women (and men) face if they wish to pursue career success. However, it has also been stressed that circumstances are by no means unchanging. In part, pro-motion procedures have become more open because of pressures to include previously excluded groups (particularly women) – although it should be noted that this 'openness' resonates positively with other aspects of currently influential managerial policies that stress the im-portance of individualism and self-development. Nevertheless, through-out the 1980s and 1990s, Equal Opportunities (EO) policies were positively encouraged by government in Britain (as indeed, they still are), and widely introduced across the organisational spectrum. As Bradley (1998: chs. 5, 6) has demonstrated, EO policies have been, to a considerable extent, effective and have had an impact amongst men and women alike. As she emphasises, it is not only middle-class women who are seeking to take advantage of new opportunities for women, but also '"ordinary" women from lower-middle and working-class back-grounds who had worked their way up from the bottom' (Bradley 1998: 92). As we have seen, individual career development is an im-portant aspect of 'high-commitment' management practices, and in any case, basic grade jobs in low-level service work (such as Shopwell) do not furnish a sufficient income to maintain an independent household, even for a single person. Political culture in Britain after the demise of 'one-nation' policies has emphasised the importance of individual-ism, self-reliance and continuous self-development. How, then, are aspirations distributed amongst the British population?

The BSA survey included a number of questions relating to careers, including the statement: 'Speaking for myself, it is important for me to move up the job ladder at work.' The answers are summarised by sex and occupational class in Table 3.1:

Table 3.1. *'Speaking for myself, it is important for me to move up the job ladder at work' by sex and occupational class. BSA/ISSP survey (percentages)*

	Professional and managerial		Intermediate		Routine and manual	
	Men	Women	Men	Women	Men	Women
Very/fairly important	64**	46**	31	23	45	21
Not (very) important	36	54	69	77	55	79
Total	100	100	100	100	100	100
N	284	280	51	133	229	200

**p < .01; significant within-gender class differences.

The data in Table 3.1 show, as might have been expected, that career aspirations are not evenly distributed. Men are more likely to want to move up the job ladder than women, and managerial and professional employees are more likely to want promotion than routine and manual employees (between-class differences in promotion aspirations were also statistically significant).[6] Other factors that we might expect to affect career aspirations are age (people towards the end of their working lives being perhaps less concerned about career development than younger people), and the presence or absence of children – there is evidence that women in particular tend to put their careers 'on hold' when they have children (Becker and Moen 1999). We have also seen that working part time will significantly affect career possibilities. However, when all these factors were analysed together using a logistic regression (on full-time employees only, see Appendix Table 3.3, p. 88) it was found that the presence of children did not have a significant impact on career aspirations, once other factors were taken into account. The important factors are class, sex and age. Men are more than twice as likely as women to think that moving up the career ladder is important. People in the managerial and professional class grouping are three times more likely to think that moving up the career ladder is important than people in routine and manual jobs.

Managerial and professional women, therefore, are more than twice as likely as intermediate and routine and manual women to want to move up the job ladder. This might be taken to imply that non-managerial and

---

[6] As described in Chapter 2, note 8, women are overrepresented in the 'Intermediate' group given that the self-employed were not included in the BSA/ISSP survey. Our subsequent discussion will focus on Professional and Managerial, and Routine and Manual, employees only.

non-professional women (and men, for that matter), are more 'family centred' (and less 'work centred') than managerial and professional men and women, as suggested by the attitudinal data summarised in Chapter 2. As has been argued in Chapter 2, 'choosing' to focus on motherhood and family life rather than pursuing an employment career may be a rational position to take up if a lack of qualifications and relevant job experience means that it would be difficult to take strategic decisions in relation to employment in the future. It should also be remembered that career opportunities are, of course, likely to be more numerous in managerial and professional occupations than in routine and manual occupations. As has further been argued in Chapter 2, the fact that women in lower-level occupations with no or lower qualifications 'balance' employment and family by leaving employment or switching to part-time work will also contribute to the deepening of material class inequalities. However, as we shall see, this strategy does have the consequence of lowering levels of work–life stress.

Work–life 'balance' is, it might be argued, a somewhat misleading phrase, in that the term 'balance' suggests that some kind of harmony has been achieved between the competing demands of employment and family life. Given the increase in women's employment, more households are combining more paid work with their family obligations, but this does not necessarily mean that a 'balance' has been gained. A distinction may be made between the practicalities of work–life arrangements and their experiential dimension. The more neutral concept of 'articulation' refers to household/employment strategies via which employment and family are combined (dual earner, one and a half earner etc.). This is a purely descriptive term, no judgement by the user is implied (as it is by the term 'balance'). Variations in strategies of work–life articulation are likely to be associated with varying levels of work–life conflict (the experiential dimension of work–life articulation). The term work–life 'balance' is conventionally used if couples, somehow or other, manage to combine dual earning with caring responsibilities. However, this does not necessarily mean that an *experiential* 'balance' has been reached. The lack of attention to the experiential dimension no doubt underpins the widespread assumption that work–life 'balance' is somehow easier for middle-class women, as they are more able to buy in domestic supports. For example:

Any sensible approach to work–life policies cannot ignore the ... phenomenon of occupational class ... Women in managerial and professional jobs with higher incomes and benefits are in a much better position to achieve a balance than their much lower-paid and insecure counterparts employed, for example, in the retail trade and textiles. (Taylor 2002a: 18)

Besides assuming that work–life balance is a 'woman's problem', thus reproducing stereotypical assumptions about the gender division of labour, this statement also gives no attention to the lived experience of combining employment with caring responsibilities – that is, the experiential dimension.

In order to explore these nuances, a work–life conflict scale[7] was constructed using four items from the BSA survey (respondents were asked to indicate for each item whether this occurred several times a week, several times a month, once or twice or never. Higher scores indicate higher work–life conflict):

I have come home from work too tired to do the chores which need to be done.

It has been difficult for me to fulfil my family responsibilities because of the amount of time I spent on my job

I have arrived at work too tired to function well because of the household work I had done

I have found it difficult to concentrate at work because of my family responsibilities

In fact, women who worked part time had significantly ($p < .001$) lower (7.04) work–life conflict scores than women who worked full time (8.00). For the sample as a whole, reported levels of work–life conflict were significantly ($p < .001$) higher for professional and managerial (7.9) as compared to 'intermediate' or 'routine and manual' respondents (7.2) – which is not surprising given that professional and managerial respondents are more likely to be in full-time dual-earner households. Professional and managerial men and women expressed higher levels of work–life conflict despite the fact that in 'work–life' terms, their working conditions were likely to be better than those of routine and manual respondents (they were less likely to lose money if they took time off work for family reasons, and more likely to have 'understanding' supervisors. See Crompton *et al.* 2003). Variations in work–life conflict by occupational class, however, would appear to be largely a consequence of the average weekly hours worked within different occupational classes. A third of full-time managerial and professional employees in the BSA sample reported working over 50 hours a week, as compared with 15 per cent of routine and manual full-time employees ($p < .001$). In summary, work–life conflict levels are higher amongst professional and managerial employees because (a) professional and managerial women are more likely to work full time, and (b) professionals and managers (both men and women) work longer hours than

---

[7] Cronbach alpha 0.73, eigenvalue 2.2, 56 per cent of variance.

people in other occupational class categories. Hours of work, therefore, are the major factor contributing to work–life conflict, as has been demonstrated in other research (see White et al. 2003; Fagan and Burchell, 2002; Berg et al. 2003).

In Chapter 4 we will be examining in greater depth the topics of both working hours and work intensification, and their impact on work–life 'balance', and in Chapter 5 we will explore a wider range of factors that contribute to work–life conflict. In this chapter, we will look more closely at how individual aspirations for promotion might have an impact on conflict for men and women.[8] The case studies of Cellbank and Shopwell have demonstrated that it is necessary to work long hours in managerial positions (as we have seen, this is confirmed by the BSA survey), as well as to achieve promotion. It was also evident that full-time work is required in order to be considered for a career position. This fact would seem to be recognised by the BSA respondents in that amongst part-time employees, who were overwhelmingly women, over 80 per cent said that it was 'not very important' for them to move up the job ladder. The analysis in Table 3.2, therefore, focuses on full-time employees, as having the most realistic chances of being promoted.[9]

People wanting to be promoted are likely to be under pressure to 'perform' at work – which will include, as we have seen, working longer hours. Managers and professionals experience more work–life conflict, and are considerably more likely to want to move up the career ladder than routine and manual employees. However, a comparison of levels of work–life conflict by class and promotion aspirations (Table 3.2)[10] suggests that career aspirations had no impact on work–life conflict in the case of managerial and professional men – both the aspiring and the non-aspiring men had similar levels of conflict.

However, in the case of professional and managerial women, aspirations for promotion, it would seem, do have an impact on conflict

[8] In any case, it is only possible to explore the impact of promotion aspirations on work–life stress for the British sample, as questions relating to individual promotion aspirations were not asked in the other countries.

[9] The analysis will be simplified by comparing managerial and professional with routine and manual workers only, and excluding the 'intermediate' category. The intermediate category (which includes clerical workers) has a majority of female employees. In their attitudes to promotion, intermediate women are similar to routine and manual employees (Table 3.1).

[10] Only under a half of routine and manual women worked full-time, and of full-time women, only twenty expressed an interest in moving up the career ladder. Non-responses on attitude questions reduced numbers to fifteen. These numbers, therefore, were simply too small to permit further analysis. Our analysis therefore focuses on men only. However, the small numbers of full-time routine and manual women who wished to move up the career ladder did not report higher levels of work–life conflict than those who did not.

Table 3.2. *Occupational class, sex, and the impact of promotion aspirations on work–life conflict (BSA/ISSP survey, full-time employees only)*

Work–life conflict scores:	Managerial and professional men Mean (SD)	Managerial and professional women Mean (SD)	Routine and manual men Mean (SD)
'very' or 'fairly' important to move up the job ladder	7.74 (2.11)	8.78 (2.4)	7.78 (2.45)
'not very' or 'not' important to move up the job ladder	7.59 (2.2)	8.03 (2.31)	6.80 (2.55)
t-value	.511	2.095*	2.371*
Df	217	170	149

*p < .05.

levels. Neither weekly hours of work, nor the presence of children in the household, varied significantly as between 'aspirant' and 'non-aspirant' professional and managerial women. A regression analysis (Appendix Table 3.4) demonstrated that the presence of child(ren) in the household has an impact on work–life conflict for women, but not for men. If we make the assumption that the presence of children may be taken as an indicator of domestic responsibilities, then the major difference between aspirant professional and managerial women and similar men would seem to lie in the impact of these responsibilities. Women still carry out a disproportionate amount of domestic work (see Chapter 6), and it would seem that this is an important factor that contributes to the significantly higher levels of work–life conflict amongst professional and managerial women who aspire to move up the job ladder.

However, a similar argument cannot be developed in the case of routine and manual men, who will share with other men the general 'male advantage' in respect of domestic work. However, a comparison of the characteristics (whether married, and whether or not they had children) of routine and manual men who wished to move up the job ladder with those who did not revealed no systematic differences between the two groups except in one important respect. Significantly more of the men who wished to move up the job ladder were service sector employees[11] as compared with those for whom promotion was not important; 56 per cent of routine and manual men in service

[11] This includes wholesale/retail trade, hotels and restaurants, transport, finance, real estate, public administration and defence, education, health and social work and other social and personal services. Non-service employment includes agriculture, fishing, mining, manufacture, gas, electricity, water and construction.

employment said that it was important for them to move up the job ladder, as compared to only a third of men in non-service routine and manual employment. Indeed, nearly two-thirds (63 per cent) of aspirant routine and manual men were service sector employees (p < .01). It may be suggested, therefore, that an explanation for the greater levels of work–life conflict amongst aspirant routine and manual men might be sought in the nature of their employment and the career paths on offer.

As we have seen from the Shopwell case study, people who wished to be promoted were expected to work long hours, and even first-line supervisors worked longer hours because of the necessity to 'cover' for absent employees. Shopwell may be considered as a reasonably typical example of low-level service work, and the BSA survey demonstrates that routine and manual men who wished to be promoted suffer negative job to home spillover. Training and career development is an important element of 'high-commitment' managerial practices, and the work–life consequences for routine and manual men who respond 'positively' to such policies appear to be negative.

As we have seen, in the past, working-class careers have been relatively restricted, and whilst middle-class incomes increased over the employment life cycle, working-class incomes flattened beyond the peak earning ages of the mid 20s to mid-30s (Westergaard and Resler 1975: 80ff.). Indeed, the relative paucity of opportunities for promotion amongst routine and manual workers in the past was one of the reasons, it was argued in contemporary case studies, for the fact that lower-level workers tended to favour and/or put their faith in collective (i.e., trade union) or general rather than individual modes of social advancement (Goldthorpe et al. 1968: 130). This does not mean, however, that opportunities for promotion were non-existent for those in routine and manual occupations. Public service bureaucracies such as the railways, post office and fire service offered working-class occupational 'careers' – for example, from engine cleaner to engine driver. Skilled craft workers (e.g., electricians, setters, fitters, and welders) experienced occupational progression, given their long on-the-job training, from apprentice, to craftsman to senior craftsman. Trade unions played their part in protecting working-class careers via skill accreditation and the negotiation of seniority rules. These kinds of occupational protections played their part in the 'search for shelters' (Freedman 1984) that were established during the period of the mid twentieth-century social compromise.

Nevertheless, case study evidence from the 1960s indicated that aspirations for promotion were not particularly high amongst routine and manual employees. However, the reasons given for negative attitudes to promotion amongst lower-level employees in the 1960s were rather different from those offered in the second millenium. A meticulous coding of the replies given by the 'affluent workers' interviewed in an influential case study generated seven different categories of reasons for not being interested in promotion, from 'too much responsibility' to 'does not want to leave workmates' (Goldthorpe et al. 1968: 124). However, none of the men interviewed in the 1960s mentioned hours of work as a disincentive to aiming for a promoted position. As we have seen, this was the major reason given by lower-level service employees interviewed in 2002.

Thus it may be argued that the reason for the greater level of work–life conflict articulated by working-class men wanting to be promoted rests in the nature of contemporary working-class careers, particularly in the service industries. As we have seen, people working in low-level service jobs are expected to work long hours if they wish to be promoted. Indeed, amongst the BSA respondents, there was hardly any difference between the proportion of managerial and professional (36 per cent) and routine and manual (33 per cent) respondents in employment who 'disagreed' that 'In my kind of work, people who want to move up the job ladder have to put in long hours.' Many women in Cellbank and Shopwell did not put themselves forward for promotion because of the extra hours that would be involved, and men, too, were mindful of the impact it would have on their family lives. Craig, who was divorced, argued that: 'Break-ups are becoming the norm now. What's the point in trying to make the family work if you've got all these pressures coming from your employment ... you are in a cycle, aren't you? Working lots of hours, the relationship breaks down, and you go into denial and and that's happening across the board. At some point you've got to break the cycle and say "Right, what can we do now to enable people to work less hours, be closer to the family and bring some stability to businesses?"' The family pressures on managers with employed partners are indeed considerable. For example, Martin, a lower-level Shopwell manager married to another Shopwell manager said that: 'My wife and I don't see each other a lot. Because of the way shifts work out we get two clear days with each other a month.'

These findings support the arguments of Grimshaw et al. (2001, 2002), who have demonstrated that a significant effect of recent changes in service sector organisations has been to open up the 'gap' in the job ladder between lower-grade employees and the first step on the promotional ladder: 'the most direct effect of the flattened jobs hierarchy has been to remove the architecture necessary for career progression' (2001: 38). Making the transition to the first rung of the managerial ladder has become increasingly dependent on individual appraisals, and

Grimshaw *et al.* argue that: 'staff with ambitions to "move up" the organisation ... know that they face an *"all-or-nothing" effort in time and energy to make the transition to a mid-level post'* (2002:109, my emphasis). Thus James, involved in 'shift parenting' with his wife, did not want promotion at Shopwell: 'I've had approaches and chances to move up here but I've never pursued it because of the kids. Before you can get up the ladder they keep you on small wages and working long hours and I can't afford to do it.' Increasing his hours would mean he had less time for childcare, and purchasing childcare was not an option given the low wages of James and his wife.

Conclusion

In this chapter, we have focused on changes in the workplace, and on the way in which employees are managed, together with the impact of these changes on organisational careers for men and women. Organisations have become more flexible with delayering, business reengineering and outsourcing, and flexible employment has increased. Occupational careers have become less stable. Re-organisation at Cellbank, for example, meant that many employees had to re-apply for the 'new' jobs that were created, as we have seen in the case of Flora.[12] With the growth of service employment, there has been an increasing focus on the need to develop organisational cultures that will ensure that the outcomes of the service encounter will be maximised by committed employees, thus ensuring organisational profitability. 'High-commitment' management practices, that seek to empower and involve the workforce, have been developed to achieve these ends. It should be noted that many employees were highly sceptical of such 'culture-building' attempts, and many at Cellbank were positively opposed to the culture of sales and targeting that had been introduced. Most Shopwell workers were not affected, for them working at Shopwell was 'just a job'. Craig was particularly insightful on the topic of Shopwell 'culture', which was vigorously promoted:

when it [Shopwell 'culture'] goes off the rails it can be engulfing and leave people behind. If there's anything to leave. Or they get confused. But at its best it's respectful of the individual, service to the customers, a striving for excellence, all those are accomplished together and they all work together in harmony ... But when it's rammed down their throats then people get confused. It's very

---

[12] This reengineering usually involved a loss of posts, as described by Zoe: 'There used to be G3 and G4 managers. I got the job as a G3 manager and then they decided to get rid of them and so we all had to apply for G4 managers, there were 15 managers going for 12 posts but I got one of them.'

powerful. It's very driving. You either do it and fit in with it or it's not for you and you leave.

In parallel with these workplace trends, gender equality has been promoted and indeed has now been 'mainstreamed' in government policies at both national and European levels. Rising levels of qualification amongst women have been associated with the increased entry of women into higher-level occupations and professions, and as individuals, women are widely accepted as the equals of men in the sphere of employment. Indeed, it has been argued that stereotypically feminine attributes such as empathy, and the capacity to form and nurture relationships, are key attributes in employment in the 'service economy'. In the flexible, individualised working environments of 'reflexive modernity', it is argued, gender differences will increasingly be eroded. Thus McInnes (1998), for example, has argued for the 'end of masculinity', and Castells (1997: 169) emphasises the attractiveness of female employees as lying in 'their relational skills, increasingly necessary in an information economy'. Castells goes on to describe a 'crisis of patriarchalism', that 'manifests itself in the increasing diversity of partnership arrangements among people to share life and raise children' (*ibid.*: 221).

Other authors have been rather more pessimistic as to the consequences of increasing employment flexibility and the growth of the 'network society' as described by authors such as Castells. In an influential text, Sennett (1998) has argued that flexible working and the end of long-term career predictability have undermined the contribution of employment to the formation of individual identities. In the circumstances of modern organisations, he argues, trust has broken down, and relationships have been fragmented, as human beings no longer have deep reasons to care about one another (Sennett 1998: 148). Sennett's argument, however, ignores gender differences as far as the impact of these kinds of changes is concerned, and it is assumed that their impact on women and men is the same (Wajcman and Martin 2002).

However, most women do not experience career development in the same way as, or have the same priorities as, most men. The playing field between men and women competing as individuals in employment may have been levelled somewhat, but women as mothers and carers, as we have seen in this chapter, face considerable difficulties. Moreover, as Lewis (2002: 348) has argued, 'too often women experience little *genuine* choice to care'. As individuals, women may be seen as equal in the sphere of employment, but normative constructs still allocate the major responsibility for care to women: 'our constructs of gendered behaviour emerged from societies in which men had far more cultural and economic power than women. The result can be described as "socially imposed altruism" (Badgett and Folbre 1999: 316). Thus although, within contemporary organisations, direct discrimination by sex is probably a relatively unusual phenomenon, as normatively 'encumbered workers' (Halford et al. 1997), even experienced and well-qualified women will face difficulties in pursuing an organisational career.

As has been argued in Chapters 1 and 2, therefore, a perspective (whether positive or negative) informed by an emphasis on increasing individualism in 'reflexive modernity' is not sufficient to understand the gendered impact of contemporary workplace change. Rather, a consideration of the total social organisation of labour and the totality of relationships of production and reproduction, employment and care has demonstrated the continuing tension between employment and caring responsibilities, together with the negative occupational consequences for women. That it is problematic to combine caring responsibilities with career success is not, of course, a new or original finding. The data analysed in this chapter suggests that these tensions are greatest for two groups who have responded 'positively' to the competitive changes of reflexive modernity, and seek advancement within increasingly individualised career structures. These are aspirant managerial and professional women, and men in routine and manual occupations who want to move up the job ladder. Much of the contemporary discussion of the problems of combining career success and family responsibilities has focused on individuals in high-flying managerial and professional occupations (Bailyn 1993; Wharton and Blair-Loy 2002). However, the qualitative data analysed in this chapter suggests that even a move out of a lower rung of the occupational ladder will be associated with increased pressures on domestic life.

In line with the contemporary emphasis on individualism in much social science, one feature of many discussions of workplace change has been a focus on attempts to change workplace behaviour from within via the development of organisational cultures and the 'enterprising self' (Rose 1989; Du Gay 1996). However, organisations do not exist in thin air, but are embedded in a wider economic and social context that can have a significant impact on them. For example, the major banks undertook significant changes in their practices in relation to the recruitment and employment of women following a reference to the Equal Opportunities Commission in the 1980s (Crompton 1989), and employers are now required to 'mainstream' gender in all their practices. Thus organisations have changed and responded to wider shifts in ideas about gender equality, and women's aspirations.

Nevertheless, in many if not most organisations, the 'ideal' career worker will still be an individual who is prepared to demonstrate their commitment to the employer by meeting organisational demands (for example, by meeting personal or group targets), even if this means working long hours.

Furthermore, organisations do not recruit undifferentiated labour, but individuals who have families, are men or women, and possess different kinds of expertise, job experience and qualifications. An older literature on labour market segmentation has argued for the advantages that may be gained by employers if they recruit from particular, non-competing, labour market sectors (Barron and Norris 1976; Doeringer and Piore 1971). In an increasingly 24/7 society, employee flexibility has demonstrable advantages for employers (Dex and McCulloch 1997; Purcell et al. 1999). From this kind of perspective, it might be argued that although Shopwell *was* 'family friendly', and *did* go to considerable lengths to accommodate its (basic grade) employees, more cynically this flexibility might be seen as a skilful adaptation to the circumstances created by a declining 'breadwinner wage' society and the requirement for 'component wages' (Siltanen 1986) in one and a half breadwinner households. In such households, workers need flexibility, particularly if they have caring responsibilities, and Shopwell was ready to oblige: 'One of my staff, her sister had cerebral palsy and was quite poorly ... her dad also works for Shopwell ... just so they could visit her ... we are now in the process of just tweaking her hours around slightly because her dad works at night and sleeps during the day ...' (HR manager Shopwell; see also Thea and Carolynne: ch. 2, pp. 47, 59).

However, as we have seen, this flexibility did not extend to those in even lower-level managerial jobs. Indeed, the evidence reviewed in this chapter suggests that current organisational policies might be seen as pulling in two directions. On the one hand, many (if not most) organisations are attempting to develop and deliver a progressive human resources agenda that values diversity and encourages employees in their personal and career development, whilst responding positively to staff combining employment and caring responsibilities. On the other hand, high-commitment management practices, together with organisational delayering and business reengineering, are setting demanding business targets and increasing workplace pressures on individuals. In Chapter 4, therefore, we will explore at greater length the changing nature of employer–employee relations, as well as current developments in both government and employer policies relating to work–life articulation.

Appendix

Table 3.3. *Logistic regression: Important to move up the job ladder at work*

	Odds ratio
Respondent's sex: male	2.026***
Age	.920***
Child in household	.885
Occupational class (Reference category: routine and manual)	
Professional/managerial	2.756***
Intermediate	.556*
Full-time employment	2.169***
Constant	4.775
N	1084

*p < .05.
***p < .001.
−2 Log likelihood 1253.712.
Nagelkerke R .342.

Table 3.4. *Multiple regressions on work–life stress, men and women, Britain*

Men only, ft

Variable	Beta	t-value	Sig.
Work hours	.209	4.641	<.001
Child in household	.057	1.252	.211
Class[a]	.109	2.428	.016
Age	−.058	−1.285	.200

Adj. r^2 = .058; ANOVA F = 8.293; p < .001; N = 332.

Women only, ft

Variable	Beta	t-value	Sig.
Work hours	.230	4.074	<.001
Child in household	.197	3.711	<.001
Class[a]	.036	.644	.520
Age	.008	.157	.875

Adj. r^2 = .083; ANOVA F = 8.474; p < .001; N = 332.
[a] managerial and professional *vs.* intermediate and routine and manual.

4   Work–life articulation, working hours and work–life policies

Introduction: the story so far

In previous chapters, we have examined in parallel a series of developments relevant to the articulation of employment and family life. The economic and normative changes associated with the emergence of the 'modern', male-breadwinner family in Britain have been reviewed, together with its slow erosion and decline. We have charted women's progress towards formal equality with men, and the associated increase in women's employment, particularly that of mothers. The role of 'preferences' and gendered moral rationalities in shaping mothers' employment practices has been critically examined. Changing attitudes to the family, and gender roles, have been reviewed, and the class and gender variations in these attitudes described. Finally, we have addressed the issue of contemporary employment and workplace change, and its implications as far as both family arrangements and women's aspirations for promotion are concerned.

A number of different themes have emerged. The significance of individual 'choice' has been recognised but it has been emphasised that 'choices' are constrained by the (rather different) inequalities of gender and class. Women's claims to gender equality have been largely accepted, and there is widespread support for more egalitarian gender roles. However, even though women may have had their equal status, as individuals, recognised as legitimate, there are nevertheless persisting normative assumptions relating to gendered responsibilities for care work (even though 'choice' may indeed play its part in the take-up of these responsibilities). The nature of employment has changed in a manner that accommodates women's dual responsibilities (for 'breadwinning' and 'caregiving'), in that more part-time and flexible work is now available (particularly in countries such as Britain). However, at the workplace, full-time employment and longer hours working are required even to move off the first rung of the job ladder. This means that as mothers and carers, most women are simply not able to compete on equal terms with most men. Thus despite formal gender equality policies in respect of employment, men still predominate in higher-level jobs. As a consequence, Britain is still a one and a half breadwinner, rather than dual breadwinner society.

We have maintained a dual focus on class and gender in our discussions. The persistence of powerful gender norms in relation to care work means that women have different kinds of external constraints, and therefore a lack of equity, in comparison to men. Class inequalities are shared by women and men alike. There are substantial class variations in both the distribution of men's and women's employment (that will serve to widen inequalities between middle-class and working-class households), and in attitudes to gender roles and the family. Middle-class women face, relatively, lower levels of external material constraints than working-class women, and are more able to exercise their choices. Thus our evidence suggests that working-class 'familialism' is (at least in part) likely to be a consequence of class inequalities. Both quantitative and qualitative research suggests that attitudinal differences, particularly between young working-class and middle-class women, are a rationalisation of the inequitable 'choices' they have made.

At the present time, therefore, work–life articulation in Britain is achieved alongside continuing gender inequality in the sphere of employment, and widening class inequalities. At the level of the individual and the household, it may be argued that this need not necessarily be a cause for concern. The majority of people, when asked a direct question, would place family life ahead of any striving for individual career success (61 per cent of men, and 75 per cent of women, in the BSA survey 'disagreed' that it was 'important to move up the job ladder at work, even if it gets in the way of family life'). Nevertheless, the 'one and a half breadwinner' work–family articulation model is by no means satisfactory. As we have seen, it is associated with widening inequalities between households, family stress associated with the increased number of hours worked by families in total and men in particular, and an unfair distribution of 'choices' between both men and women, and women in different occupational classes. These problems are amongst the reasons for the increasing importance that 'work–life balance' has assumed as a policy issue. In this chapter, therefore, we will be reviewing a range of research evidence relating to employers' work–life integration provisions as well as scrutinising recent policy developments in Britain. We will also continue with our investigations, initiated in Chapter 3, of the effect of recent changes in workplace organisation and management, particularly their impact on working hours and work intensification.

Bringing in the state

Much of the research on employment and work–life 'balance' originates in the United States – see, for example, Hochschild's (1997) widely cited case study of the 'failure' of family-friendly policies in an organisation also committed to 'high-commitment' management practices. That employer-related policies should be a focus of concern in the US is not surprising. As Evans (OECD 2000: 12) has noted, in comparison with many European states, the US has 'relatively low levels of public provision for childcare and relatively low levels of statutory family leave benefits, stemming partly from the belief that the State should not interfere in family life and in the organisation of enterprises. A good deal of responsibility thus rests upon firms, and there is considerable interest in how they respond' (see also Gornick and Meyers 2003: 143). There was a very rapid increase in the employment of women in the US from the 1970s, and indeed, since the mid-1970s there have been more dual-worker than 'traditional' (i.e., one-earner) families (Bailyn 1993: 5). Between 1960 and 1998, in the US the proportion of married women with children less than 6 years old who were in the workforce increased from 18.6 per cent to 63.7 per cent (Freeman 2000). Indeed, Freeman argues that the 'unprecedented rate' at which employment opportunities for women were opened up in the US is one of the major factors contributing to the success of the (flexible, deregulated) US economy in the 1990s (see also Hutton 2001).

Flexible, deregulated employment in the US is also associated with extreme income inequality. Although the US has the highest per capita income in the world, the bottom 10 per cent of the income distribution in the US ranks only thirteenth (Freeman 2000; Hutton 2002: 25). Many women are sole earners, or have joined the labour market because their family could not subsist without two incomes. As noted, the US is also characterised by a lack of state welfare provision. Welfare provision is residual, acting as a 'safety net' for only the very poorest, and is highly privatised (Esping-Andersen 1990). Thus employer-provided social insurance and pension provision is crucial – when it is available. With no statutory protection, employees in the US may have existing benefits reduced or withdrawn even when in employment. As Zweig (2000: 90) has noted, 'Leaving welfare and Medicaid for a low-paying job with no medical benefits is hardly a rational economic choice.' However, welfare 'reforms', notably the removal of Aid to Families with Dependent Children (AFDC) and its replacement in 1996 by the Personal Responsibility and Work Opportunity Reconciliation Act (PRWORA) and Temporary Aid to Needy Families (TANF) removed many of the poor from the welfare rolls and into low-level, unprotected, employment. An example of such employment would be Wal-Mart, the largest supermarket in the US, which is non-union and pays its workers $9.64 an hour, as compared to the $15.98 union average.[1]

A number of parallels may be drawn between Britain and the United States in respect of these trends. British women, particularly mothers, have also been entering employment in ever-greater numbers. The rate of increase has lagged slightly behind that of the US, but the overall picture is very similar. Two-earner couples of working age were the norm in the US by the 1970s, but in Britain this norm was not established until the 1980s (51 per cent by 1981, 60 per cent by 1991, census data. See Rake et al. 2000). By 2001, 57 per cent of mothers with a child under 5 in Britain were in employment (Dench et al. 2002), as compared to (as we have seen) 68 per cent (1998 figures) in the US. In a number of other respects, British labour market and welfare policies are also closer to those of the US than the rest of Europe. For example, Gornick and Meyers' (2003) comparative policy analysis of dual-earner family policies and their outcomes consistently ranks Britain, along with the US and Canada, as making the least generous provisions and having the most negative outcomes for families.

The British government has done much to promote employment flexibility, and indeed, in debates within the European Union, British governments have argued that the deregulation of employment in Britain is the major factor contributing to the success of the British economy, as compared to European partners (considerable caution needs to be exercised in respect of these kind of arguments, as the most recent evidence suggests that average job tenure has increased, and turnover decreased, between 1992 and 2000 (Taylor 2002b)). However, elements of the government's approach to welfare in Britain also have US parallels – indeed, Esping-Andersen (1990) groups the US and the UK as 'liberal' welfare states, offering means-tested benefits to only the poorest. These kinds of policies have not changed radically under the 'New Labour' government. Indeed, in 1998 the incoming New Labour government, in an echo of PRWORA, cut benefits to lone parents as well as introducing a 'New Deal'. The New Deal promotes paid work as the best long-term route to financial independence for all citizens. In 1999 Prime Minister Blair declared 'the end of the something-for-nothing

---

[1] See *Guardian* 29 Nov. 2003: 'US shoppers join counter revolution: Benefits battle could be one of most critical strikes in American labour history.'

welfare state', and the government introduced compulsory work-focused interviews for virtually all benefit claimants.

These kinds of comparisons should not be overdrawn. Britain still has a free National Health Service at the point of delivery. The levels of benefit for the poorest have been raised since 1997 (a National Minimum Wage has been introduced, alongside Child and Working Family tax credits),[2] and overall poverty (defined as 60 per cent of median income) has fallen by 1 million (Hills 2004; Sutherland *et al.* 2003). Nevertheless, a broad distinction may be drawn between, on the one hand, a rather more regulationist, 'European' approach to employment and welfare on the one hand, and a deregulationist, flexible, Anglo-US approach on the other (see also Chapters 5 and 8).

One feature that the UK shares with the US is the relatively long hours worked by employees (indeed, Britain is the only country with partial exemption from the European Working Time Directive). Average working hours in Britain are the highest in Europe (1737 hours a year) and average working hours are even higher in the US (1957 hours a year, see Freeman 2000, OECD 2002). Much of the work–life debate in the US was stimulated by Juliet Schor's (1991) influential study, *The Overworked American*, which argued that, contrary to the widespread assumption that hours of work were falling in advanced or 'post' industrialism, they were in fact rising in the US. As hours worked are, as we have seen in Chapter 3, highly significant for the quality of work–life articulation, we will briefly examine recent perceptions of work and working hours in Britain, drawing on both qualitative (JRF) and quantitative (BSA) data.

Working hours and work intensification

Hours worked by employees vary considerably between different countries. OECD data (*Employment Outlook* 2002: Table F) suggests a huge variation between 1346 hours a year (the Netherlands) and 2447 hours (Korea). However, these data include part-time employees, which would have the effect of greatly reducing 'average' hours in countries with high rates of part-time employment (and rates of part-time employment are indeed very high in the Netherlands). Individual-level data gives a more robust indicator of hours actually worked by employees. As can be seen from Table 4.1, the hours worked by British full-time employees (men and women) are the highest in Europe (Table 4.1 gives data for some

---

[2] Tax credits and the minimum wage are also features of US policy.

Table 4.1. *EU comparisons: Average hours usually worked per week by full-time employees, by sex; working time arrangements, couples with children (percentages)*

	Men (hours per week)	Women (hours per week)	Couples with children: % 1 earner	Couples with children: % both ft	Couples with children: % man ft, woman pt
UK	44.9	40.6	29.8	28.6	40.0
France	38.2	36.9	36.0	45.4	16.3
Norway	39.0	37.6	n.a.	n.a.	n.a.
Finland	40.0	38.2	n.a.	n.a.	n.a.
Portugal	41.1	39.2	26.5	66.5	7.0
EU 15	40.8	38.6	n.a.	n.a.	n.a.

Sources: Working hours, Labour Force Survey, 2002; working time arrangements, Franco and Winqvist 2002 (data for 2000).
n.a. data not available.

of those European countries that will be included in our comparative analysis in subsequent chapters). However, as Clarkberg and Merola (2003: 35) have argued, 'Debates that centre on the measurement of individual-level averages are missing the point – the time squeeze is largely a family-level phenomenon.' That is, in a household with caring responsibilities beyond the maintenance of adults alone, it is the total hours spent in employment by adults that will impact on caregiving capacities. Thus in relation to work–life articulation, the household, rather than the individual, should be the unit of analysis. Table 4.1, therefore, also includes data on household working time arrangements (where available).

Table 4.1 demonstrates, as would have been expected, that the most frequent household arrangement for couples with children in Britain is the one and a half breadwinner model, whereby the man works full time, and the woman part time. However one and a half worker households are by no means the norm amongst European countries. Besides the UK, the one and a half breadwinner arrangement is most prevalent in the Netherlands, as well as Belgium, Germany and Luxembourg. In all other countries, two full-time earners are the norm. In the UK, Germany and the Netherlands, the presence of children has a significant positive impact on the level of women's part-time working in dual-earner households (Franco and Winqvist 2002). From the data in Table 4.1, therefore, we would expect considerable variations in the actual 'time squeeze' both between and within countries. Individual working hours are lowest in France (a consequence of national legislation on the 35 hour working week, see Bishop 2004), but proportionately more couples with children both work full time than in Britain. Although the UK has the longest working hours, it also has the highest proportion of one and a half earner households, which will reduce the impact of the time squeeze on families. Portugal has lower individual working hours than Britain, but a very high proportion of both parents working full time. These variations demonstrate the very real significance of what Fagan (2001) has described as national 'working-time regimes', which should be taken into account in any attempt to understand both 'preference' and 'choice' in respect of men's and women's employment.

Britain, therefore, is characterised by a working-time regime that involves long hours for those who work full time, but the time squeeze on households will be reduced by the prevalence of part-time working amongst women, although, as we have seen in Chapter 2, this particular version of a national working-time regime is associated with widening class inequalities. There is a widespread perception amongst people in Britain that this country has a 'long hours culture'. This is in part a consequence of the long hours actually worked by (full-time) individuals, as well as the increase in hours worked within the household given the rising levels of women's employment. The extent to which average working hours in Britain have actually risen in recent years may be debated (Green 2001), but it is incontestable that a majority of people think that they have increased. A recent survey (the 'Employment in Britain' survey, see Taylor 2002b) demonstrates a sharp decline in satisfaction amongst employees with the hours they work between 1992 and 2000. Amongst managerial and professional employees, satisfaction with hours worked declined from 36 per cent to only 16 per cent over this period, and for unskilled workers, satisfaction fell from 34 per cent to 15 per cent (these data are for men only, a similar pattern is found for women and other occupational groups). When asked why they work longer hours, the majority of respondents in the Employment in Britain survey said that their jobs had got more demanding. This perception was reported across the whole range of occupations, from professionals and managers to routine and manual workers (however, routine and manual workers were considerably more likely to say that they worked long hours to earn extra money).

Work intensification, therefore, was the major reason given by the respondents in the Employment in Britain survey for their perceived increase in working hours. In Britain (and other countries), a number of factors have contributed to the intensification of work. Technological developments such as IT have increased the flexibility with which organisations source, produce and distribute their products, calling for a corresponding increase in employee flexibility. In Britain, the economic impact of globalisation has been considerable, as reflected in the high inflow into the UK of Trans National Companies (TNCs), that can shift production and resources globally, leading to increasing insecurity at work.[3] Shareholder power (via stock market liberalisation) has increased, and cost-cutting through redundancies and work intensification is seen as a quick-fix strategy for increasing profitability and thus meeting shareholder demand. These developments reflect the growing significance of neoliberal policy responses to global changes:

The neoliberal economists of the late 1970s and early 1980s argued that inflation results from increases in the money supply . . . They claimed that unemployment was caused not by deficiencies on the *demand side* of the economy . . . but by those on the *supply side*. In their opinion, the reason unemployment remained so high was because of the inflexibility of the labour market and, in particular, the failure of wages to make sufficient downward adjustment. (Ladipo and Wilkinson 2002: 35–6)

Thus, as has been noted in Chapter 2, from the end of the 1970s neoliberalism has been increasingly influential in shaping labour market related policies in Britain and the US. British workers have never enjoyed particularly strong legal protections, and changes in the 1980s (such as the weakening of redundancy protections) reduced these further, bringing British workers closer to the 'employment-at-will' circumstances of the US. Unemployment (and other) benefits were relatively reduced (the link between relative earnings and benefit levels was removed, and replaced by a link to prices), and entitlements to unemployment pay brought down (e.g., a time limit of six months was set for entitlement to full unemployment benefits). There has also been a deliberate change in the structure of ownership in Britain with the privatisation of the public sector. Many enterprises have been sold to the private sector (gas, telecommunications, water, rail etc.). The services that remain (health, education, national and local government) have been commercialised, and contractual (or quasi contractual) market mechanisms introduced. These kinds of changes have intensified work levels and increased feelings of job insecurity – although, as we have seen, employment in Britain is probably more secure than is perceived by individual employees.

Nevertheless, feelings of insecurity will make a contribution to a willingness to 'go along with' employer requirements that increase levels

---

[3] For example, at the present time (2003) call centre jobs are being moved to the Far East.

of work intensity. As Rubery *et al.* (2003) have argued, it is in the interest of employers to work towards a 'results-based' employment relationship that maximises employee output. Through flexible scheduling and variable shifts, employers act so as to eliminate work time when opportunities for effort are low and maximise work time when opportunities for effort are high. Higher up the occupational ladder, salaried workers not entitled to overtime pay may simply have their workloads increased. Rubery *et al.* (2003) have described these processes as aspects of the increasing 'commodification' of the employment relationship (see also Esping-Andersen 1990). If commodification is high, the employment relationship only exists when labour effort is being expended. Both state regulation and collective bargaining have in the past intervened to modify the employment relationship away from a purely employer-led model, but as Rubery *et al.* demonstrate, recent changes in workplace practices, associated with the 'high-commitment' management practices discussed in the last chapter, are placing increasing pressures on employee time.

In Rubery *et al.*'s case studies of six large service sector organisations, 'working time' emerged as a major issue. All of the organisations studied had extended opening or operating hours to respond to perceived customer or client demands. The range of new strategies that targeted working time to increase productivity included flexible scheduling for full-timers to target labour hours to the peaks of customer demand, cutting core hours of work for part-timers, linking time schedules to tighter job specifications, extending operating hours without increasing staff numbers, and expecting staff to take overtime as time off in lieu. In addition, more and more lower management and supervisory staff were being placed on contracts with no rights to paid overtime. These practices reduced the 'porosity' of the working day and increased work intensity.

As we have already seen in Chapter 2, similar practices were under way (if not already in place) in Shopwell and Cellbank (the discussion that follows will also draw on interviews with employees in Local Government carried out as part of the JRF project). Shopwell stores were open for very long hours (some were open for 24 hours) and achieved working time flexibility via the extensive employment of part-time staff on variable shifts. First-level supervisors (also on variable shifts) were expected to work unpaid overtime when necessary (see Grace, p. 72). Cellbank was also in the process of extending hours of opening. Cellbank made extensive use of part-time staff and expected unpaid overtime from managers; non-managerial staff were expected to take time off in lieu. In addition, as we have seen in Chapter 2, the introduction of performance-related pay ('targets') has also increased work intensity. Flexible working, which included Saturday working without an overtime premium, was being introduced in some areas. In Local Government, employees were under constant pressure as the result of budget cutbacks, as well as initiatives such as 'Best Value' (where council departments have to demonstrate that the service they provide could not be provided more cheaply by the private sector).

In the JRF research, information was gathered on contracted hours, and all interviewees were in addition asked to state their 'usual' hours of working. Nearly a half of the 126 respondents interviewed in the JRF research reported that they regularly worked longer hours than contracted; 41 reported working unpaid overtime, 16 (all Shopwell employees) worked longer hours to earn extra money (on a regular basis). All Cellbank managers interviewed, and all Shopwell managers, worked regular unpaid overtime, some non-managerial Cellbank employees also worked unpaid overtime in order to meet their targets. Both councils operated flexitime systems, and most council employees used flexitime to compensate for extra hours worked. However, most council managers also reported that they worked unpaid overtime. All interviewees were asked whether or not they thought that 'people worked longer hours these days'. The majority of interviewees thought that working hours had in fact increased. Those who thought that working hours had *not* increased usually saw this as a consequence of strategies designed to maximise employee output without increasing costs (as Rubery and her colleagues would put it, to increase the 'commodification' of the employment relationship):

RACHEL (Cellbank): I don't think so [*that people work longer hours*] because I can cast my mind back 12 years ago and I would often be there until six o'clock at night on busy days. And now you're not because the bank doesn't want to pay overtime. They want you out the door. When there was overtime, people did tend to work longer. You work harder now . . . I'd say definitely they get their money's worth now.

Amongst those who did think that people now worked longer hours, one reason given was material pressures: 'greed, probably', 'lifestyles have changed so you need better incomes coming in', 'more things now, more mod cons, mortgages'. As Flora put it: 'I think we are very materialistic these days and we all want the playstations and everything for the children and everything for the home, but we have to work so hard for it.' Not surprisingly, the answers of many Shopwell employees reflected the long hours opening of the stores 'Society has now made it that it is part and parcel of the norm. You have a six-day week, work 30,

40 hours a week. There isn't a lot of family life for people because this is what society is making it. We must rush, we must have what they've got' (Grace).[4]

However, it was striking that, in the main, the reasons that interviewees gave for believing that 'people work longer hours than they used to' related in a very direct fashion to the kinds of changes in both the employment relationship, and the employment context, that have been reviewed and discussed in relation to Rubery et al.'s research findings. In Cellbank, the introduction of Saturday working (which also changed core hours for permanent staff) without an overtime premium was unpopular:

SHIRLEY: I am having to work on a Saturday and have never had to do so since I was 16, now we have to. It used to be voluntary and you got paid but now it's all day and no pay and you get another day off in the week, but I'm on my own then, my husband doesn't get that day off.

NATALIE: At one time there was a lot of overtime but now we've got flexible working. It means a longer working day and some Saturday working. It was voluntary to sign the flexible contract but you had to move your days and change your hours otherwise you'd have to change branches. People are not happy about it.

Other employees, particularly in Shopwell, also complained of 'unsocial' hours:

LAURA: I think they [i.e. 'people'] work odd hours. There's no social life. Today I'm here for 10 hours, from 10.30 a.m. to 8.30 p.m. By the time I get home it's 9 p.m. so it's taking your life away from you.

These examples demonstrate that, as Rubery et al. have argued, one impact of flexible working is that the time boundary between 'work' and 'non-work' becomes increasingly blurred and contested.

In the councils and in Cellbank, many interviewees commented on the way in which changes to working practices had increased the intensity of work. In Cellbank, staffing in branches had been cut and individual targets introduced:

SCOTT: Without question [people work longer hours these days]. Because we are spread very thinly. The targets aren't always achievable during the day, so a lot of people stay and do telesales in the evening.

---

[4] Another reason given for 'people working longer hours' was the desire for promotion. This has been discussed in Chapter 3 and will not be pursued further here.

BILL: Yes [people work longer hours these days]. In the bank environment there is more pressure on them to achieve their targets. And you will find that that added to the staffing being reduced in branches, they haven't got enough hours in the day to do their job as well as they need to do.

PHILIP: I think there's a fear factor, which may put you under more pressure than you need to be . . . I think it's expected. And you feel that if you don't put in that amount of work you could jeopardise your own position. If others are seen to do it and you don't follow suit it can isolate you.

In the councils, budget cuts and initiatives such as 'Best Value' have increased the pressure:

TERRY: The threat that the whole IT service would be contracted out and that it would be run in quite a different way in the future. There is quite a lot of pressure to do those hours, to perform, to meet project deadlines and impress the management without necessarily being compensated in any way other than as some way of securing or prolonging your job so it wasn't contracted out. So I think a lot of pressure does come from the threat of competition and I do see that is why people are working longer hours.

PATSY: People definitely work longer hours. More is expected of you, and the level of staffing is much lower so there really aren't enough people to do the work . . . I have suffered from depression caused by stress. Many of my senior colleagues are in the same boat. There is an awful lot of pressure on you, mainly caused by government initiatives.

These kinds of interviewee responses, therefore, contribute to the growing body of evidence to the effect that, in Britain, work intensity has increased considerably (Burchell *et al.* 2002; Green 2001; Rubery *et al.* 2003; Taylor 2002b), and most of those interviewed in the JRF research thought that working hours had increased as well. Similarly, in the BSA survey, 58 per cent of men, and 55 per cent of women in employment, agreed that 'people in my kind of job are expected to work longer hours these days than they used to'. Only 25 per cent of men, and 28 per cent of women, 'disagreed' that people are expected to work longer hours. There was some variation by social class (65 per cent of male professional and managerial, as compared to 52 per cent of routine and manual, thought that people had to work longer hours). Not surprisingly, those respondents who worked the longest hours were the most likely to think that longer hours were expected nowadays, and this was particularly marked for women. Amongst women who worked more than 40 hours a week, 70 per cent thought that people in their kind of job were expected to work longer hours, and for women who worked more than 50 hours a week, the percentage rose to 83.

Table 4.2. *Couple work-hour strategies, BSA/ISSP survey*

Work-hour strategy	His work hours	Her work hours	Percentage (total)	% (Child in household)
High commitments	Over 40	Over 40	12	7
Dual moderates	35–40	35–40	16	9
Neotraditionalists	Over 40	Under 40	33	38
Alternate commitments	One partner works less than 35 hours, the other works no more than 40		19	18
Traditionalists	Over 35 hours	None	20	27
			100 (830)	100 (434)

However, as has been argued above, it is the total of working hours within the household that has the greatest impact on the 'time squeeze' experienced by families. Couple households in the BSA sample were therefore classified according to their working hour strategies (see Moen 2003: 19). These are described in Table 4.2.[5] As can be seen, a third of the respondents were in couple working arrangements that would be classified as 'neotraditional', where the man works over 40 hours a week, and the woman works less than full time.

As would have been expected on the basis of the data presented in Chapter 2, there was considerable class variation in couple working hour strategies: 34 per cent of managerial and professional respondents fell into either the 'high-commitment' or 'dual moderate' category, as compared to 21 per cent of routine and manual respondents. Just over a half of the respondents in partnerships had a child under 16 in the household, and not surprisingly this also had an impact on the proportions falling into the different categories, as can be seen from Table 4.2. The impact of couples' different work-hour strategies on attitudes to work–life 'balance' is considerable, as can be seen from Table 4.3.[6]

---

[5] The basis of the classification varies from that of Moen 2003. Long hours have been defined as more than 40 hours a week, short hours as under 35. A further category of 'traditionalists' has been added of households of working age where one partner (the woman) was not in employment. Moen's study only included dual-earner couples. Moen included a further category, 'crossover commitments', where the woman worked long hours and the man worked shorter hours. As there were only nine cases in the BSA sample, this category has been excluded.

[6] Crossover couples have been omitted from Table 4.3, because of small numbers. Traditionalists have also been omitted. The data given are for individual respondents, therefore only dual-earner respondents have been included.

Table 4.3. *Respondents' work–life conflict*[a] *mean scores by couples' work-hour strategies and 'agreeing' that 'in my kind of job people have to work longer hours these days': BSA/ISSP survey*

	N	Mean[b]	Agree people have to work longer hours these days (%)[c]
High commitments	83	8.52	83
Dual moderates	102	7.16	45
Neotraditionalists	221	7.51	56
Alternate commitments	132	6.78	58
Traditionalists	81*	7.59	52
Total	619	7.44	57

*This category will include male respondents only.
[a]see Chapter 3, p. 79; [b]Anova F 8.306 $p < .001$; [c]χ^2 $p < .001$.

'High-commitment' respondents stand out from all other groups in thinking that working hours have got longer, and they also have a significantly higher mean work–life stress score than all other groups. There are no significant differences in the mean scores of respondents in the other groups, but it is of interest that the scores for traditionalists and neotraditionalists, where the man will be working long hours, are higher than either the dual moderates or alternate commitment categories. Clearly, households where both partners are working long hours are under the most significant pressure – but the traditionalist and neotraditionalist scores suggest that even one long-hours partner in a household makes for more difficulties in work–life articulation.[7] As White *et al.* (2003: 188) have demonstrated, actual hours worked are 'by far the strongest explanatory variable' in seeking to explain negative job-to-home 'spillover'.

In this section, we have explored a range of evidence relating to working hours, work intensity and work–life 'balance' in Britain. As individuals, British employees work the longest hours in Europe, but the prevalence of part-time work amongst British women means that on average, the *total* of working hours in the household is lower than that of countries such as Portugal, where both partners tend to work full time. Case study, quantitative and qualitative evidence all suggest that a majority of employees in Britain think that working hours have increased, as has work intensity. Household working hours have a

---

[7] In fact, the total average hours worked by 'neotraditionalist' households (76) was slightly greater than in 'dual-moderate' households (75), given the very long hours worked by men in neotraditionalist households. Men in 'traditional' households also worked long hours – an average of over 49 a week.

significant negative impact on capacities to achieve work–life balance. This kind of evidence, together with the data relating to careers presented in Chapter 3, suggests that changes in the employment relationship are making it more, rather than less difficult to achieve work–life balance in Britain. In the next sections, therefore, we will examine the kinds of policies that are being developed by employers with a view to improving work and family articulation.

Work–life articulation: employers, states (and families)

Although 'the family' is by convention seen as a 'private' sphere, there is a long history of state intervention in many of its aspects. For example, in the area of population policy, states have sought both to increase fertility and to limit family size, as in the 'one child' policy in China. The state has acted to protect those individuals within families who might be vulnerable to neglect or violence, particularly women and children. Welfare states (to varying degrees) provide support for families in need (Saraceno 1997). States, however, do not act in isolation and contemporary welfare 'regimes' have three interacting elements, labour markets (employers), families and the state (Esping-Andersen 1999: 4). Both welfare and labour market regimes have an important impact on capacities for work–life articulation, and this will be explored further in Chapter 5. Controls on working hours (or their absence, as we have seen above in the British case) will have an obvious impact on family life. Another of the more high-profile aspects of these supports (or lack of them) is the degree of assistance provided to parents and other carers in paid employment, such as maternity and paternity leaves, and childcare and eldercare assistance.

In our exploration of the context of work–life articulation in contemporary Western societies, we have so far addressed mainly the topic of changes in employment, and the employment relationship. The state is an important player in this field – but considerably more so in some nation states than others. In those states such as Britain and the US, where supports for those in need are relatively minimal, the potential for assistance from employers assumes greater significance, as do wider family supports.[8] In neoliberal labour market regimes, moreover, governments are usually reluctant to intervene in the employer–employee relationship (Gonyea and Googins 1996). As Glass and Estes (1999:

---

[8] For example, the extent of firm-based provision of 'family-friendly' benefits in the Nordic countries is low, given the high level of state provision of these benefits (see Evans 2001: 23).

Table 4.4. *Policy developments in the UK (see Dex and Smith 2002)*

1998 Working Time Directive. A maximum of 48 hours a week, and 3 (now 4) weeks annual leave (this brings UK in line with EU regulations. Note that in UK, employees may 'opt out')

1998 National Child Care Strategy (DfEE 1998)

1999 National Strategy for Carers (DoH 1999)

1999 Parental Leave Directive (Employment Relations Act 1999, bringing UK in line with EU regulations). Working parents have the right to take 13 weeks unpaid leave for each child up to the age of 5

1999 Time off for Dependants. The right to take a reasonable amount of time off work for emergencies (Employment Relations Act 1999)

2000 Part-time Work Directive (agreed 1997, bringing UK in line with EU regulations). Part-time workers should receive no less favourable treatment than full-time workers in respect of employment-related benefits

2000 Work–life Balance: changing patterns in a changing world (DfEE). A discussion paper aimed at widening the extent of flexible working

2000 Work and Parents: competitiveness and choice (DTI 2000, green paper)

2001 Work and Parents Taskforce (DTI) to consider 'light touch' arrangements giving employees the right to flexible working

2001 Employment Act: From April 2003: extension of maternity leave, increase in maternity pay, right to 2 weeks paternity leave, right to request reduced hours.

2005 Further increases in maternity leave announced, right to request reduced hours extended to carers. Employers to be enabled to offer £50 tax-free towards childcare expenses

291) have argued in the case of the US: 'In the United States, to a far greater extent than in Western Europe's social democracies, employers have been allowed to vary in the degree of responsiveness they show to workers' family obligations.'

Although Britain would be categorised as a 'liberal' welfare state, British welfare and labour market policies are to some extent constrained by European-level agreements. In other respects – notably that of the key benefit of free health care – Britain is closer to Europe than the US, and support for public services has remained at a high level (see Hutton: ch. 9). Table 4.4 summarises the initiatives taken by the New Labour government since its election in 1997. As can be seen, a number of policy improvements simply bring the UK into line with EU regulations, demonstrating the significance of EU membership for British work–life policies.

Nevertheless, British government strategies in respect of work–life articulation have many parallels with those to be found in the US. In particular, there is a noteworthy reluctance to 'interfere' with the business enterprise or to do anything that might be seen as challenging managers' 'right to manage'. For example, the DTI Work and Parents Task Force raised the possibility of introducing a *right* for both parents to work reduced hours when the mother's maternity leave ends (DTI 2000: 34). In the original Green Paper, the possibility was also aired that an employee's request might be refused if it caused harm to the business; and exemptions might be given for small businesses (*ibid.*: 56). The legislation finally introduced in the Employment Act of 2001 gave parents a right to 'request' flexible or reduced working hours only, and the employers' duty was limited to giving the request 'serious consideration'. Similarly, in the US in the early 1990s 'the version of federally mandated parental leave that ultimately was signed into law shortened the originally proposed leave and contained provisions that exempted small businesses and employees in any business whose job duties were considered essential to the organisation's operation' (Glass and Estes 1999: 291). Work–life articulation policies in relation to employers in Britain and the US, therefore, would appear to operate largely at the level of exhortation, rather than regulation.

Identifying and defining a work–life employer policy is by no means straightforward. What is included will depend on the particularities of national contexts – for example, in the US, assistance with tuition fees for relatives is included as a work–life benefit (Berg *et al.* 2003). Evans (OECD 2001: 10) defines work–life or (family-friendly) policies as 'working arrangements, introduced voluntarily by firms, which facilitate the reconciliation of work and family life'. However, it is not always obvious which arrangements are positive from a work–life perspective and which are not. For example, flexible working, which is widely regarded as having work–life benefits, is also of considerable advantage to employers (as we have seen in the example of Cellbank above, where an increase in flexible working was imposed by the employer. See also Dex and McCulloch 1997; Purcell *et al.* 1999). As Evans (2001: 10) argues, 'The test of whether or not a practice is family-friendly or not must ultimately depend on the appreciation of the families concerned.'

The three major categories of work–life policies facilitated by employers are: allowing leave or absence from work for family reasons (emergency leave, extended maternity/paternity leave, career breaks, etc.); changes in work arrangements introduced for family reasons including flexible work of all kinds (a reduced working week, flexitime, job sharing, term-time work, working from home, etc.) and practical help with caring responsibilities (workplace nurseries, help with childcare costs, help with eldercare costs, etc.). Evans (2001: 41) also identifies a fourth category of supports which is 'relevant information and training' that includes information packs, refresher courses, lists of childcare facilities, etc. In

Britain, short-term leave arrangements for family reasons, and changes to work arrangements, are the most frequently occurring work–life arrangements, and few employers offer direct practical assistance. For example, under 5 per cent of British firms have workplace nurseries (Evans 2001: 47).

Some firms are more likely to offer these policies than others. Recent research (Dex and Smith 2002; Evans 2001; Forth *et al.* 1997; Glass and Estes 1999; OECD 2001) has demonstrated that larger firms are more likely to offer policies, and across a wider range, than smaller firms, and work–life policies are more likely to be found in the public sector than in the private sector. The prevalence of work–life policies in the public sector is in part because of the pressures on government to be seen as a 'good' employer, but also because levels of trade union membership are relatively high, and workplaces with a recognised trade union are more likely to have family-friendly working arrangements (Dex and Smith 2002: 12).

A number of factors have been identified as contributing to whether employers offer work–life policies or not (Dex and Smith 2002: 10). These include *institutional pressures* such as those that have already been mentioned in the case of the public sector. Other institutional pressures identified by Dex and Smith include a high proportion of female employees and the 'bandwagon effect' of human resource policies such as 'high-commitment' management and high-profile equal opportunity policies (see also Evans 2001; Osterman 1995). *Resource constraints* include size (smaller establishments finding it more problematic to cope with individual absences and changed working practices), and whether firms had market and recruitment difficulties. Finally, *individual incentives* are important, particularly if employers wish to recruit and retain skilled and qualified employees, or particular categories of employee, such as married women with children (Appelbaum *et al.* 2003 describe this as a 'rational choice' employer perspective). In fact, more skilled and qualified employees are more likely to be offered family-friendly work–life arrangements such as being able to work from home, or the opportunity to reduce and/or change hours, than lower-level employees, and firms employing a high proportion of such employees are more likely to offer policies (Dex and Smith 2002; see also Glass and Estes 1999). A picture emerges, therefore, of the 'model employer', from a work–life articulation perspective, as being large, unionised, having good human resource policies and 'high-commitment' management, a high proportion of female employees and/or a highly skilled and qualified workforce. However, to what extent do employees take advantage of these policies, and how effective are they in achieving positive work–life articulation?

There is a range of evidence that suggests that many employees do not, in fact, take up the work–life policies offered by even the most 'enlightened' of employers. One problem of take-up relates to the mismatch between the range of policies on offer and employees' awareness of them. For example, a DTI survey of working parents suggested that a third (34 per cent) of working parents were not sure whether their employer provided parental leave or not (DTI 2000: 44). Dex and Smith (2002: 20) also report a 'substantial amount of mismatch between employers' claims and employees' perceptions of their access to . . . various policies'. Employees most likely to be in need of these policies (for example, people with caring responsibilities, or a long-term illness or disability) were more likely to be aware of them (see also Still and Strang 2003; Yeandle *et al.* 2003). However, even when employees *are* aware of the policies offered, they may nevertheless not take advantage of them.

As Lewis (1997: 18) has argued, positive work–life and/or family-friendly policies can coexist uneasily with other organisational values. Managers may place a greater value on employees who do not allow family commitments to intrude in their working lives, and long hours in the workplace may be seen as an indication of organisational commitment. As we have seen in Chapter 3, employees wishing to respond 'positively' to individualised promotion opportunities often do not feel able to take up 'family-friendly' policies, and managers are often constrained to work long hours. Lewis identifies two major barriers to a culture change in a family-friendly direction: subjective senses of entitlement, and organisational discourses of time. In her research (in a manufacturing company, a public sector organisation and an accountancy firm), family-friendly provisions were often seen as being 'perks' rather than a basic right (women were more likely than men to feel 'entitled' to these provisions but less likely to feel 'entitled' to a career), and long hours working was seen as a measure of commitment to the organisation. Individual managerial and supervisory discretion (both *de jure* and *de facto*) is often central to the implementation of policies such as short-term leave, or the ability to change or reduce working hours (Valcour and Batt 2003; Yeandle *et al.* 2003). Thus even if an organisation has policies available, supervisory discretion means that they may not be equally available to all employees.

CHARLES: My immediate line manager is one of the ones without children, and he can be quite difficult. It's not an obvious thing, but I think it can be quite uncomfortable asking for time. But then his manager has got two kids and she's more understanding . . . so what we tend to do, we tend to bypass him and go straight to her!

ZOE: People at my level, one manager in particular doesn't want children and is career-minded and sees kids as getting in the way. They say they understand because Cellbank tell them to but they don't understand really. They groan about the kids being ill again.

As we have seen in Chapter 3, many employees do not use work–life policies (such as part-time working) for fear of jeopardising their career prospects. Indeed, for women like Flora and Peggy, both in managerial positions, the choice was stark:

PEGGY: I'm a bit stuck at full time at the moment. I keep getting told that I'd be selling myself short if I went part time. The bank does have flexible hours but the higher up you go you're not encouraged to take advantage of it.

Flora, as we have seen in Chapter 3, had taken voluntary redundancy rather than increase her hours of work following reorganisation. It would seem to be taken for granted that supervisors and managers will work longer hours than contracted if necessary, and as we have seen in our discussion of working hours above, most appear to do so. On the other hand, as 'valued employees', managers may also be able to achieve more flexibility in their day-to-day working hours.

It is also the case that the intensification of work itself, via downsizing and re-engineering, can make it more difficult for employees to use the work–life policies available. This can be a particular problem if the working unit is small and colleagues will be affected by individual absences:

BETH (Cellbank): It depends on [my daughter]; when she was ill we were short staffed on some days so I couldn't, take time off, well I could but I wouldn't, but the last time she was off was on a Friday and we're not short staffed so it wasn't so bad. I always try to avoid taking time off when we're short staffed; I feel like I'm letting colleagues down.

ISOBEL (Council): We are so pushed and they have cut the staffing levels right down. To get the work done a lot of people stay late. We are on flexitime whereby you build up time and you can take the day off. But I do know a lot of people who don't get the chance to take their days off, purely because they want to keep on top of the work.

Thus as Eaton (2003: 147) has argued: 'Flexibility *formally* offered by the employer is insufficient as an indicator of flexibility available to the employee. Many employers limit flexibility to a small portion of the workforce or workday . . . The culture of the workplace can determine whether work–family benefits are available and to whom; in some cases, using policies is discouraged or has negative career effects.'

If employees are unable, for whatever reasons, to take advantage of work–life policies, then their effectiveness in achieving work–life articulation must obviously be called into question. However, much of the argument for the introduction of work–life policies has emphasised the importance of the 'business case', as well as the potential benefits for individual employees. It is assumed that these kinds of benefits will increase the attractiveness of particular employers to employees (by becoming the 'employer of choice'), and that employees will not only appreciate these benefits but be more highly motivated and committed to the organisation as a result. Indeed, as we have seen (Dex and Smith 2002), in Britain the presence of better than average work–life policies is associated with 'high-commitment' management, that seeks positively to nurture and encourage the identification of the employee with the goals of the organisation. Dex and Scheibl's (1999) review of the literature relating to the impact of family-friendly policies on business performance comes to a largely positive conclusion, although disadvantages were greater in smaller and medium-sized companies. Dex and Smith (2002: 42) found positive effects from having family-friendly policies on employee commitment in private sector companies (but not in the public sector). Such policies were also seen to be cost effective (in most cases), and brought about increases in performance (although the effects were small).

Increasingly, therefore, it is being argued that the introduction of work–life policies by employers represents a 'win–win' scenario from which both employers and employees will benefit. Good work–life policies, it would seem, are becoming a marker of leading edge companies characterised by the 'best' managerial practices that also facilitate worker autonomy, flexibility and control. However, this positive scenario also has its critics. In her case study, Hochschild (1997) has demonstrated how 'work becomes home and home becomes work'. That is, the demands of 'high-commitment' work practices (in an organisation with excellent family-friendly policies) were such that employees were spending longer hours at work, and less and less time with their families. Hochschild's research was based on a single case, and has been challenged empirically. Berg et al. (2003, see also Osterman 1995) have argued (via their research in steel, clothing, and medical electronics and imaging industries in the US), that 'high performance work practices – the opportunity to participate in decisions, informal training, pay for performance, and good promotion opportunities – all have a positive effect on work–family balance . . . Whereas Hochschild's view of high-performance workplaces may hold for professionals and managers, it does not appear that it can be generalised to nonsupervisory workers' (Berg *et al.* 2003: 184, 185).[9]

However, White *et al.* (2003) have argued that the British case demonstrates otherwise. Their analysis of the Employment in Britain survey (1992 and 2000) found that appraisal systems, group working practices, and individual incentives (all aspects of 'high-commitment' management practices) all increased negative job-to-home spillover. Thus they suggest that: 'There may . . . be . . . practices that employers regard as important for their own success which may exacerbate the work–life balance problem irrespective of the positive contribution of family friendly policies' (White *et al.* 2003: 176). White *et al.* found that opportunities to work flexibly reduced negative job-to-home spillover, particularly for women, but the major factor that exacerbated negative job-to-home spillover was working hours (Berg *et al.* 2003 also found that long weekly hours and involuntary overtime reduced workers' ability to balance work and family responsibilities). Another finding of White *et al.*'s was that the way supervisors use their discretion (that is, whether supervisors are seen as fair or unfair) had an important impact on negative spillover – and 43 per cent of respondents did *not* think that their supervisor treated all employees fairly. Given the importance of supervisors, and supervisory discretion, in implementing work–life policies, this finding serves to reinforce Eaton's arguments that work–life policies will only make a contribution to organisational commitment if they are capable of being used.

Summary and conclusion

In this chapter, we have further explored the contemporary articulation of employment and family life by examining in greater depth current changes in the employment relationship, as well as the kinds of policies that are being developed by some employers in order to assist their employees in combining work and family. Much of the empirical evidence reviewed in this chapter suggests that high-commitment management practices such as performance-related pay and the setting of targets, and performance appraisals, together with other strategies that

---

[9] One problem in evaluating the effectiveness and impact of work–life policies will be that employees at different stages of the life cycle will require different kinds of policies – help with childcare provision, for example, is of little value to the child-free. The demand for policies within particular organisations will vary by the type of employee predominating (Glass and Estes 1999). For example, the incidence of work–life policies in the construction industry in Britain is low, no doubt reflecting the fact that this sector is a largely male preserve (Dex and Smith 2002).

increase work intensity, including changes to working time, organisational delayering and reengineering, have a negative impact on work–life articulation. Employee-led flexibility, as well as work systems that give people a greater sense of control over their working lives, can have a positive impact. However, even though the evidence in respect of all aspects of these management practices is not absolutely conclusive (Berg *et al.* 2003, for example, found a positive association between pay for performance and work–life balance for non-supervisory workers in the companies they studied), one feature that, not surprisingly, has a negative association with work–life balance in all of the research reviewed and presented in this chapter is long hours working. Our evidence suggests that, in Britain, new employment practices have resulted in an increase in working hours (for a substantial minority of employees) together with an increase in work intensification and perceived insecurity.

It would seem, therefore, that some aspects of current trends in the workplace are making it more, rather than less, difficult to combine employment with caring responsibilities. This is paradoxical because as Moen (2003: 3) has argued, there is already a mismatch between the current reality, in which employees are increasingly likely to have caring responsibilities, and the work-hour and career policies and practices 'developed in response to the needs of the first (US) workforce of mostly young, mostly white working-class and middle-class men, located for the most part in (unionised) and white-collar jobs in the manufacturing sector in the first half of the twentieth century'. Increasing workplace pressures can only increase the tensions that already exist between outmoded institutions and the changing nature of the workforce. However, as we have seen, there have also been attempts to respond to these tensions, most notably via the development of flexible employment (although this has contributed to the maintenance of gender inequality), and employers have come under increasing pressure to develop positive work–life balance policies.

Employer-provided work–life policies will be of particular importance for employees in national contexts in which statutory protections and state supports for family life are relatively lacking, such as Britain and the United States (Canada, Australia and Japan are other examples of advanced and prosperous societies where statutory family supports are weak). However, cross-nationally comparative data indicates that in countries with low levels of statutory support and regulation, 'voluntary' provision by employers of supportive work–life policies falls very far short of making up the 'deficit' in state supports (Evans 2001; OECD 2001). Countries with low levels of statutory supports, such as Britain, Ireland and the United States, also have relatively low levels of employer-provided supports as compared to countries such as Germany and Austria. The lowest incidence of extra-statutory employer-provided work–life policies is in fact found in the Nordic countries, where national provision is highest, and the state (as in, for example, Sweden) has deliberately taken over a good deal of the caring role of the family. The highest level of employer supports is found in countries where there are medium levels of statutory supports, such as Germany, Austria and the Netherlands.[10] Evans (2001: 30) has suggested that this pattern might indicate that 'national legislation tends to encourage private provision up to a point, and then tends to displace it'. Whatever the explanation of these trends, however, it remains the case that employees in countries with the lowest level of state supports – that is, countries broadly characterised by neoliberal labour market policies – appear to suffer a 'double disadvantage' as far as work–life policies are concerned. Universalistic national protections and provisions are weak, and governmental reluctance to interfere in the employers' 'right to manage' means that supportive policies remain at the discretion of employers.

In addition, the impact of changes to employment practices and the employee relationship that impinge negatively on work–life articulation is likely to be greater for employees with only weak or negligible institutional work–life supports – either statutorily or employer provided. In such cases, the third element in the welfare 'triangle' – the family – is likely to come under increasing pressure. In subsequent chapters, we will be examining whether and to what extent statutory supports do have a positive impact on capacities to achieve work–life articulation. For the moment, however, we would note that there is some evidence that even statutory supports have their limits, given the pressures brought about by competitive capitalism and the building of individual careers. For example, research has shown that Scandinavian policies directly aimed at softening or ameliorating the contradictions between family and employment, and encouraging men to take on a more active involvement in family life, do not appear to have been completely successful (Hojgaard 1997; see also Haas and Hwang 1995). Hojgaard's case studies (of three Nordic organisations) suggest that organisational career cultures in practice render this impossible:

---

[10] France is a particular case here, lying around the middle of the distribution. Levels of childcare provision in France are historically high, as are state supports for working mothers, but France has not adopted the gender 'equality agenda' to the same extent as many other countries (see Crompton and Le Feuvre 2000).

It is a commonly held view by the men in all three companies that career and family are incompatible . . . In the ministry it is the fight for the good and prestigious work tasks and the ability to be available at all times that are complicated by family obligations . . . In the medical firm it is the size of the workload necessary for pursuing a career that will hurt the family, and in the bank it is the feeling of not living up to the norms prescribed for a serious career maker that is felt to be the obstacle. (Hojgaard 1997: 256)

This kind of evidence has led some authors to argue that the most important factor in seeking to adapt to the new realities of employment and family life brought about by the increasing employment of women is to focus on organisational change, particularly changes to the organisational 'culture' (Bailyn 1993; Lewis and Lewis 1996). This will involve efforts to 'challenge and modify all organisational practices based on assumed separation between work and family lives so as to empower men and women to make optimum contributions in both spheres . . . to adapt organisational policies and structures to enable people to manage multiple demands in work and family with maximum satisfaction and minimum stress' (Lewis 1996: 8.9). However, it is a moot point as to whether the kinds of workplace pressures that inhibit individual empowerment and create pressures for family life are best described as 'cultural' and therefore, in theory, amenable to normative transformation. As Kerry (a Cellbank manager) put it, when she was asked what improvements might be made to make her organisation more 'family-friendly':

KERRY: More staff. More staff would take the pressure off of a lot of people, because your workload . . . we could stay here until 7 p.m. every night doing our workload, but that's not helping our family life. But no one's going to say you've got the workload of another person, let's give you somebody. It doesn't happen. But that's the squeeze that goes on in all the companies. Because looking at your bottom-line profit, people are expensive.

In policy terms, Cellbank was a 'family-friendly' organisation, but competitive pressures also made it family 'unfriendly'. Although, therefore, it might be important to change organisational cultures, this objective might be problematic to achieve in the absence of external regulation of some kind. Indeed, as Drago and Hyatt (2003: 143) have argued, it is likely that 'markets will not induce an optimal mix of work–family policies in the absence of (government) intervention'. They focus in particular on childcare, which, as they argue, is the one type of work–family policy not found bundled with other work–family policies, or common in high-commitment workplaces, because 'it is not profitable for employers to foot the bill for it'. Abstractly, it is the case that capitalism undermines the family form via its indifference to the 'private' lives of the labour power it purchases (Seccombe 1993: 19), and as Beck has remarked, 'The market subject is ultimately the single individual, "unhindered" by a relationship, marriage, or family' (1992: 116). Even though a completely unregulated (or 'self-regulating', Polanyi 1957) market is itself a fiction, there are, nevertheless, considerable national variations in the extent to which markets are regulated by governments and other interest groups (such as employers and trade unions), as well as by prevailing normative prescriptions. In the next chapters, therefore, we will extend our investigations of the contemporary rearticulation of employment and family life via a comparison of national policy contexts characterised by contrasting levels of regulation and statutory supports in respect of labour markets, employment and the family.

5   States, families and work–life articulation

In Chapter 4, it has been argued that contemporary managerial and labour force policies in the US and the UK are serving to increase work intensity as well as working hours. All other things being equal, these kinds of employment policies will be likely to make the practicalities of work–life articulation more difficult. It has been argued that these kinds of pressures are a consequence of managerial approaches influenced by neoliberal thinking, that seek to increase productivity by reducing the 'porosity' of the working day via a number of strategies. These include reducing the numbers of employees, removing or modifying entitlements to paid overtime, introducing targets for employee performance, and tightly scheduling worker availability to meet peaks and troughs of demand. Simultaneously, employers may also seek to enhance employee 'commitment' by offering a series of benefits that can include generous work–life policies. However, case study and other evidence suggests that many employees do not feel able to take advantage of these policies because of increasing workplace pressures. In Britain and the US, governments have imposed relatively few restraints on employers and managers' 'right to manage'. Indeed, the lack of regulation of the British and American labour markets is often contrasted (favourably) with the 'over-regulated' European norm. However, state policies (or regulation) have a significant impact on the structuring of both gender and class, as well as work–life articulation. In this chapter, therefore, we will first examine more closely the question of the impact of state policies on class and gender inequality. We will then explore the impact of different policies on work–life articulation, focusing in particular on the topic of work–life stress.

Similarities and difference in societal regimes

Since the collapse of 'state capitalism' (often called 'state socialism'), market capitalism has become global. Seemingly inexorable, and common, trends are sweeping the world (Strange 1997). Nevertheless, it is something of a truism to note that 'capitalisms' are not all of a piece, and there are many different varieties of 'capitalism'. As far as the organisation of work and family life is concerned, national differences remain of considerable significance. As has already been argued, a common emphasis in the 'varieties of capitalism' literature is that 'self-regulating markets' do not exist independently (as is assumed by liberal economic theory), but are 'embedded' in sets of institutions that bestow a distinctive character on particular markets. 'Markets' are, in fact, better understood as configurations of institutions, often described by the term 'regime'. The particular manner in which family and employment are articulated (and, as we shall see, whether this articulation is experienced positively or negatively) will vary according to different kinds of institutional regimes, including production regimes, welfare state regimes, and, as we have seen in Chapter 4, working-time regimes.

Regime typologies are useful heuristic devices through which the impact of characteristic 'bundlings' of institutions and behaviours may be assessed. Although the foci of regime typologies will vary, all of these approaches share the assumption that institutions may be seen as 'intervening variables' that mediate between assumed causal factors and their effects (for example, the impact of different kinds of childcare provision on women's employment patterns). No single paradigm or regime typology will encompass all of the issues we discuss in this book, and we will be drawing upon a variety of different frameworks. First, we discuss national production regimes, which are closely linked to national labour market regimes. These in turn are intertwined with working-time regimes. Finally, we discuss welfare state regimes. Production, labour market and working time-regimes will all serve to shape the kinds of jobs available to men and women (for example, and most obviously, a regime of long working hours is likely to have a negative impact on work–life articulation). Welfare state regimes will vary in the kinds and extent of supports they make available to men, women and families – to take another obvious example, there are extensive variations in the extent to which states offer assistance with childcare.

One major contrast that has been drawn is between 'coordinated' and 'uncoordinated' market economies (Soskice 1999; see also Hutton 2002). These two types of 'production regime' reflect different sets of institutional frameworks in relation to production. Coordinated market economies (CMEs) are characterised by the availability of long-term company finance, cooperative industrial relations systems and coordinated wage bargaining, extensive initial (vocational) training of the young, and 'intercompany systems that enable substantial technology and standard setting cooperation to take place between companies' (Soskice

1999: 107). Examples of CMEs would include Germany, Sweden and Japan.[1] In contrast, uncoordinated or liberal market economies (LMEs) are characterised by short-term financing, deregulated labour markets and general education systems together with strong competition, and limited cooperation, between companies. Examples of LMEs include Britain and the United States. Employment relations in LMEs are not, of course, completely 'marketised'. Indeed, in the liberal market economy of the United States, employers have been at the forefront of attempts to build the kinds of social relations necessary for production 'in-house' by applying social engineering technologies such as 'high-commitment' management and corporate culture building (Crouch and Streeck 1997: 9).

An extensive debate has attempted to assess the relative merits of contrasting regime types. During the 1960s, 1970s and 1980s, CMEs appeared to be not only more successful in generating economic prosperity, but also to a considerable extent to have resolved some of market capitalism's inherent tendencies towards exploitation and class conflict (Hirsch and Goldthorpe 1978; Streeck 1989). In Britain, the 1960s and 1970s were the years of 'Butskellism' and the 'social contract', as discussed in Chapter 2. In CMEs, unemployment tended to be low and the wages of 'standard' (male) workers were protected. Material inequalities were, as a consequence, reduced. However, during the 1980s and 1990s, many coordinated market economies were increasingly characterised by declining productivity and rising unemployment. As we have seen in Chapter 4, it was argued by neoliberal economists and policy-makers that the kinds of labour protections characteristic of CMEs kept wages artificially high and placed restrictions on the development of the employment flexibility required in order to compete nationally in global markets. Indeed, within Europe, neoliberal economic and labour market policies have become increasingly influential and indeed, are in the ascendant.

Notwithstanding these shifts in policy emphasis, labour markets are still subject to a greater degree of regulation in coordinated market economies. Regulation has often sought to protect 'good breadwinner' jobs – for example, by placing restrictions on the development of part-time work. Thus the protection of 'breadwinner' jobs may inhibit the expansion of 'women's' (i.e., flexible, part-time) employment.

---

[1] Soskice argues that the Northern European and Japanese CMEs constitute two subtypes, in that the former is industry coordinated and the latter group coordinated, as in the Japanese *Keiretsu*.

'Standard' full-time working hours will be influenced by both national regulation and collective bargaining. During the post Second World War period of rapid economic growth and rising rates of productivity, across Europe there was a widespread, collectively negotiated, reduction in average weekly hours of work. This process slowed (and indeed was reversed) from the 1970s, as regulated working-time reductions have been more difficult to negotiate in circumstances of slower economic growth, increased competitiveness, and reduced union bargaining power (Fagan 2002). In the EU, the shortest working week is established by regulation in Denmark, the Netherlands, France and Belgium (Fagan 2002: 74).

Gender is a major factor affecting weekly hours of work as women work shorter hours than men in all countries. The self-employed work longer hours than the employed, and managerial and professional employees work longer hours than routine and manual workers. Tax and social security regulations will also generate incentives and disincentives relating to working hours. As labour markets become more flexible, the proportion of shorter hours (i.e., part-time) jobs will increase – although at different rates in different countries. Within Europe, long hours working amongst employees is concentrated amongst British men, 28 per cent of whom worked more than 48 hours a week in 1994 (Rubery et al. 1998: 79). There is more dispersion in weekly hours of work in Britain than in any other European country, a reflection of both long working hours amongst men and short part-time hours amongst women (both features of the relatively unregulated British labour market. See Bishop 2004). In these respects, Britain is closer to the US than most other European countries (see Gornick and Meyers 2003: ch. 6).

Both the regulation of working hours, as well as employment protections such as rules relating to health, safety, unfair dismissal and so on represent governmental attempts to protect their citizens by restricting and regulating the potentially destructive power of private ownership and control (i.e., capital). Such protections have often been achieved only as a consequence of trade union struggles. The major elements of citizenship protections, however, are located in the institutions comprising social citizenship. Social citizenship has been classically defined by Marshall (1948: 11) as 'the whole range [of rights] from the right to a modicum of economic welfare and security to the right to share to the full in the social heritage and to live the life of a civilised being according to the standards prevailing in the society'. Thus, in general, social rights give citizens a claim on economic resources if they are unable to find (or incapable of finding) employment, as well as equipping citizens for adult life through education and training. As in the case of labour market and working-time regimes, the actual extent to which social rights are guaranteed and/or provided by the state varies considerably from society to society – that is, states are characterised by different 'welfare regimes'.

Classic liberals would confine citizenship to the formal (negative) civil and political rights necessary to protect individual freedom. In a return to classic liberalism, the neoliberal new right accords primacy to market rights over all other forms of citizenship rights. Indeed, the new right argues that the promotion, by governments, of a more positive notion of freedom as the ability to participate in society as full citizens is not legitimate. It is argued that as social rights imply a claim on resources, they are categorically different from civil and political rights (Lister 2003: 16). Thus attempts to 'roll back' state welfare provision and expenditure are also integral to the neoliberal critique of, and prescriptions for, economic and social policy. Welfare spending is seen not only as a drain on national resources, but also as further impeding the workings of the market. As Lister (2003: 17) has argued: 'Social citizenship rights also promote the "de-commodification of labour" by decoupling the living standards of individual citizens from their "market value" so that they are not totally dependent on selling their labour power in the market. This, of course, is one reason why neoliberals, for whom the market rules supreme, resist their development.'

Nevertheless, despite the growing influence of neoliberal prescriptions, there remain considerable contemporary variations in both the nature and extent of national welfare provisions. Recent empirical research on welfare states has been largely comparative, 'focusing on the causes and consequences of the "natural experiments" with different types of public policies that have taken place in the Western countries' (Korpi 2000: 129). As described in previous chapters, Esping-Andersen's threefold classification of welfare state regime types – conservative (or state corporatist), liberal (offering only minimal protections), and social-democratic universalist – has been enormously influential. 'Liberal' welfare state regimes, in which state assistance is reserved only for those in greatest need and individualised market solutions for welfare are favoured, are, not surprisingly, usually associated with uncoordinated or liberal market economies (LMEs). Coordinated market economies (CMEs) can be associated with both conservative (for example, Germany) and universalist (for example, Sweden) welfare state regimes. In conservative welfare regimes such as Germany, social protections are channelled through the main family earner (usually the 'male breadwinner'), social insurance is compulsory and breadwinner jobs highly protected, through, for example, the coordinated wage bargaining and cooperative industrial relations system that characterises the coordinated market economy in that country.

Social democratic or universalist welfare regimes are also found associated with coordinated market economies, but in these cases, welfare provision is seen as a universal right rather than being closely linked to paid employment. Both liberal and social democratic welfare regimes will tend to encourage employment amongst women. The former encourages low wages and discourages market barriers (and in the absence of state provision, the resources for welfare provision must be earned, thus stimulating women's employment), the latter generates extensive employment for women via the state's provision of welfare services. In contrast, as we have seen, conservative regimes protect 'breadwinner' jobs (thus excluding 'outsiders' such as women), and assume that welfare will be provided within the family, thus discouraging women's employment.

Welfare regimes and feminist debates

As has been noted in Chapter 1, Esping-Andersen's analysis has generated an extensive corpus of feminist-inspired critical research and debate (Bock and Thane 1991; Lewis and Astrom 1992; Sainsbury 1994). One major feminist criticism of Esping-Andersen (1990) was that his primary focus on the state and the labour market failed to take into account the contribution of the family and unpaid caring to welfare provision (Leira 2002: 24). Alternative categorisations of 'caring regimes' have been proposed that incorporate an explicit recognition of the role of unpaid caring in welfare provision (e.g., Millar and Warman 1996). In his recent work, Esping-Andersen (1999) has acknowledged the significance of family care, and has introduced the notion of 'familialistic' welfare regimes – that is, welfare regimes in which family provision of welfare plays a major role. Conversely, welfare regimes are 'defamilising' to the extent that the state takes on 'traditional' family responsibilities. Mapping the 'familial' dimension onto his original classification reveals the social democratic welfare states to be the most 'defamilising', and conservative or corporatist regimes to be the least, liberal regimes being located, in terms of familialism, between the two extremes.

Esping-Andersen may have recognised the contribution of unpaid family care to welfare arrangements, but as many feminist authors have argued (e.g., O'Connor et al. 1999: 20), an explicitly gendered analysis is not in fact a goal of Esping-Andersen's work. His focus remains on women as workers rather than on gender relations as such, and he is interested in relations among states, markets and families because of the implications of caregiving responsibilities for women's capacities to bear children and to enter paid employment, rather than in women's aspirations for equality. Indeed, as Esping-Andersen himself has stated, he is 'not interested in women *per se*' (Esping-Andersen 2000: 759).

Nevertheless, in his most recent work Esping-Andersen (2002) does address the topic of women's equality, and he has argued for the need for a 'new gender contract' in the building of 'new welfare states' that will reflect new social realities. Modern (European) welfare states, he argues, are in crisis because of a series of exogenous 'shocks' – including an ageing population, economic globalisation that brings with it the reduction of social benefits and pressure on wages in order to enhance competitiveness, and growing family instability. As he argues, it would seem that, therefore: 'if, as in most of Europe, welfare states are committed to uphold existing standards of equality and social justice, the price is mass unemployment; to reduce unemployment, Europe appears compelled to embrace American-style deregulation' (Esping-Andersen 1999: 3).

Thus Esping-Andersen argues that women's employment is the most important element in any attempts to address the crisis of the modern welfare state and indeed: 'women are the vanguard force of change in the new economy' (Esping-Andersen 2000: 759). If women's employment increases, then the demand for services (no longer supplied by the stay-at-home woman) will rise, thus creating more employment. Rising employment will increase or maintain levels of taxation, allowing for the long-term maintenance of benefit levels. In order for this win–win scenario to be successful, he argues, it is important that services are no longer provided within the family, as in, for example, conservative (or 'familialist') welfare states such as Germany or Spain. In order to make services more affordable, there will have to be some downward pressure on wages ('Conservative' job protections make the cost of services in continental Europe high. See Esping-Andersen 1999: 113). Moreover, Esping-Andersen argues that modern welfare states must re-focus their priorities away from the protections associated with the breadwinner model (such as employment status protection and pension maintenance) and towards those most in need. Those most in need are dual-earner families with young children (on whom the future of welfare ultimately depends), and the young (poorly educated) unemployed.

This refocusing of priorities, he argues, must also address the problems of entrapment that are found in liberal regimes – notably because of poverty in childhood and low-wage, low-skill jobs in adulthood (or no jobs at all). 'Guarantees against immobility' need to be introduced by the removal of risks associated with marital instability and low skills. These include support for families of all kinds, including universally available childcare provision, and enhanced training and educational provision. Esping-Andersen's solution to the crisis of state welfare, therefore, borrows elements from all three regime types – bringing down the cost of services (liberal), increasing direct family supports (social democratic) and investing heavily in education and training (conservative and social democratic). The extent to which this solution is in practice achievable may be debated – not least because, as Esping-Andersen himself argues, nation states find themselves bound by 'path dependency'. That is, existing institutional arrangements will heavily determine individual national trajectories.

'Gender equality', therefore, has become 'the lynchpin of any post-industrial equilibrium' (Esping-Andersen 2002: 6). Some of Esping-Andersen's prescriptions, such as, for example, the provision of universal and affordable childcare, have been a central aim of feminist struggles for many years. However, in a number of other respects, it may be suggested that Esping-Andersen's analysis and prescriptions for economic regeneration and welfare state reform will serve to perpetuate gender inequality as well as being antithetical to work–life articulation. For example, he argues that an increase in the sharing of domestic work by men (particularly childcare) would simply encourage family-based service provision and therefore not make a contribution to employment generation. For similar reasons, any reductions in working hours that would also increase the likelihood of family self-servicing and therefore a reduced hours or employment sharing strategy (such as the 35 hour week in France) is not necessarily positive as far as job creation is concerned (Esping-Andersen 2000; but see Bishop 2004). However, as we have seen in Chapter 4, long hours of employment work within dual-earner households do not make a positive contribution to work–life 'balance'. Moreover, as women predominate in the kinds of service sector jobs for which wage reductions are being advocated by Esping-Andersen, any such reductions would reinforce material inequalities between men and women (thus reinforcing the 'rational' choice made by men in partnerships to put their efforts into market work rather than care work).

A further questionable assumption made by Esping-Andersen is that policy may be guided by *women's* (not men's) 'preferences', as Hakim has argued (Esping-Andersen 2002: 72–3). Most women, he argues, aim for a dual-role combination of employment and motherhood (Hakim's 'adaptives'). Thus equity – or fairness – will be achieved by a combination of institutional supports (most particularly, universal childcare) that facilitate this combination, together with the availability of 'mother' (note not 'father') 'friendly' employment. He draws on the example of the Nordic countries, which have been extremely successful in drawing mothers into employment as a consequence of both high levels of child-care provision as well as the creation of 'mother-friendly' job opportunities in the public sector (Esping-Andersen 2002: 76). One consequence of this combination, however, is high levels of occupational segregation in the Nordic countries, where women as employees are concentrated in the 'public ghetto'.[2] Therefore, as Esping-Andersen notes, gender neutrality or equality in employment has not been achieved.

Whether or not indexes of occupational segregation are appropriate as measures of gender inequality is itself a debatable point.[3] For the moment, however, we would point to the fact that this preference-based approach takes the gender division of labour between market and caring work as being an unproblematic 'given', and it is assumed that it is women who desire dual roles, not men. 'Preferences', as argued in Chapter 2, are a dangerous guide to policy given that they are liable to be shaped by habit, low expectations and unjust background conditions. Women may often seek 'mother-friendly' employment given their conventionally assigned caring responsibilities and the enduring power of the ideology of domesticity. 'Mother-friendly' employment may thus be 'preferred', but it is at least arguable that women might actually 'prefer' not to have to make a 'choice' between marginalised 'mother (or family-)friendly' employment and 'standard worker' 'mother- (or family-)unfriendly' employment. As Esping-Andersen (2002: 91) observes, the marginal preference of a competitively exposed firm would, if costs were equal, favour male workers over (protected) female employees. Moreover: 'Everywhere, the greater risk associated with female employees would spur a rational manager to favour men when promoting employees to higher echelon functions' (ibid.).

Contemporary discussions of welfare state reform, therefore, advocate a move away from a 'male breadwinner' and towards a 'citizen worker' model (Lewis 2002). However, as Lewis argues, the kind of change in

---

[2] Esping-Andersen's major preoccupation here is with the question of fertility. The supports provided for mother's employment in the Nordic countries have resulted in the maintenance of fertility rates. In contrast, in the conservative, familialist, welfare states (e.g., Italy, Spain), where employed mothers have few supports, fertility rates have fallen dramatically, and people are having fewer children than they would prefer. During the 1990s recession, and cutbacks in 'mother-friendly' public sector employment in Sweden, fertility rates fell, particularly amongst less educated women.

[3] See Blackburn et al. 2000. It may be argued that the most significant 'equality indicator' is the gender wage gap, rather than the extent of occupational segregation, and the wage gap is lower in the Nordic countries than in less 'segregated' countries such as Britain. It is also possible that in some rich countries where women have few civil rights (such as Gulf Arab states), the provision of generous but separate facilities for men and women may result in relatively low levels of occupational segregation.

welfare states that is being advocated by current reformers – that is, of 'recasting the central work/welfare relationship in order to promote labour market activation and "make work pay"' (Lewis 2002: 333) is not, in practice, being accompanied by the kinds of changes needed to properly address the question of the work of care. Esping-Andersen does advocate universal childcare provision, but this is a necessary, but not sufficient, answer to the problem of gender inequality, as can be seen in the example of the Nordic countries discussed above. Children need to be delivered to and collected from daycare, and daycare schedules tend (unavoidably, as daycare workers have homes and families too) to be rather rigid and not always responsive to the demands of new forms of flexible working. Unpaid caring suffers from Baumols' 'cost disease' (Esping-Andersen 1999: 56) for the same reasons as paid service employment, in that it often cannot be provided in a shorter time period without reducing the quality of the care.

However, the changes brought about by the development of 'high-commitment' (or 'high-performance') management strategies have, as we have argued in Chapter 4, brought about increases in work intensity and working hours that will have a negative impact on capacities for work–life articulation amongst both men and women, particularly in dual-earner households. Gallie (2002: 97) has demonstrated that across Europe there has been a 'sharp intensification of work effort, posing serious risks of work stress and tension between work and family life'. 'High-commitment' and 'high-performance' management strategies have come about in part because of the perceived need for social engineering in order to moderate workplace conflicts, as well as in order to increase organisational competitiveness and maximise employee integration. Cooperative, high-performance work systems have increased work intensity, particularly in competition-driven, private sector employment.

Addressing the question of care within a gender equality framework, therefore, means not only the provision of alternative (i.e., non-family) care arrangements, but also facing up to the realities of contemporary workplace developments that make employment 'carer-unfriendly' for both men and women. Esping-Andersen has placed, in his discussions of welfare state reform, much emphasis on the need to create the circumstances in which individuals can avoid 'entrapment' in either poverty or low-level employment – or even no employment at all. However, policy proposals based on women's assumed preferences for care – even via the 'dual roles' model – make it unlikely that women can avoid the 'entrapment' of responsibility for caring work. The goal of gender equality is indeed an ambitious one, but our discussion suggests that it is unlikely to be achieved unless something is done about the nature of employment itself. To continue to work with assumptions that are grounded in shaky 'theories' about women's 'preferences' is likely to perpetuate gender inequality.

Welfare regimes: their impact on gender and class

Feminist criticisms, therefore, have focused on the lack of attention that was given to the significance of women's unpaid labour and family care in mainstream debates on the welfare state. These kinds of arguments paralleled the wider feminist critique, developed from the 1970s, of mainstream approaches to the analysis of inequality within the social sciences. These were dominated by class analysis, in which class was defined with reference to employment and the class (employment) structure was seen as male (e.g., Blau and Duncan 1967; Goldthorpe 1980/87). This approach located the origins of inequality within the 'public' sphere, and effectively naturalised gender inequalities within the family (Acker 1973; Crompton 2002). Similarly, analyses of the welfare state were focused largely on its contribution to the amelioration of class, rather than gender, inequalities (Land 1986).

Until the 1970s, therefore, on the whole, mainstream social science reflected, in a rather uncritical fashion, the ideologically gendered *status quo*. For as Orloff (1999: 325) has argued: 'common cultural assumptions and ideological preferences about gender – most often about the gender division of labour and women's economic dependency – have been embedded in all Western systems of social provision'. Most pervasive and obvious has been the assumption, initially incorporated into all state welfare models, that women would specialise in caring work whilst men would specialise in market work, and that women would be economically dependent on men.

Nevertheless, despite these common assumptions, different welfare regimes have been demonstrated to have very different impacts on gender equality and inequality. In Scandinavia, it has been argued that universalist social democratic welfare regimes may be seen as constituting a 'state feminism', in that the state has consciously developed policies with the aim of achieving equality for women (Brandth and Kvande 2001; Hernes 1987). In an analysis (drawing on data up to the 1990s), Korpi (2000) has demonstrated the differential consequences of welfare regime types for both class and gender inequalities. He demonstrates that welfare regimes vary in the extent to which they offer general family supports, dual-earner supports, or are characterised by market-oriented policies that offer but little by way of support to families (Korpi 2000: 144).

General family supports, directed at the (nuclear) family, may encourage the reproduction of a relatively traditional division of domestic labour, particularly if they are aimed directly at women. General family supports include cash child allowances (including 'cash-for-care' arrangements, see Leira 2002: ch. 5), family tax benefits to children and non-employed spouses, and care provision for older children. Even if such supports are ostensibly gender neutral, they are still more likely to be taken up by women rather than men given the persistence of the ideology of female nurturing. Dual-earner supports identified by Korpi include public daycare for young children (aged 0–2), paid maternity and paternity leaves, and public home help for the elderly. They are more likely to encourage women's employment than general family supports, through their attempts to shift care work from unpaid to paid work (i.e., public sector provision) as well as within the family. In contrast, market-oriented state policies are characterised by the relative absence of either general family or dual-earner supports.

Korpi found that levels of gender inequality are lowest in 'encompassing' welfare states providing high levels of dual-earner supports (the Nordic states). These states are also characterised by high levels of women's employment. Conservative or corporatist welfare regimes (such as Germany, Belgium and Italy) providing general family supports tend to be associated with relatively high levels of gender inequality, and low levels of women's employment (given that social and employment protections are directed at the male breadwinner/provider in such regimes. See Esping-Andersen 2002). Basic security or 'liberal' regimes (such as the UK and the US) tend to be associated with moderate levels of gender inequality, and relatively high levels of women's employment (although high levels of class inequality), given that there are relatively few barriers to women's employment in the labour markets of such regimes.

Korpi's analysis also emphasises the significance of (national) cultural differences in shaping gender and family policies. The Catholic Church has promoted (and still promotes) a highly traditional (and essentialist) model of women and the family. In 1971 an encyclical of Paul VI warned against 'the misinterpreted equality which denies the differences God himself has created and that deny the woman's special and especially important role in the heart of the family and society' (cited in Korpi 2000: 149). In countries where (Catholic) confessional parties have been influential, general family support policy models have predominated. Left-leaning political parties have generally been more sympathetic to women's equality claims, and as we have seen, in Scandinavia, where left parties have been influential, dual-earner supports have been developed. An absence of either sustained left or confessional party influence is generally associated with market-oriented gender policy models.

Dominant political and religious ideologies, therefore, have been of considerable significance in shaping policies that have affected both class and gender inequalities. Nevertheless, in respect of gender inequality, there persist significant variations even within similar regime types. O'Connor et al.'s (1999) comparison of four 'liberal' welfare states (Canada, the US, Australia and UK) suggests that national cultural variations in both models of motherhood and the sexual division of labour have resulted in variations in outcomes in respect of both women's employment and employment/family articulation. In particular, these liberal regimes are characterised by variations in the importance accorded to the 'sanctity of motherhood', reflected in policy differences in which the status of motherhood is seen as a justification for protection from the 'sanctity of the market' (Orloff 1999: 347). Social policies in Britain and Australia have historically offered more support for (collective) social rights supportive of traditional arrangements relative to the sexual division of labour. In the US, and to a lesser extent Canada, there has been more of an emphasis on (individual) civil rights, as well as on the primacy of the market. As Appelbaum et al. (2003) have noted, in the US: 'regulation of the employment relationship has emphasised equal employment opportunity – equal treatment in the workplace, equal access to opportunities for organisational advancement and leadership – for employees, female or male, who function in the workplace as if they are unencumbered by home or care giving responsibilities' (emphasis in original). In the US, the strength of economic liberalism has resulted in the triumph of the market over the sanctity of motherhood, and motherhood as such carries with it little by way of market protections, as we have seen in Chapter 4.

In summary: state policies will have an important impact on the manner in which families manage the articulation between employment and family life. National controls on average weekly hours worked will have the effect of securing more 'family' time. Variations in the extent and nature of labour market regulation will affect the kinds of jobs available (whether mainly full time, or full time and part time) and thus the possibilities of different employment–family combinations. Perhaps most importantly, states also vary in the nature and extent of welfare supports they offer to families, and the support given to different family models. In the next section of this chapter, therefore, we will, using ISSP survey data, explore the impact of these national variations in policy on work–life conflict, using the same measure as used in Chapters 3 (see p. 79) and 4.

Work–life conflict: cross-national comparisons

This comparative analysis draws on ISSP Family 2002 data for six countries: Britain, the US, France, Portugal, Finland and Norway. These countries represent markedly contrasting national policy models, which might be anticipated to have an impact on levels of work–life conflict and the manner in which work–life articulation is achieved. In both the US and Britain, economic and political liberalism has been influential recently, and these countries would be described as 'liberal' within Esping-Andersen's typology. Both Finland and Norway are universalist Scandinavian welfare states. Portugal might be described as familialist, and France would be characterised as a corporatist or conservative welfare regime. However, as we shall see, France has developed policies in respect of women's employment that are at some variance from those more usually associated with conservative family policies.

As we have seen in this and previous chapters, governments in both Britain and the US have embraced neoliberal economic and social policies. There are, of course, important differences between the two countries, in that the extent of universal protections is greater in Britain than in the US, most notably in respect of health care. Nevertheless, both countries are characterised by labour markets that are relatively unregulated, and considerable (and widening) income inequality (see Hills 2004; it should be noted that New Labour has introduced a national minimum wage). Standard weekly working hours tend to be long, although there is plentiful part-time work available in both Britain and the US. In 1999, over 60 per cent of mothers in couple families in Britain and the US were employed, although the employment rate of mothers with a child under six was rather higher in the US (62 per cent) than in Britain (56 per cent) (see OECD 2001). In Korpi's analysis of state family supports, both countries are in the lowest category of both general and dual-earner family supports. In both countries, childcare provision is largely marketised. In the US, parents have been given tax relief on childcare expenses for many years (Dex and Shaw 1986). Some tax concessions have also recently been granted in Britain, but in this country childcare is more often provided via other family members (Paull *et al.* 2002).

The British and US cases stand in stark contrast to the situation in the Scandinavian countries. The Nordic states all rank high as far as support for the dual-earner family model is concerned, with good provision of public daycare services and eldercare, as well as paid parental leave and caring entitlements (Korpi 2000). Norway has in the past been seen as somewhat exceptional amongst the Nordic countries, in that the provision of state childcare services developed later than in other Nordic states (Leira 1992). However, childcare provision in Norway increased rapidly during the 1990s, and the government aims to achieve universal coverage by 2005 (Ellingsaeter 2003; Leira 2002). In contrast, Finland developed universal childcare services from the 1960s and 1970s onwards, and Pfau-Effinger (1999) argues that the culture of 'state motherhood' in Finland is highly supportive of mothers' full-time employment. Both countries also offer 'cash for care' (that is, direct cash payments to parents). 'Cash-for-care' policies have sometimes been seen as supporting more traditional family arrangements, as it is usually the mother who takes up such benefits. However, employment levels amongst both Finnish and Norwegian women are high, at 67.3 per cent in Finland and 73.8 per cent in Norway. Weekly hours of work are regulated (at 40 hours) in both countries, and both countries are also characterised by low levels of income inequality. In Norway, part-time work is highly protected, with the same rights (pro rata) as full-time work (Torp and Barth 2001). Part-time work in Finland is less protected and part-time jobs are seen as less advantageous, and a high proportion of Finnish women (in comparison to Norwegian women) work full time.

Within Europe, France is also characterised by a high level of state childcare provision (Hantrais 1990, 1993). French family policy has sought to channel supports directly to families with children, and nearly all French children between the ages of three and six, and a substantial minority of two year olds, attend state nursery schools. There is further state provision for under twos in *crèches collectives*, as well as tax relief on childcare expenses. In France, much of the support for mothers' employment has been pro-natalist in its inspiration, rather than being concerned with women's equality as such (Jenson 1986). Nevertheless, childcare supports in France have done much to help women into employment, particularly full-time employment (Dex and Walters 1989). Lewis (1992) has described France as a 'modified male breadwinner' state, in which women have benefited, albeit indirectly, from the care and support directed at children, and 56.4 per cent of French women are in employment, the majority of whom work full time. Hours of work in France are also regulated, and since 1998 the Aubry laws have progressively sought to introduce a 35 hour working week.

Portugal also has a relatively high (61.2 per cent) level of women in employment, and the level of full-time employment amongst Portuguese women is also high. Under the Salazar regime (that lasted until 1974), women in Portugal were legally subject to their husbands and formally barred from a wide range of occupations. However, as Portugal was a country of out migration, women were needed in the labour force at home. Colonial wars drained resources away from the 'home' country, and two incomes were in any case required in order to keep families out of poverty (Portugal has one of the lowest *per capita* wage rates in Europe). The level of state welfare spending in Portugal is low and families are legally responsible for the support of their kin. Portugal would be described by Esping-Andersen (1999) as a 'familialistic' welfare state, and therefore not particularly supportive of women's employment (although levels of full-time employment amongst Portuguese women are high). Only low levels of state provided childcare are available – although (and perhaps as a legacy of the past corporatist dictatorship) the level of childcare provision by employers is relatively good (OECD 2001). Hours of work in Portugal are regulated at 40 hours per week.

The six countries under examination in this chapter, therefore, show considerable variation in the nature and extent of supports they offer to dual-earner families. The two Nordic welfare states offer the most substantial level of support, and Britain, the US and Portugal the least. France might be placed somewhere in between the two extremes. Although France is by no means a 'universalist' welfare state, nevertheless, the level of childcare support offered to mothers is relatively extensive and of long standing. To the extent that state supports for dual-earner families serve to reduce work–life conflict, therefore, we might expect that levels of work–life conflict will be lowest in the Scandinavian countries and highest in Britain, the US and Portugal, with France located somewhere in between. Hours of work will also have an important impact on work–life conflict, so we will first examine variations in working hours between the six countries, as reported by the respondents to the ISSP survey.

Although some of the country samples are rather small, Table 5.1 nevertheless reflects, in broad outline, the characteristics of the different working-time regimes, as outlined in this chapter, in the different countries. In all countries, women are considerably more likely to work part time than men, but the extent of part-time work amongst women shows extensive variation. Part-time work amongst women is most common in Britain, followed by the US, and is least common in Finland and Portugal, where full-time dual-earner families are the norm. The British

Table 5.1. *Employees by country by sex by full time/part time; women working part time under 20 hours a week (ISSP surveys, percentages)*

	Britain		US		Finland		Norway		France		Portugal	
	M	F	M	F	M	F	M	F	M	F	M	F
Full time	94	66	87	73	93	86	97	77	99	79	96	85
Part time	6	34	13	27	7	14	3	23	1	21	4	15
N	688	668	357	395	347	330	480	435	496	538	321	252
% p-t > 20 hours		46		29		44		27		29		28

Table 5.2. *Country by average weekly working hours: full-time men and women only (ISSP surveys, percentages by column)*[a]

	Britain		US		Finland		Norway		France		Portugal	
	M	F	M	F	M	F	M	F	M	F	M	F
Under 20	0	0	1	1	0	0	0	0	0	0	3	3
20–34	3	12	5	7	2	10	2	14	4	16	2	6
35–44	44	61	40	55	76	86	57	68	65	72	56	69
45+	54	27	54	38	23	4	41	18	31	12	39	22

[a]Full-time/part-time work was self-reported which may explain the short 'full-time' hours reported by some respondents.

sample is also characterised by a high level (nearly a half of all female part-time workers) of short hours part-time working (short hours part-time working in Finland reflects the 'poor' quality of part-time work in that country).

In all countries, however, the majority of both men and women work full time. Table 5.2 describes the reported weekly working hours of the full-time men and women in the ISSP sample. It can be seen that reported hours of full-time work are substantially longer, for both men and women, in Britain and the US than in the other countries.

The extent of national regulation, therefore, clearly has a significant impact on working hours, and we might anticipate that longer working hours will have a negative impact on capacities to achieve positive work–life articulation. In fact, a comparison of means of work–life conflict indicated that the reported levels of conflict were significantly lower for respondents working under 20 hours a week, and significantly higher for respondents working over 45 hours a week.

Table 5.3. *Work–life conflict by working hours (ISSP pooled sample), all respondents*

Working hours	N	Mean	S.D.
Under 20	295	6.4766	2.138
20–34	692	7.1511	2.365
35–44	2568	7.1863	2.330
45+	1282	8.0854	2.511

ANOVA F = 59.870, df = 3, p < .001.

Table 5.4. *Work–life conflict by country: full-time and part-time respondents, ISSP surveys*

Country	N	Mean	S.D.
Britain	1032	7.54	2.37
US	736	7.79	2.66
Finland	703	6.88	2.07
Norway	857	6.95	2.16
France	1007	7.52	2.46
Portugal	522	7.74	2.80

ANOVA F = 19.6, df = 5, p < .001.
Post hoc tests showed that Finland and Norway reported significantly lower work–life stress scores than all other countries (p < .001).

Part-time work, therefore, is significantly associated with lower levels of work–life conflict. In couple households, it will usually be the woman who works part time, and we might expect that this will make a contribution to reducing levels of work–life conflict in 'one and a half' breadwinner societies such as Britain. Table 5.4 describes mean scores of work–life conflict by country for all employees. However, it may be seen that mean conflict scores are significantly lower in Finland, where full-time employment is the norm for both men and women and the majority of couples are dual earning, than in Britain, the US, France or Portugal. Indeed, Finland and Norway, the two Scandinavian countries, stand out as reporting significantly lower mean levels of work–life conflict. This suggests that supportive state policies may indeed be 'making a difference' as far as the combination of employment and family life is concerned.

Cross-national variations in the extent of part-time work, particularly amongst women, will have an impact on aggregate national conflict levels. Given the extent of national variation in levels of part-time work

Table 5.5. *Work–life stress by country: full-time respondents only (ISSP surveys)*

Country	N	Mean	S.D.
Britain	814	7.726	2.370
US	569	7.835	2.594
Finland	622	6.881	2.066
Norway	753	7.013	2.176
France	886	7.613	2.475
Portugal	479	7.699	2.787

ANOVA $F = 22.225$, df = 5, $p < .001$.
Post hoc tests showed that Finland and Norway reported significantly lower work–life stress scores than all other countries ($p < .001$).

amongst the six countries, this factor is controlled for by excluding part-time employees from subsequent analysis. A comparison of levels of work–life conflict for full-time employees by country, however, suggests that in explanations of the extent of work–life conflict, hours of work, although clearly very important, are by no means the whole story. Table 5.5 shows that reported levels of work–life conflict were indeed high in Britain and the US, where working hours are on average longer than in the other countries. However, levels of work–life conflict are relatively high in France, a country where working hours are considerably shorter than in Norway (although not Finland).

Indeed, in relation to work–life conflict, Finland and Norway emerged as a distinctive grouping when compared to the other countries. As we have seen, the Nordic welfare states rank high on the level of supports they offer to dual-earner families, and Finland and Norway also rank high on the level of general family supports on offer. It may be suggested, therefore, that as Gallie (following Maurice *et al.* 1986) would put it, a 'societal effect' is in operation in the Scandinavian countries. Gallie's (2003) comparative investigation of the quality of working life in Europe found that in the Scandinavian countries, respondents (to a European-wide survey) reported a significantly higher quality of work task than in other European countries. He argues that this finding may be attributed to the cumulative impact of Scandinavian policies (from the 1970s onwards) directed at the enhancement of variety, autonomy and decision-making amongst employees. In a similar vein, it may be suggested that supportive work–family policies in Finland and Norway have had a similar, and positive, impact in reducing levels of work–life conflict in these countries.

When the impact of working hours on conflict was compared for individual countries, it was found that even at higher levels of working hours (i.e., 45 hours or more), conflict levels were still lower in Finland and Norway than in the other countries (although very few people report working more than 45 hours a week in Finland). It was still possible, however, that there might be country-specific sample variations in other individual level factors that affect work–life conflict, and that these might have an impact on the variations in stress scores by country. For example, women report higher levels of work–life conflict than men. Individuals with a child in the household report higher levels of conflict than those with no resident children, and managerial and professional employees report higher levels of conflict than routine and manual employees. However, when these different factors were controlled for in a multiple regression analysis (Appendix Table 5.6, p.138), the 'societal' difference between Finland, Norway and the other countries still persisted. That is, living in Finland or Norway was associated with a significantly lower level of work–life conflict than living in the other countries.

In the case of the Scandinavian countries, therefore, this evidence suggests that a 'societal effect' is in operation. In Finland and Norway, state policies have been directed not only at improving the quality of working life, as Gallie's research has demonstrated, but also at the support of dual-earner families and thus 'positive' work–life articulation. Past and present government policies in both countries are also characterised by a high level of support for policies of gender equality. The empirical findings presented in this chapter, however, suggest that France still remains something of a puzzle. In Korpi's comparative analysis, France ranks high on general family supports and relatively high (only just below the Scandinavian countries) on dual-earner supports. Average hours of full-time work in France are relatively low – in fact, Table 5.2 above suggests that they are the second lowest of all of the countries in the ISSP samples (after Finland). As we shall see in Chapter 6, it would appear that another important factor affecting levels of work–life stress – the domestic division of labour – has a particularly negative impact for French women, and this has a significant effect on conflict scores.

Summary and conclusions

In this chapter, the differential impact of government policies on inequalities, including gender inequalities, as well as on capacities for work–life articulation, has been examined. Despite the current popularity of theories of globalisation, which tend to downplay the importance of 'national' differences, state policies still have an important impact on the lives and well-being of their citizens. Amongst the advanced Western societies, Britain and the US are rather distinctive in being two countries most affected by the influence of neoliberal economic and social policies – although in many other respects, it has been argued that Britain is still closer to Europe than to the US (Hutton 2002). The impact of neoliberal prescriptions in respect of employment will be to resist the introduction of policies that attempt to regulate employment conditions in respect of matters such as wages, job security and working hours. At the other pole of governmental regulation are Northern European coordinated market economies such as the German Federal Republic, in which the wages, job security and working hours of 'core' or 'standard' workers have historically been highly regulated – often at the cost of excluding 'outsiders', including women, from protected employment.

Nevertheless, in the 1950s, 1960s and 1970s, attempts at labour market regulation did serve to lower levels of inequality for those 'standard workers' – usually men – in the labour force. As a parallel strand of research and commentary on welfare provision has demonstrated, there was also considerable variation in the extent to which states offered welfare and other benefits that have been associated with the development of social 'citizenship', and which also serve to reduce inequality. Neoliberal governments will be inclined to resist the introduction of welfare protections, not least because they will interfere with the workings of the 'self-regulating' market at both the national and individual levels. The nature and extent of state welfare provision has had a significant impact on women, particularly the level of women's employment, as was highlighted in Esping-Andersen's (1990) analysis.

However, from its initial publication, Esping-Andersen's work was subject to extensive criticism from feminist social policy analysts. They criticised his regime typology for paying little or no attention to the significant contribution made to welfare provision by the unpaid caring work of women within the family.[4] In part as a consequence of these criticisms, contemporary debates have undergone a dramatic shift and women's economic behaviour is now seen as central to welfare state

---

[4] The 'gender blindness' of Esping-Andersen's analysis was a reflection of the 'gender blindness' of social science research more generally. For example, empirical research on social mobility drew on 'men only' samples (e.g., Blau and Duncan 1967; Goldthorpe 1980).

regeneration in Europe. However, despite this recent shift, Esping-Andersen's analysis still incorporates gender stereotypical assumptions relating to women's 'preferences' – in particular, that women will 'choose' mother-friendly employment. If changes in employment, such as reduced and flexible hours working, continue to be largely directed at, and taken up by, women, then the broad contours of gender inequality are unlikely to undergo any fundamental change, as is argued by Fraser (1994).

Fraser (1994) engages in a 'thought experiment' in relation to gender equity and welfare reform. As she demonstrates, neither 'universal breadwinner' (that is, full employment for both men and women) nor 'caregiver parity' (that is, economic recompense for domestic carers) welfare models would actually achieve gender equity. The 'universal breadwinner' model, as we have seen, would seem to be emerging as the preferred model in contemporary discussions of welfare reform (Esping-Andersen 2002; Lewis 2002). It would maximise labour market participation for both men and women, and care work would be shifted from the family to the market and the state. However, as Fraser argues, the 'universal breadwinner' model has a number of disadvantages as far as gender equity is concerned, not least because it gives primacy to men's traditional arena of activity – employment – and simply tries to help women 'fit in' to this mould (Fraser 1994: 605). 'Caregiver parity' attempts to 'make [gender] difference costless' – that is, to give child-bearing, childrearing and domestic work an equal status (and reward) to market work (Fraser 1994: 606). Thus, within this model, most care work would still be carried out within the household, supported by public funds. However, caregiver parity would be very unlikely to result in income equality (with 'market' workers), and would tend to consolidate the gender division of domestic labour. Thus Fraser argues that gender equity is only likely to be achieved if men become 'more like women' – that is, people who combine both primary care work as well as paid employment. That is, gender – at least in respect of those aspects that relate to the division of labour between the sexes – needs to be deconstructed.

Fraser argues, therefore, that welfare reforms are unlikely to achieve gender equity unless some kind of gender shift takes place in the 'private' sphere of the family and household. However, as we have seen, Esping-Andersen argues that an increase in the amount of household work carried out by men would only serve to inhibit job creation, and that women will continue to 'choose' to specialise in care work and/or 'mother-friendly' employment. In short, Esping-Andersen does not advocate any fundamental reordering of the gendered division of labour, other than to increase women's participation in market work.

Nevertheless, it is important to recognise, as Korpi's work amply demonstrates, that national variations in labour market and welfare regimes do have a very substantial impact on gender inequalities, as well as on capacities for work–life articulation. The impact of these policies has been explored empirically via survey evidence drawn from six countries characterised by very different labour market and welfare regimes. As was anticipated, weekly (full-time) hours worked were considerably longer, for both men and women, in the relatively unregulated labour markets of Britain and the US. Long hours of work contributed significantly to levels of work–life conflict. However, respondents in Finland and Norway, the two Nordic states in our 'sample' of countries, emerged as reporting the lowest levels of work–life conflict even when a number of significant factors including working hours and the presence or absence of a child in the household were controlled for. It is very clear, therefore, that national policies can have a substantial impact on capacities for work–life articulation, and the evidence presented in this chapter supports arguments as to the existence of a positive 'societal effect' (Gallie 2003) in the Scandinavian countries.

In respect of the kinds of changes that are required in order to adjust to the new realities brought about by the increased employment of mothers and women's transformed economic and social claims, therefore, the evidence of this chapter serves to reinforce the arguments developed in previous chapters as to the negative effects of simply 'letting the market decide', as would be implied by neoliberal policies. At the same time, however, the case of France suggests that there may also be limits to the positive impact of state regulation as far as work–life articulation is concerned. The French government has (successfully) acted to reduce average weekly working hours, and state childcare provisions in France are good as compared to those in Britain, the US and Portugal. Nevertheless, reported levels of work–life conflict in France are higher than in the Scandinavian countries, and indeed, when the impact of weekly hours of work and the presence of child(ren) in the household are controlled for, are actually higher than in Britain, the US or Portugal. In Chapter 6, therefore, we will examine in greater depth a further important topic that will crucially affect work–life articulation – that is, the nature of the household arrangements, and the domestic division of labour, between men and women, and the possibilities and potential for 'deconstructing gender' in respect of the division of labour within both market and family work.

Appendix

Table 5.6. *Regression on work–life conflict (all countries, ISSP samples)*

Variable	Beta	t-value	Sig.
Living in Britain[a]	−.022	−.908	.364
Living in Finland[a]	−.126	−5.693	<.001
Living in France[a]	−.018	−.772	.440
Living in Norway[a]	−.128	−5.416	<.001
Living in USA[a]	−.013	−.571	.568
Hours worked	.197	11.861	<.001
Being female	.109	6.407	<.001
Child in household	.099	6.232	<.001
Age	−.044	−2.757	<.01
Professional class[b]	.053	2.805	<.01
Intermediate class[b]	−.002	−.090	.928
Constant		21.492	<.001

[a]Portugal as reference case.
[b]Manual class as reference class.

6   Households, domestic work, market work and happiness

The 'breadwinner' model of the articulation of employment and family life assigned women to domestic work and the family. As described in previous chapters, the naturalism of this gender arrangement or division of labour was extensively challenged by second-wave feminism. Nevertheless, an essentialist ideology of domesticity, that assigns domestic responsibilities and self-sacrificing motherhood to women, has proved to be remarkably persistent (Williams 2000). A major feminist objective that was articulated during the 1960s, 1970s and 1980s was to encourage men to play a greater part in domestic work and childcare – summed up in the popular slogan of the time: 'the personal is political'. As with women's involvement in market work, so men's involvement in domestic work has also changed. However, most of the narrowing of the gender gap in respect of domestic work has come about because of women's declining involvement, rather than men's increased participation, in domestic work. In this chapter, recent trends in time use and the domestic division of labour will be examined cross-nationally. A number of other relevant issues will also be addressed, including the impact of variations in the domestic division of labour on work–life conflict. We will return in particular to the case of France, where, as described in Chapter 5, levels of work–life conflict are relatively high despite good state supports for employed mothers and non-excessive working hours. We will also examine the impact of domestic traditionalism on general and family happiness, particularly for women.

Time use and the domestic division of labour

As discussed in Chapters 4 and 5, the question of 'time poverty' has attracted increasing attention in recent years. The extent to which hours worked by individuals in paid employment have increased or not has been substantially debated (Green 2001; Schor 1991). Aggregated data using time use diaries for six countries (including the US) suggests that at an averaged individual level, weekly hours of market work for men have

luced slightly since the 1960s (Sullivan and Gershuny
although average individual weekly working hours may
:d in Western countries (and in some cases, such as
ally have been reduced, see Bishop 2004), the overall
's employment means that in aggregate, working hours
.. ac the level of the household. In the US, for example, total
couple working hours increased from 52.5 per week in 1970 to 62.8 per
week in 1997 (Jacobs and Gerson 1998: 455). As many have argued (Moen
2003; Sullivan and Gershuny 2001), more people are *feeling* overworked
(despite the lack of an increase in individual working hours) because
'families can no longer rely on the unpaid support of a woman at home,
yet the structure of work has not changed sufficiently to accommodate the
transitions in workers' private lives' (Jacobs and Gerson 1998: 450).

Two different sets of theories, the first largely economistic or material,
and the second largely normative, have been developed to explain the
nature of and trends in the division of domestic labour between men and
women (Baxter *et al.* 2004; Bianchi *et al.* 2000). Economistic/material
theories stress the significance of both time availability and relative
resources within the household. Time availability models suggest that
those household members spending most time in market work (usually
men) will have the least time available for household work. Those
spending most time in market work will also bring the most resources
into the household, and as a consequence, their superior relative material power will also result in their spending less time on housework (Blood
and Wolf 1960). Furthermore, neoclassical economists (Becker 1991;
Mincer and Polachek 1974) have argued that the household as a unit will
operate to its best advantage if men specialise in market work and
women specialise in caring and domestic work. According to these kinds
of theories, therefore, women's increased involvement with market work
(which will both reduce the time they have available as well as increasing
the resources they bring into the household) should be followed by
men's increased involvement in domestic work.

These kinds of rational economic accounts of the division of domestic
and market labour have been challenged by normative theories. Feminists have argued that the allocation of the primary responsibility for
housework to women itself constitutes a symbolic re-enactment of
gender relations, as the roles of wife and mother are intimately tied to
expectations for doing housework (West and Zimmerman 1987). Thus
order and cleanliness within the home are reflections on women's competence as a 'wife and mother' – but not on men's competence as a
'husband and father' (Bianchi *et al.* 2000: 195). According to these
arguments, given that the construction and reconstruction of gendered

identities is the major factor in the determination of who does domestic work, its allocation is not necessarily rational and women will almost invariably do more of it, even when in full-time employment.

These two competing explanations may be evaluated in the light of recent trends relating to the time spent by men and women on housework. Cross-national data, as well as detailed information for the US (Bianchi et al. 2000; Sullivan and Gershuny 2001), indicates that women's hours of household work declined considerably from the 1960s to the 1980s. In the US: 'women spent about 30 hours doing unpaid household work in 1965, over six times the 4.9 hours men spent in housework. Women's housework hours dropped to 23.7 hours per week in 1975, 19.7 hours per week in 1985, and reached a low of 17.5 hours per week by 1995. Men's hours increased to 7.2 hours in 1975, 9.8 hours in 1985, and levelled off at 10.0 hours in 1995' (Bianchi et al. 2000: 206). Thus there has been a considerable convergence between men and women in the hours spent on housework, but this has been largely as a consequence of women reducing their domestic work hours. Data from a range of other countries shows a similar trend, that is, a considerable reduction in the hours devoted to housework by women, together with a (smaller) increase in housework hours amongst men (Baxter et al. 2004; Gershuny et al. 1994; Sullivan and Gershuny 2001).

Clearly, therefore, women's entry into paid employment has been associated with a reduction in the hours they spend on household chores. However, it should not be forgotten that, on average, women still spend about twice as many hours on housework as do men. There are, of course, variations around the average. As we shall see, there are considerable cross-national variations in the hours spent in household labour, as well as in the housework 'gender gap'. Older people spend more time on housework than younger people, and married women spend more time on housework than non-married women, even those women living in non-married partnerships. There is some evidence that men in 'non-traditional' (i.e., not married) households spend more time on housework than married men, and that couples who marry after a period of living together also have less traditional housework arrangements, perhaps suggesting a slow process of change in the domestic division of labour as 'non-traditional' household relations proliferate (Baxter et al. 2004). Women who work full time spend less time on housework, although women who work part time do proportionately more. The presence of children increases housework hours (more for women than men), and men with higher levels of education tend to do more housework. Finally, wives with a more egalitarian gender ideology do less housework (Bianchi et al. 2000: 217).

The empirical evidence of change in the gendered domestic division of labour over time, therefore, offers support for both rational/economistic and gender ideology theories. As women have increased their hours spent in employment, so their hours of domestic work have declined, and men's hours have increased somewhat. However, gender continues to explain more of the variance in hours of domestic work than any other factor, and women still carry out considerably more domestic work than men. The slowing down of men's contribution over the last decade suggests that some kind of plateau may have been reached (a similar slowing down may also be noted in the distribution of domestic tasks, see Crompton *et al.* 2003). This suggests that any future change may also be very slow. Nevertheless, these empirical trends indicate that, since the 1960s, both structural changes in women's employment patterns, as well as changing attitudes to gender roles, have had an impact on the domestic division of labour. What is not revealed in the trend data, however, are the attitudes and perceptions of the men, women and households who have been going through these changes. For there is by no means universal agreement as to the beneficial impact of changes in gender roles and the domestic division of labour.

Neoconservatives have targeted 'feminism' (usually unspecified) as responsible for the increase in single parenthood and family dissolution, as well as problems for family life more generally: 'these massive changes in gender roles have not been the unambiguously good thing that some feminists pretend. There have been losses accompanying the gains, and these losses have fallen disproportionately on the shoulders of children . . .' (Fukuyama 1999: 120; see also Morgan 1999). Massive social disruption, Fukuyama suggests, can only be averted if women somehow rediscover their innate nurturing capacities and devote themselves to the care of their young children (Fukuyama 1999; Kristol 1998). As Williams (1991: 82) has suggested, this essentialist (i.e., gender-specific) assignment of the virtues of caring and nurturing to women brings with it the threat of a loss of these capacities to society as a whole if traditional gender roles are transformed: 'Decoded, the message is that the continued subjection of women is a key force standing between America and the paltry, alienating consequences of possessive individualism.'

More insidious, perhaps, has been the expression of an essentialist backlash in the emergence of populist conservative feminism. Popular works such as *Men are from Mars, women are from Venus* (Gray 1992) emphasise the emotional and interpersonal differences between men and women, with women as empathic carers and men as competitive fixers. Equally populist texts such as *The Rules* (Fein and Schneider 2002) and *The Surrendered Wife* (Doyle 2001) urge a gender traditionalism in intimate relationships as the road to gender harmony. The validity of these assumptions is usually asserted as commonsense 'truth', rather than being supported by systematic empirical evidence.[1] In the following sections of this chapter, therefore, we will first, examine cross-national variations in the gendering of the domestic division of labour, and second, the impact of variations in domestic traditionalism on both work–life conflict and family and general happiness.

Cross-national variations in the domestic division of labour and its impact in Britain, Finland, France, Norway, the US and Portugal

Although the family is by convention a 'private' sphere, it is also widely represented as being the major building block of society itself. For example, in Britain, the New Labour Green Paper *Supporting Families* (1998) states that 'family life is the foundation on which our communities, our society and our country was built'. Nevertheless, there will be a potential tension between the rights of the state and rights within families, particularly those of the senior adults. Historically, state policies in respect of the family have tended to endorse the rights and authority of the husband over the wife (Pateman 1989). In Portugal under the corporatist dictatorship, for example, wives were held responsible for domestic duties and legally subject to their husbands, and in France, an attenuated legal framework of 'private' (i.e., domestic) patriarchy persisted into the 1960s (Crompton and Le Feuvre 2000).

However, in other countries, particularly in Scandinavia, 'second-wave' feminism has had a considerable influence on policy, and as Anttonen has argued, Scandinavian universalism 'has been important in the process of feminising social citizenship' (2002: 75). Thus in the later decades of the twentieth century, in the Scandinavian countries, state provision for dual-earner family support and childcare were developed in a political context which was seen as making a positive contribution to women's equality (described as 'state feminism'; see Hernes 1987). Moreover, family policies have not been directed simply at mothers, but at mothers *and* fathers. In the Nordic states, therefore, state supports for dual-earner families have been accompanied by efforts to encourage men to undertake a greater share of domestic work, particularly in respect of childcare.

---

[1] This style of argument is entirely compatible with gender essentialism, which emphasises the innate and natural character of differences between the sexes. The attributes specific to each gender are held to be of an intrinsic nature closely associated with physical or physiological differences.

In Norway, for example, a paternity quota (or 'daddy leave') was introduced in 1993. This reserved four weeks of parental leave for the father, not transferable to the mother, and to be forfeited if not taken up. As Brandth and Kvande (2001: 256) have argued, this policy 'may be considered an approach by which the state feminism system pushed fathers into active fatherhood', and was explicitly developed to 'facilitate the equal sharing of family work between men and women' (*ibid.*: 264). There has been a sharp increase in the take-up of this 'compulsory' leave in Norway, as compared to the take-up of the 'voluntary' leave entitlements that are also available (Brandth and Kvande 2001). Nevertheless, the impact of 'state feminism' on the domestic division of labour in the Scandinavian countries does not seem to have been particularly successful. Gershuny's and Sullivan's comparison of the distribution of the domestic division of labour in contrasting 'liberal' and 'social-democratic' regimes suggests that men do not make a greater contribution to core domestic labour in social democratic countries as compared to 'liberal' countries (Gershuny and Sullivan 2003: 217). Their data suggests that variations by sex in the division of domestic work are more affected by cross-nationally 'universal' factors, such as educational levels, rather than regime type.

In contrast to the Scandinavian countries, in neither Britain, the US, France nor Portugal is there evidence of state policies that explicitly encourage men to take on a larger share of domestic work. Data from the US shows that in general, men do more housework when their wives work longer hours in market work, in line with time-availability models of changes in the gender distribution of domestic work (Bianchi *et al.* 2000: 215). Both gender role attitudes, and level of education, affect men's participation in domestic work. We might expect there to be gendered national variations in the domestic division of labour, therefore, according to the extent of women's employment as well as in relation to gender role attitudes.

Within the ISSP samples, there was considerable national variation in attitudes to gender roles, as is demonstrated in Table 6.1. Amongst the European countries, Portugal is the most traditional, with a third of respondents agreeing that 'a man's job is to earn money, a woman's job is to look after the home and family'. The Scandinavian countries are the least gender traditional. Britain, France and the US are very similar, with around a fifth of respondents expressing 'traditional' gender role attitudes.[2]

---

[2] The same question was asked in all countries, but the response categories were different in the US. In the US, there was no differentiation in the category 'disagree', whereas in

Table 6.1. *Gender role attitudes and women's full-time work in Britain, Finland, France, Norway, US and Portugal (ISSP surveys: respondents in full-time employment only); employment rates of mothers of young children*

	% 'agreeing' that 'A man's job is to earn money, a woman's job is to look after the home and family' (ISSP samples)	% women in employment working full-time (ISSP samples)	Employment rate of all mothers with a child under 6 (1998/9)[a]
Britain	18	66	55.8
Finland	12	86	58.8
France	22	79	56.2
Norway	10	77	72.8
USA	22	73	61.5
Portugal	34	85	70.6

[a]OECD 2001, Table 4.1

However, there would not seem to be a consistent association, by country, with conservative gender role attitudes and the extent of women's full-time employment. Portugal, where respondents express the most conservative gender role attitudes, has one of the highest proportions of women working full time, and the extent of women's full-time working is also high in the Scandinavian countries, where gender role attitudes are the least traditional. It would seem, therefore, that at the aggregate national level, 'generalised' gender role attitudes are not a reliable guide to women's paid employment behaviour. What, however, of the impact of gender role attitudes on the other major element in the 'total organisation of social labour' – unpaid domestic work?

Table 6.2 describes the mean hours of household work reported by respondents, and their estimates of their partner's household work hours, for the ISSP samples in each country. It is immediately apparent that the gendered distribution of hours of household work is most traditional in Portugal, where respondents also profess the most traditional gender role attitudes (Table 6.1). In general, both men and

Europe and the Scandinavian countries, 'disagree' and 'strongly disagree' were differentiated. Thus, in the US, a quarter of the respondents reported that they 'neither agreed nor disagreed', a higher proportion than in any of the other countries. The data reported in this table, therefore, uses exactly comparable categories for all countries, that is, 'strongly agree' and 'agree' combined.

Table 6.2. *Mean weekly hours of reported household work (not including childcare and leisure time activities, partners' household work hours reported by respondent, ISSP surveys)*

	Britain		Finland		France		Norway		USA		Portugal	
R sex:	M	W	M	W	M	W	M	W	M	W	M	W
Men	7.7	5.3	6.8	6.1	6.5	4.2	5.2	4.1	8.4	5.4	7.2	5.6
Women	15.3	13.5	13.0	13.7	13.6	13.0	11.4	11.7	13.6	12.7	24.2	26.4
Total	23.0	18.8	19.8	19.8	20.1	17.2	16.6	15.8	22.0	18.1	31.4	32.0
Women's reported share of hh work in relation to men's	2.0	2.5	1.9	2.2	2.1	3.1	2.2	2.9	1.6	2.4	3.4	4.7
Difference between male and female reported shares	.5		.3		1.0		.7		.8		1.3	

women report that women do the larger share of household work, but there are considerable differences in reporting between the sexes with regard to the extent of men's sharing. Men report more hours of household work than women's reported hours of their partners' (assumed to be male) household work in all six countries. In general, men report more aggregate hours of household work than women claim their partners do, with discrepancies between the sexes of nearly four hours a week in Britain and the US. The bottom two rows of Table 6.2 summarise the respondents' reports of the relative hours of household work carried out by men and women in their own households. For example, British men report that their partners do twice as many hours of household work as they do, but British women report that they do two and a half times as many hours as their partners. French men report that their partners do twice as many household hours as they do, but French women report that they do three times as much. In all countries, men report a more egalitarian sharing of hours of household work than do women, with the largest gender variations in estimates being in France and Portugal.

It would appear, therefore, that there is a cross-nationally universal tendency for men to report a higher level of gender egalitarianism in respect of housework than women do – and this gender difference is also found in relation to the reporting of domestic tasks in the ISSP samples. Nevertheless, there are, clearly, considerable cross-national differences in reported hours of household work by country. Portuguese respondents report an average of 31.6 total hours of household work per week as compared to only 16.1 hours in Norway. Indeed, women in Portugal report that they carry out nearly five times as much domestic labour as Portuguese men – a similar pattern to that of the US in the 1960s and 1970s. These variations will reflect country differences in norms relating to the gender division of household work, as well as in income levels that will affect access to labour-saving household appliances and other services – and Portugal is the poorest of the six countries under discussion here. They may also reflect national (cultural) variations in both the levels of cleanliness that are considered appropriate, as well as preferences for particular kinds of accommodation, cuisine and furnishings – but it is impossible to gauge the impact of these factors from this data. The case of Portugal, however, suggests that gender role traditionalism can have a significant impact on the gendered division of household work, although not on the extent of women's paid employment.

Notwithstanding these country variations in hours of household work, there are also cross-national continuities in the gendered division of domestic labour by household type. Further analysis of the ISSP samples (not reported here) found that in all countries, total reported hours of household work are lower when both partners work, and higher in 'traditional' households, in which the man works full time and the woman does not. In all countries, women working full time carry out fewer hours of household work than women working part time, and hours of household work are the greatest amongst married women not in paid employment.

The exploration of cross-national variations in the gendered allocation of household work was extended further by computing a domestic division of labour (DDL) index from five questions from the ISSP survey:

In your household, who usually does the:
Laundry
Cares for sick family members
Shops for groceries
Household cleaning
Prepares the meals
(always me, usually me, about equal, usually spouse/partner, always spouse/partner)

By convention, these would be considered 'women's' tasks. Scores were allocated in accordance with this assumption. Thus a 'most

Table 6.3. *Mean scores of domestic division of labour (DDL) for each country (ISSP surveys: respondents in full-time employment only)*

	N	Mean (SD)
Britain	514	18.61 (3.23)
Finland	452	18.23 (2.67)
France	575	19.23 (3.22)
Norway	545	18.19 (2.67)
USA	335	17.60 (3.70)
Portugal	276	20.49 (3.18)
Total	2363	18.81 (3.08)

ANOVA F = 42.67; p < .001.

traditional' score (where all of the tasks are usually carried out by the woman) would be 25.[3] Average scores for all six countries are given in Table 6.3.

Respondents in the US report the least traditional DDL, followed by the Scandinavian countries, then Britain. As with hours of household work, men tended to report a less 'traditional' division of domestic tasks than did women. As we have seen, in the Scandinavian countries there have been government-sponsored efforts to persuade men to engage in a wider range of household tasks, particularly childcare, and the relatively less traditional mean DDL reported in these countries might provide modest further support for the argument that a 'societal effect', resulting from the impact of state-sponsored policies, is in operation. However, in neither Britain nor the US, where respondents also report a DDL below the mean, has there been any attempt by governments to shift the domestic division of labour in a less traditional direction.[4] Respondents in France did not profess particularly 'traditional' attitudes to gender roles (unlike respondents in Portugal), and the level of childcare supports provided by the French state is relatively generous. However, the domestic division of labour would appear to be rather traditional in France (and French women reported that they spend three times more

[3] DDL scores ranging from 5 to 25; higher scores indicate more traditional DDL. Factor analysis showed 1 factor, Eigen value 2.699, explaining over 54 per cent of the variance. Cronbach's alpha for all 5 items = 0.7860.

[4] As with hours of domestic work, men reported a less 'traditional' division of domestic tasks than women. The largest (2 points plus) gender discrepancies were found in France, the US, and Portugal. In the US, the gender discrepancy was over 3 points (the largest), so it is possible that the low 'traditionalism' scores in the US are an artefact of the overreporting of domestic tasks by men in that country.

hours on domestic work than their male partners). Indeed, in respect of the domestic division of labour, *post hoc* tests on the DDL index showed that France is closer to Portugal (which has the most traditional division of domestic labour) than to Britain.

Notwithstanding these cross-national variations, a similar range of factors impact on domestic gender traditionalism (or a lack of it) in all six countries. These factors are the same as those that have been identified in previous research on this topic, and are summarised in the regression in Appendix Table 6.7, p. 162. Age, having a child in the household, a lower level of education, part-time working amongst women, and less liberal gender role attitudes were all significantly associated with a more traditional division of domestic tasks (adding country to the model in Table 6.7 only increased the variance by 4 per cent).

Nevertheless, Tables 6.2 and 6.3 both demonstrate that, although similar factors might be affecting the extent of gender traditionalism in the different countries, some countries are more traditional than others. Both Portugal, and to a lesser extent France, report a more traditional division of household tasks than the other four countries. The division of domestic work within the household might be expected to have an impact on work–life conflict, particularly for women. Adding the DDL variable to the regression in Table 6.7 demonstrated that a more traditional division of domestic labour was, indeed, associated with higher levels of work–life conflict. However, a separate analysis by individual country showed that a more traditional DDL was a significant predictor of work–life conflict only in France (Table 6.8, Appendix, p. 162). As discussed in Chapter 5 (Table 5.4, p. 132), reported levels of work–life conflict in France are also relatively high, which was a rather surprising finding given the extensive state supports for childcare, and the shorter working hours, in France. It would seem, therefore, that in France, the gender division of domestic work might be a rather contentious issue.

We have used the ISSP samples to examine cross-national variations in both the hours of domestic work carried out by men and women, as well as the extent of gender traditionalism in the allocation of household tasks. In general, the findings serve to support Gershuny's and Sullivan's (2003) arguments that when 'liberal' and 'social democratic' nation states are compared directly, variations in state policies do not appear to have a highly significant impact on the division of domestic work within the household. There is little variation in both hours and allocation of domestic tasks, in relation to gender non-traditionalism, between the two Scandinavian countries and the two countries characterised by liberal market regimes and non-supportive work–family policies (i.e., Britain and the US). The allocation of domestic tasks is most traditional in France and Portugal (although hours of domestic work are not particularly high in France). A high level of gender role traditionalism in attitudes will no doubt make a significant contribution to traditionalism in respect of domestic work in Portugal. However, the case of France is rather puzzling. Gender role attitudes are markedly less traditional in France than in Portugal, and there is a long history of practical state supports for working mothers in France. Moreover, more traditionalism in respect of the division of domestic tasks is also associated with higher levels of work–life conflict in France. In the next section, therefore, the case of France will be examined in more detail.

Domestic labour, attitudes and behaviour: the case of France

Until the relatively recent past, Franco-British cross-national research has tended to focus on the rather different employment patterns of French and British women. As a consequence of both the French state's support for working mothers, as well as the non-availability of part-time work in France, women in France had fewer childrearing breaks (and thus more continuous employment), and were more likely to be in full-time work, than women in Britain. Thus until the 1980s French women tended to perform rather better, in labour market terms, than British women, and were more likely to be in professional and managerial occupations (Hantrais 1990). However, as Gregory and Windebank (2000) have argued (and as has been argued in this book), a focus on employment as the principal form of 'work' leads to a rather narrow conceptualisation of 'progress' in gender relations. Indeed, as the similarities between the 'liberal' and 'social democratic' states in respect of the domestic division of labour suggest, 'state social policy alone provides a poor understanding of the similarities and differences in women's *unpaid* work situations' (Gregory and Windebank 2000: 179, my emphasis).

Thus past research has argued that, despite a long history of state support for working mothers, and family-directed benefits, both gender stereotyping in respect of employment, and the domestic division of labour, are more conventional (or traditional) in France than might be expected (Crompton and Le Feuvre 2000; Windebank 2001). Explanations of this gender traditionalism have drawn in particular on French thinking about 'difference' and 'equality', which is imbued with Republican universalism. In France, universal 'equality' is associated with the rejection of 'difference'. Thus, any claims to special treatment by particular groups is seen as a claim for unequal (i.e., more advantaged) consideration.[5] For example, although French women have equal rights to men in employment, the implementation of these policies has not been accompanied by any special measures (i.e., affirmative action) to redress previous gender imbalances in employment and the labour market.[6] In some contrast to other national contexts (for example, UK, Scandinavia and the US), the topic of 'equal opportunities' has not had a particularly high profile in France. Perhaps as a consequence, attitudes to the gendered division of labour – for example, as revealed by perceptions of 'suitable' jobs for men and women – are rather conventional in France (at least in comparison to the British case, see Crompton and Le Feuvre 2000).

Gregory's and Windebank's comparative research has demonstrated that in the UK, there is slightly more gender equality in domestic work times than in France, despite the fact that French women are more likely to be working full time.[7] Further evidence of an embedded gender traditionalism in France would seem to be confirmed by the evidence of a relatively traditional division of domestic labour described in Tables 6.2 and 6.3 above. In a similar vein, Windebank's qualitative comparative study of domestic labour and parenting in Britain and France found that French men contributed less than British men:

in the French sample, there were numerous men who were available to look after children during the week when their partner was employed (e.g. teachers who did not work in the school holidays or on a Wednesday afternoon) but nevertheless, did not take responsibility for childcare even when they were free. This was not the case in any of the British sample where sequential scheduling of jobs was used to minimise formal childcare provision . . . (Windebank 2001: 287)

Windebank suggests that the greater involvement of British men in childcare and domestic work is in fact a consequence of the greater flexibility in labour markets, and lack of support for childcare, in Britain as compared to France. She suggests that British men have been in a sense 'forced' into domesticity in order to enable their partners to work. Paid work is becoming, increasingly, a financial necessity for British households (a parallel argument might be developed in relation to the United States). In contrast, French men have been enabled to 'fall back' on state childcare provision if their partners are in employment. That is,

---

[5] This position has guided recent legislation on the wearing of religious symbols in state (secular) schools, in particular, headscarves for Muslim girls.
[6] In 1983, the Loi Roudy attempted to persuade companies to develop gender equality programmes, but with limited success. See Crompton and Le Feuvre (2000).
[7] See Gregory and Windebank 2000: 51. Data are for 1984 and 1986.

state support for childcare in France has, historically, been largely directed at *mothers*, thus serving to reinforce gender traditionalism even when women are in paid employment. In contrast, in the Nordic countries, childcare supports have been seen as important elements in efforts to bring about gender equality (Lewis and Astrom 1992).

To summarise, therefore, aggregate data indicate that with women's entry into employment, their hours of domestic work have fallen considerably, and men's hours have increased somewhat. These are universal trends and, at the national level, the extent of gender traditionalism in domestic work varies according to factors that are also cross-nationally universal. Thus age, level of education and the presence of a child in the household have an impact on domestic traditionalism in all of the country level ISSP samples. Although in all of the six countries examined in this chapter, women carry out by far the larger proportion of domestic work, the ISSP data also indicate substantial cross-national differences in the extent of domestic traditionalism that are not to be explained by individual country variations in the 'universal' factors that have been identified in the discussion above. A complete explanation of levels of DDL traditionalism, therefore, will vary from country to country. In the UK and the US, there are few external (state) supports for dual-earner families. In the case of Britain, Gregory and Windebank (2000) have argued that men are therefore constrained to give more support to their partners in their domestic tasks, given the increasing necessity for two incomes in contemporary families. A similar argument might be developed in the case of the US, where, it will be remembered, women work longer hours than in Britain. In Scandinavia, men do not carry out substantially more by way of domestic work than men in Britain and the US despite 'official' encouragement to do so. Nevertheless, the presence of generous state supports for dual-earner families in Scandinavia does not seem to have resulted in men carrying out *less* household work, as Gregory and Windebank have argued is the case for French men in particular.

French and Portuguese respondents report the most 'traditional' domestic division of household tasks. Portugal is characterised by a much greater traditionalism in gender role attitudes than France, which will contribute to an explanation of the highly traditional gender division of domestic work in that country. In France, traditionalism in respect of domestic tasks would appear to be 'embedded' despite a relatively high level of professed gender role liberalism. Against the background of these cross-national differences, the links between domestic traditionalism and work–life conflict were examined. It was found that a more traditional domestic division of labour is associated with greater work–life conflict, particularly in France. In the next section, therefore, we will explore further the associations between work–life conflict, gender role attitudes and the domestic division of labour.

Attitudes, work–life conflict and the domestic division of labour

The processes whereby a more 'traditional' domestic division of labour might contribute to work–life conflict are likely to be complex. It might be anticipated that at an individual level, attitudes to gender roles will have an impact – for example, a highly 'traditional' domestic division of labour might not be a source of stress if both parties are of the opinion that this is 'the right thing to do'. Women (and men) tend to report that the division of domestic work in the home is 'fair' – even though women do far more domestic work than men (Baxter 2000). Context, too, will be important – for example, the presence of a (nationally) supportive work–life context might well (all other things being equal) make domestic responsibilities less onerous, particularly for women. The amount of time spent on domestic work is also likely to contribute to conflict. It was found that for the pooled sample, for full-time women, but not men, the more hours spent on domestic work, the higher the level of work–life conflict.[8]

As we have seen, respondents in France report relatively high levels of work–life conflict (despite a 'favourable' national childcare context), as well as a significantly more 'traditional' division of domestic labour than in Britain, Finland, Norway and the US. It would seem that the question of domestic labour might be more of an issue in France than in the other five countries. However, French women do not, on average, carry out significantly longer hours of domestic work than women in Finland, Norway the US or Britain (Portuguese women carry out significantly more hours of domestic work than women in the other five countries). Another possibility, therefore, might be that a contradiction between attitudes and practice in relation to domestic work might be a source of conflict. For example, an individual might have 'liberal' or 'non-traditional' gender role attitudes, but be involved in a rather traditional domestic division of labour, and this might be a source of resentment.

The possibility that reported contradictions between gender role attitudes (whether more or less 'liberal') and the domestic division of labour

---

[8] For women, hours of domestic work are significantly associated with the DDL scale – i.e., the more 'traditional' the division of domestic labour, the longer the hours of household work for women.

Table 6.4. *Means of work–life stress for congruence categories (ISSP pooled sample, respondents in partnerships only, full-time employees only)*

	N	Mean (S.D.)
Congruent liberal	661	7.14 (2.21)
Inconsistent	1110	7.53 (2.46)
Congruent traditional	671	7.83 (2.51)
Total	2442	7.46 (2.42)

ANOVA F = 13.88; p < .001.
Post hoc tests showed that congruent liberals had significantly lower work–life stress scores than either inconsistents or congruent traditionals.

(whether more or less 'traditional') might be a source of conflict will be explored by developing a combined measure of gender role attitudes and the domestic division of labour. Responses relating to gender role attitudes (Table 6.1) were dichotomised and cross-tabulated with a dichotomised version of the DDL scale (Table 6.3). This generated four categories which were combined into three as follows: (1) 'congruent liberals', those respondents with more liberal gender role attitudes, and a less traditional division of labour; (2) 'inconsistents' – that is, a combination of both more liberal gender role attitudes, more traditional division of domestic labour and less liberal gender role attitudes, less traditional division of domestic labour; and (3) 'congruent traditionals', those respondents with less liberal gender role attitudes and a more traditional division of domestic labour. The means of work–life conflict for the different congruence categories are given in Table 6.4.

Congruent liberals report a significantly lower level of work–life conflict than the other two groups. A lack of consistency in attitudes and behaviour would seem to result in higher levels of conflict, but (and contrary to what has been suggested previously), congruent traditionalism is associated with an even higher level of conflict for full-time employees. A separate analysis by country showed that in all six countries, congruent liberals had consistently lower levels of work–life conflict, although the difference was not always statistically significant. This finding serves to support the more general argument that work–life 'balance', as indicated by level of work–life conflict, is an outcome of the allocation of work in the home, as well as in the marketplace. It suggests that those respondents who have achieved a 'congruent liberal' balance in respect of their domestic lives are also likely to have achieved more of a work–life 'balance'. It has been argued above that the question

Table 6.5. *Means of work–life stress for congruence categories, France (ISSP survey, full-time employees only, respondents in partnerships only)*

	N	Mean (S.D.)
Congruent liberal	123	6.52 (2.19)
Inconsistent	240	7.82 (2.51)
Congruent traditional	165	7.90 (2.40)
Total	528	7.54 (2.47)

ANOVA F = 14.31; p < .001.
Post hoc tests showed that congruent liberals had significantly lower work–life stress scores than both other groups.

of gender traditionalism in the domestic sphere might be particularly acute in France, given the potential for tensions between liberalism in respect of gender role attitudes, but traditionalism in respect of domestic work. This suggestion is further confirmed in Table 6.5, which demonstrates that in France, congruent liberal respondents report a markedly lower level of work–life conflict than the other two groups.[9]

In summary, evidence from this six-country analysis of the ISSP samples tends to confirm existing findings relating to the gendered division of domestic work. Women carry out more domestic work than men, and similar, cross-nationally universal, factors have been found to affect levels of gender traditionalism in respect of domestic work. Little variation in domestic traditionalism was found as between 'social democratic' (Finland, Norway), and 'liberal' (Britain, US) states, as Gershuny and Sullivan have demonstrated. Nevertheless, there were some differences in the extent of domestic traditionalism amongst the six countries under consideration, in that the domestic division of labour was more traditional in France and Portugal. It has been argued that domestic traditionalism in Portugal is in some large part a consequence of the rather conservative gender role attitudes that prevail in that country. In the case of France, it has been argued that persisting domestic traditionalism is more of an unintended consequence of historic state supports for working mothers, which have had the effect of taking the pressure off men to engage in domestic work.

---

[9] An analysis for full-time employed French women only revealed an even larger contrast, with work–life conflict scores of 6.8 for congruent liberals, 7.8 for inconsistents and 8.8 for congruent traditionals.

If this logic of argument in respect of the French case is a correct one, then it may be suggested that a similar (relative) lack of domestic traditionalism in 'liberal' and 'social democratic' nation states may in fact derive from different combinations of factors.[10] Men in Britain and the US, it may be argued, have been constrained to offer more domestic support to their employed partners given the lack of external supports for dual-earner families. However, men in the Nordic countries offer similar levels of domestic support to their partners, despite the availability of state-sponsored supports for dual-earner families. This argument suggests that 'state feminist' policies in the Nordic countries may, indeed, have had a modest effect on the gendered division of domestic labour in the Scandinavian countries.

Gender role attitudes and reported levels of happiness amongst men and women

The next issue to be addressed in this chapter is the question of whether traditionalism in domestic and gender roles is associated with greater happiness, particularly family happiness, for men and women. As discussed in the first sections of this chapter, populist conservative feminism, which is rooted in essentialist assumptions about 'natural' differences between men and women, has argued that women will achieve greater happiness and life satisfaction if they assume a traditional role in relation to men, particularly in the domestic sphere. Life and family happiness were measured using three questions from the ISSP survey: 'If you were to consider your life in general, how happy or unhappy would you say you are, on the whole?'; 'All things considered, how satisfied are you with your family life?'; and the attitude statement 'My life at home is rarely stressful.' There were country-specific variations in the answers given to these questions, but they did not follow a consistent pattern. US and British men and women were more likely to say that they were 'completely' or 'very' happy than men and women in the other four countries. However, Finnish and French men were more likely than men in the other countries to say that life at home was rarely stressful. Finally, British and US men were more likely than men in other countries to say that they were satisfied with family life, as were women in Britain, Finland, Norway and the US.

It was not possible, therefore, to identify particular national 'happiness regimes'. However, was there any systematic association

---

[10] Pickvance (1995) has described this as 'plural causation'.

between gender liberalism (or traditionalism) and general or family happiness? Adapting[11] the couple working arrangement classification used earlier (see Table 4.2, Chapter 4), respondents in partnerships were divided into four categories as follows: (a) both working full time (41 per cent); (b) man full time (over 40 hours a week), woman part time (22 per cent); (c) both working shorter hours, that is neither works more than 40 hours a week and one works less than 35 hours a week (21 per cent); and finally (d) households in which the man worked full time and the woman was not employed (16 per cent). Category (b) may be described as a 'neotraditional' division of market work between men and women (Moen 2003), and category (d) as traditional. Respondents in these household categories were evaluated against the three life and family happiness questions, with rather interesting results.

There were no significant differences between men and women in the different household types as far as the level of general satisfaction with family life was concerned. However, men in traditional households were somewhat more likely (p < .05) than men in the other household categories to say that they were 'completely' or 'very' happy with life in general (there were no significant differences between women in the different household categories on this question). On the third question – whether or not life at home is stressful – there were no significant differences between men in different household categories, but women in traditional households were significantly (p < .001) *less* likely than women in the other household categories to report that they did not find family life stressful. It would seem, therefore, that traditionalism in household arrangements might possibly bring some marginal advantages as far as men are concerned, but there is no evidence that gender traditionalism in the balance of family and employment work is associated with greater happiness for women.

Populist conservative feminism, however, does not (necessarily) argue that women should not take up or reduce their input into paid employment. Its focus is more on the domestic sphere and interpersonal relationships between men and women. The ISSP data does not provide much information on the nature of interpersonal relationships (apart from a question on conflict over domestic work). However, the congruence categories described above do give a reasonable indication of gender traditionalism (or otherwise) in the domestic arrangements of

---

[11] Across most of Europe, 35 hours a week would be considered as 'full-time'. Thus 'full-time' hours were set at 35 hours a week for dual full-time couples. This adaptation of the 'Moen categories' introduced in Chapter 4 was made for analyses of the pooled sample given the considerable variation in reported working hours by country.

Table 6.6. *Life and family happiness for men and women by congruence categories (ISSP pooled sample, respondents in partnerships only, percentages)*

		Congruent liberal	Inconsistent	Congruent traditional	Total
'completely' or 'very' happy with life in general[a]	Men	48	48	49	48
	Women	57	45	48	48
'completely', 'very' or 'fairly' satisfied with family life[b]	Men	94	93	93	93
	Women	97	89	87	90
'strongly agree' or 'agree' that life at home is rarely stressful[c]	Men	58	59	61	59
	Women	53	43	45	45

[a]Men: n.s., women $p < .001$: [b]Men: n.s., women $p < .001$: [c]Men: n.s., women $p < .001$.

the respondents' households. Table 6.6 summarises the measures of life and family happiness by congruence categories, separately for men and women.

It can be seen that for women, but not for men, a combination of gender role liberalism together with a less traditional allocation of domestic work is significantly associated with enhanced life and family happiness and satisfaction. It would seem, therefore, that contrary to the assertions of feminist conservatives, for women, domestic gender traditionalism is *not* associated with an enhanced level of personal and family happiness. Repeating the analysis on an individual country basis revealed that, in all countries, it was the women with the least traditionalism in their domestic lives (i.e., the congruent liberals) who reported the highest levels of personal and family happiness.[12]

A possibility that might be considered is that even if gender traditionalism in the domestic sphere does not increase women's happiness, it might, nevertheless, reduce levels of conflict between partners. In the ISSP data sets, a limited exploration of this possibility was available via a single question relating to disagreement between partners about the

---

[12] An analysis by country resulted in some rather small cell sizes – for example, there are low numbers of 'congruent traditional' women in Finland and Norway. The difference between the 'congruent liberal' women and the other two categories was not uniformly statistically significant by country, but nevertheless, their happiness scores were uniformly higher.

sharing of domestic work. An analysis of this question suggested that there was little difference between congruent liberals and congruent traditionals: 74 per cent of congruent liberal, and 77 per cent of congruent traditional women reported that they 'rarely or never' disagreed about domestic work. The 'inconsistent' respondents, both men and women, were significantly ($p < .001$) more likely to disagree about the sharing of domestic work, raising the intriguing possibility that an apparent conflict between attitudes and behaviour might be directly reflected in disagreement between partners.

However, a separate analysis by country and sex revealed a rather confusing picture. In Finland, the US and Portugal there was no significant association between congruence categories and the reported extent of domestic conflict. In Norway, female traditionalists reported significantly less conflict, and in Britain, the inconsistents reported significantly ($p < .05$) more conflict. Interestingly, in France, congruent liberal women reported significantly ($p < .001$) less conflict than the other two groups. Overall, however, these cross-country variations suggest that the grounds on which it might be argued that inconsistent attitudes and behaviour in relation to gender roles and domestic tasks result in a greater level of conflict between partners are not very strong. On the other hand (and this is the more important point), these findings do indicate that a greater level of gender role traditionalism does *not* bring about a reduced level of domestic conflict.

It is not being claimed that the data available from the ISSP surveys has facilitated an exhaustive exploration of the links between traditionalism in gender relations and personal happiness for women. Nevertheless, the evidence we do have suggests that for women (but not for men) gender traditionalism in attitudes and/or practice (as indicated by gender role attitudes and the domestic division of labour) is not associated with greater general or family contentment and happiness, but indeed, the opposite. There is some slight indication that men find a traditional division of domestic labour more agreeable in that those men with non-employed partners are somewhat more likely to say that they are 'completely' or 'very' happy with life in general, but this evidence is by no means conclusive. There can be no doubt that the considerable shifts in gender roles and the relationships between the sexes that have been taking place over the last half-century will have brought about considerable upheavals in the personal lives of many women and men. However, it would seem to be misleading, as gender conservatives have argued, to suggest that these transformations have brought with them any greater unhappiness for women.

Discussion and conclusion

In this chapter, recent evidence relating to changes in the domestic division of labour between men and women has been examined, and the association between domestic traditionalism and work–life conflict has been explored. In respect of domestic work, a wide range of evidence offers support to both time availability and normative (feminist) accounts of the gendered division of household work. As women have increased their share of market work, so men's share of household work has increased, but women still carry out the greater proportion of domestic work, even when in full-time employment. A comparative analysis of ISSP data from the same six countries discussed in Chapter 5 served to confirm the general trends already demonstrated in other research on the domestic division of labour.

In all six countries, women carried out more household work than men, and were involved in a wider range of domestic tasks (although men's reports of their domestic involvement was higher than women's in all countries). Cross-nationally universal factors affected traditionalism in domestic work in all six countries, including the extent of the woman's employment, age, marital status, educational level, and the presence or absence of children. There was also no real evidence of greater domestic traditionalism in 'liberal' as compared to social democratic states – where governments have actively sought to increase men's involvement in the domestic sphere. However, there was a higher level of domestic traditionalism in France and Portugal, particularly Portugal. The extent of domestic gender traditionalism in France might seem surprising given the long history of state support for mothers' employment in that country – and indeed Williams (2000: 49) draws a favourable contrast between France and the United States in this regard.

However, others have argued (Crompton and Le Feuvre 2000; Gregory and Windebank 2000) that state supports for childcare in France, whilst obviously helping mothers, have had the (perhaps unintended) effect of relieving fathers from the obligation to assist with domestic work and childcare. The example of France suggests that the rather similar levels of domestic traditionalism in the liberal and social democratic countries may have rather different origins. In liberal regimes, men have been forced to help their employed partners, given a lack of external supports. In the Nordic countries, however, men provide a similar level of assistance despite the fact that external (state) supports are available. Given that gender role attitudes are the most liberal in the Nordic countries, and that governments have also pursued active policies to encourage men to participate in domestic work and childcare, it may be that there is further (modest) support for a 'societal' effect in the Nordic countries.

For the pooled ISSP sample, the presence of domestic traditionalism was found to be associated with a higher level of work–life conflict. The respondents (men and women) identified as congruent liberals – that is, characterised by both liberal gender role attitudes and a less traditional gender division of domestic labour – reported lower levels of work–life conflict in all countries. Thus it would seem that a balance between employment and family life is facilitated by lower levels of domestic traditionalism at home, as well as (as was argued in Chapter 5), the level of external state supports for dual-earner families. In France, domestic gender traditionalism would appear to have a particularly significant impact. Moreover, for the pooled sample, gender liberalism in the domestic sphere would seem to be associated with a higher level of domestic and family happiness for women (if not men). This finding runs counter to conservative 'feminist' assertions that women will be happier if they are involved in conventional (i.e., male-dominant) gender arrangements in the domestic sphere.

Two major points, therefore, emerge from the debates and evidence summarised in this chapter. The first is that for full-time employees, lower levels of domestic traditionalism have a positive impact on levels of work–life conflict. The second is that women appear to be happier with lower levels of domestic traditionalism. Both of these findings lend general support to arguments (such as those of Fraser 1994 and Williams 2000) that the positive 'way ahead' is for men to become more 'like women' – that is, people who combine family care and paid employment. Nevertheless, the prevailing organisation of market and family work in market societies still pits women against each other (and a large proportion of men) (Williams 2000: 145). Women who have made the (often painful and difficult) choice to behave as 'ideal workers' – that is, as full-time employees, often working long hours – are often seen as rejecting the caregiving role that is chosen by the 'ideal women' who have prioritised caregiving in their lives. As Williams (2000: 147) puts it: 'Any mother with a full-time career fights gender wars every day . . . Mothers at home, and their defenders, have a substantial investment in the notion that "working mothers" take on an impossible task, and ultimately fail to meet their children's needs.' As discussed in the first sections of this chapter, neo-conservatives such as Fukuyama (1999) have also developed similar arguments in respect of employed mothers. Many full-time homemakers feel that second-wave feminism, with its emphasis (particularly in the US) on equal opportunities in the workplace for women, has contributed to the downgrading of the status of the full-time housewife. In Chapter 7, therefore, we will return again to the problematic question of the 'choices' made by women in respect of employment and the family – the contexts in which these choices are made, the consequences of these choices, and the extent to which the notion of 'choice' might or should serve as a guide to policy-making.

Appendix

Table 6.7. *Multiple regression: predictors of traditional DDL (pooled sample)*

Variables	B	Beta	t-value
Being married	.613	.088	5.099***
Being a woman[a]	1.679	.262	15.187***
Child in household	.764	.119	6.720***
Lower education	1.417	.211	12.222***
Age (older)	.024	.086	4.655***
Liberal gender role attitudes	−.969	−.132	−7.663***
Woman works full time	−.624	−.088	−5.145***
(Constant)	16.696		53.511***

Adjusted r^2 = .169; ANOVA F = 86.742; $p < .001$.
***$p < .001$
[a]This reflects the 'over' reporting of domestic work by men, and the 'under' reporting of men's domestic input by women.

Table 6.8. *Multiple regression on work–life conflict for France (full-time respondents only)*

Predictor variables	B	Beta	t-value
Age	.026	.108	2.475*
Working hours	.085	.298	6.825***
Professional/managerial class[a]	.260	.052	1.070
Intermediate class	−.280	−.051	−1.022
Being female	.739	.150	3.149**
Child in household	.616	.123	2.934**
DDL	.078	.102	2.363*
Constant	.830		.946

*$p < .05$; **$p < .01$; ***$p < .001$; ANOVA F = 12.747; $p < .001$. Adjusted r^2 = .138.
[a]Manual class was the reference category.

7   Class, family choices and
       women's employment

In this chapter, we return to some of the issues that have already been discussed in Chapter 2 – in particular, the topic of family 'choices' in relation to employment (particularly mothers' employment) and its relationship to class. First, we will explore the role of the family in the reproduction of class inequalities. Many have argued that both 'class' and 'the family' are no longer relevant concepts in 'reflexive modern' societies characterised by increasing individuation and choice, but it will be argued here that despite the considerable changes that have taken place over the last half-century, material and cultural family class practices can still be identified that contribute to the persistence of class inequalities.

Using the ISSP data, we will also critically reexamine Hakim's 'preference theory'. This has argued that, increasingly, women's employment patterns are an outcome of the choices made by different 'types' of women. The ISSP data suggests some grounds for thinking that a minority of women are indeed predisposed to domesticity, but, in all countries, both the attitudes and behaviour of women towards employment would seem to be shaped by a wide range of structural factors rather than the exercise of free 'choice' alone. We also examine the factors that shape attitudes to women's employment, whether in a conservative or more 'liberal' direction.

In the final section, the ISSP data is used to explore the complex interactions between occupational class, attitudes and mothers' employment. Less well-educated women, in the lower occupational categories, are less likely to be in employment when their children are young. This class-associated pattern of behaviour will serve to reproduce, and even deepen, class inequalities, but this may be justified by the argument that lower occupational groups are characterised by more conservative attitudes to the employment of mothers, especially when their children are young. Whilst it is not disputed that attitudinal factors will play some part in shaping mothers' employment patterns, it is argued that it is also necessary to emphasise the constraints on 'choices' in respect of employment for less-educated and less-qualified – in short, working-class women.

Class and the family

As has been described in Chapter 1, many contemporary social theorists argue that 'class' is now a redundant concept. As Beck (2002) has put it, social class is a 'zombie category', which is 'dead but still alive'. The past bases of collective identities, he argues, are no longer relevant, and society has been 'individualised'. Thus Beck (2002: 202) states that: 'Individualisation is a concept which describes a structural, sociological transformation of social institutions and the relationship of the individual to society . . . freeing people from historically inscribed roles . . . Individualisation liberates people from traditional roles and constraints . . . individuals are removed from status-based classes . . . Social classes have been detraditionalised.' Beck asserts that with the coming of 'reflexive modernity', a radical break in the nature of social organisation has taken place. This book is somewhat sceptical of the notions that a radical break has occurred with the coming of 'reflexive modernity', and that class is a 'zombie category'. Nevertheless, it will be argued that we do need to adopt a rather different approach to the analysis of class (particularly one that is different to the once hegemonic 'employment aggregate' tradition of quantitative class analysis, see Erikson and Goldthorpe 1992; Wright 1997) in order to comprehend the changes that are taking place in respect of structured social inequality, employment and the family.

The starting point of this approach to class inequality, as Bottero and Irwin (2003: 463) have argued, involves the recognition of 'the mutuality of value and material social relations'. This does not mean that values and norms cannot be distinguished from material factors for the purpose of explanatory analysis. However, it does mean, as Devine (2004: 182) has argued, that 'any theory of class reproduction must acknowledge that social, cultural and economic resources are mutually constitutive of each other', and 'constructions of social difference shape both material inequalities and inequalities of recognition' (Bottero and Irwin 2003: 465). That is, in order to understand processes of differentiation by class, social classes cannot be adequately conceptualised as economic or material categories alone, but are also characterised by cultural and normative practices that themselves serve to maintain differentiation from other classes.[1] Social

---

[1] There is no intention here to return to debates relating to whether classes 'in themselves' can be identified independently of classes 'for themselves' (see e.g., Braverman 1974). Indeed, class practices, values or social arrangements may be so deeply embedded that they remain unarticulated in any conscious sense. A similar argument may be developed in respect of gender. See Yancey Martin 2003.

interactions, cultural practices and lifestyles are not randomly distributed, but have orderly and consistent patterns that are also hierarchical. As Bottero and Irwin (203: 471) argue: 'Since hierarchy is embedded in the most intimate social relationships, and "social location" and "culture" are united in the structured nature of everyday social practices, hierarchical practices emerge as "second nature", unremarkable and unremarked.'

Although the concept of class has been hotly contested and the subject of a variety of definitions, one area of agreement between disputants would be that the family remains as a, if not the, major transmission agent of class reproduction and therefore persisting inequality. Most obviously, families conserve, and pass on through inheritance, wealth and property. Even in the absence of substantial property or wealth, families also have a central role in securing cultural and educational capital (or a lack of it) on behalf of their children. This stark and continuing reality is probably the major reason why the concept of class has never been absent from the discourse of sociologists working in the field of education and related issues such as social mobility (e.g., Ball 2003; Bourdieu 1990; Devine 2004; Goldthorpe 1996; Halsey et al. 1997; Reay 1998). Even when governments have made conscious attempts to achieve equality of educational opportunity (for example, in Britain via the provision of universal secondary education from the 1940s followed by the introduction of comprehensive schooling from the 1960s), class inequalities of educational outcomes have proved to be remarkably persistent.

As a whole range of empirical studies have demonstrated, middle- and upper-class parents will go to considerable lengths in order to ensure that their children acquire the appropriate educational credentials that will lead to success in the labour market. In some countries, such as Britain and the United States, an elite education can simply be purchased at school and, increasingly, at university level. Even in the absence of direct purchase, however, parents can seek to ensure access to 'good' public (or state) schools by making sure that they live in an area with access to such schools (where housing will invariably be more expensive), or sending their children out of the area to better schools (Ball 2003; Devine 2004). Well-educated middle-class parents can also provide individual tuition for their children, or pay for it privately, in order to gain entry into the 'right' school where selection is competitive, or make up for perceived deficiencies in preparation for examinations. More generally, there is the persistence of what Bourdieu has described as 'habitus', that is, the mental structures and dispositions that parents inculcate in their children that may be seen as encompassing the unremarked 'everyday social practices' described above in our discussion of class. Habitus generates 'things to do or not to do, things to say or not to say, in relation to a probable "upcoming" future' (Bourdieu cited in Ball 2003: 16). Thus from a relatively early age, children acquire (or do not acquire) behaviours appropriate (or not appropriate) for educational success.

The continuing reproduction of class-related educational inequalities does not mean, of course, that no individuals from relatively disadvantaged backgrounds ever achieve educational or occupational success, or that none from advantaged backgrounds ever fail to do so. Indeed, in advanced capitalist societies, the broad pattern of change in the occupational structure has served, via the expansion of higher-level managerial and professional jobs, to ensure a considerable degree of upward social mobility. Nevertheless, class differences in relative social mobility, transmitted largely through family background, still persist (Marshall *et al.* 1997). However, despite this kind of evidence, theorists of individualisation have argued not only that 'class' is a redundant concept, but also that processes of individualisation within the family are major factors driving the individualisation of society more generally. In respect of the family, Beck and Beck-Gernsheim (2002: 86) argue that what was once a 'community of need' is becoming, increasingly, an 'elective relationship' (see also Giddens 1991). Traditional family arrangements, it is argued, were constituted in inequalities between men and women, as well as the 'feudal' division of labour that allocated domestic work to women and market work to men. Women's claims to equality have radically destabilised this traditional structure, as is reflected in increasing rates of divorce, partnership breakdown, and declining fertility, as women have themselves become individualised and increasingly able to exercise their choices. As a consequence, family relationships are in flux and 'there is no given set of obligations and opportunities, no way of organising everyday work, the relationship between men and women, parents and children, which can just be copied' (Beck 2002: 203).

However, as our discussion of family practices in relation to education has demonstrated, families still continue as 'communities of need' in that patterns of interdependence still persist, particularly as between parents and children. Past periods of fertility decline in the nineteenth and twentieth centuries, as has been argued in Chapter 2, need to be seen as the outcome of not just individual decision-making, but of wider shifts in social relationships and patterns of interdependence. During the nineteenth century, children moved from being an economic benefit to an economic cost, and the emergence of the 'male breadwinner' wage and associated norms served to underline parental responsibilities to children. Similarly, contemporary fertility decline and deferral of childbearing has to be understood as taking place within a context in which the level of resources deemed to be 'adequate' for child support has increased, in which households have become more dependent on the earnings of women, and in which paid work has assumed considerably more importance in women's lives (Irwin 2003). Interdependencies have not vanished in 'new' family 'communities of choice', rather, they have been restructured and are in the process of re-negotiation.

The extent to which the reproduction of characteristic family behaviours has disappeared, as is claimed by Beck, may also be disputed. For example, the research of Mitchell and Green (2002) demonstrates that although the young (working-class) mothers they interviewed might be to some extent described as 'individualised' in their dealings with the fathers of their children, they retained strong ties with their families of origin, their mothers in particular. Mothers and other female relatives were heavily relied upon for practical and material help, and their advice was often preferred over that of healthcare professionals. Indeed, in many respects, the young mothers' relationships with their own mothers closely resembled the mother–daughter relationships described in Young and Willmott's (1962) classic investigation of working-class kinship carried out over half a century ago.

Britain has the highest rate of teenage pregnancy in Europe. Indeed, it is of interest that teenage pregnancy rates are generally higher in countries characterised by 'neo-liberal' welfare regimes, and highest of all in the US (see Gornick and Meyers 2003: 80). Empirical research in Britain on teenage pregnancy has demonstrated the overwhelming influence of class and family on young women's decision-making (Lee et al. 2004). Social deprivation (or class) has a strong influence on teenage conception rates, as well as their outcomes (i.e., whether the pregnancy is continued or terminated). Lee et al. demonstrate a clear, and statistically significant, relationship between abortion proportions and a number of social deprivation measures. That is, termination of teenage pregnancy was much *less* likely to occur in areas of greater social deprivation (as measured by proportions of dependants of family credit claimants and national geographical indexes of deprivation):[2]

---

[2] The ONS (Office of National Statistics) area classification, that groups together local authorities that have similar socio-economic and demographic profiles.

Areas that rate highly in regard to social deprivation also have higher conception rates, meaning that many young women from such areas will comprise a significant proportion of the total *number* of under-18 abortions. However, the research . . . clearly shows that they are *relatively less likely* to have an abortion than young women from areas that are not as socially deprived. (Lee *et al.* 2004: 15, emphasis in original)

Qualitative interviews conducted as part of the same research revealed that young women's decisions depended on the economic and social context of their lives, rather than on abstract moral views. Young women who saw themselves as having a secure and positive future opted for termination:

There was no question of me keeping it because I knew I was going to go to university . . . I didn't want a baby . . . I'd had a good education and I had a career path to go down, it was all laid out for me. (Lee *et al.* 2004: 18)

However, young women from insecure backgrounds, with poor employment prospects, saw pregnancy and motherhood as 'an escape route from a future characterised by lack of achievement and lack of direction' (*ibid.*). In these cases, family influences (and family supports) were crucial. One young mother reported that her mother had said that 'whatever you decide I'll stick by you' but that 'she don't agree with them [abortions]' (Lee *et al.* 2004: 44). Young women who continued with pregnancies often lived in communities in which abortion was generally disapproved of (as well as being socially deprived areas), and young motherhood was commonplace (Lee *et al.* 2004: 46). In short, despite arguments and claims as to increasing 'individualisation', class and community would appear to be of considerable significance in the shaping of young women's family decisions.

This kind of evidence, together with the example of the reproduction of educational advantage discussed above, demonstrates that many family behaviours remain broadly structured by class location.[3] Nevertheless, within families, individuals today *do* have more 'choices' to make than hitherto, largely because of the changes in the wider economic, employment and normative contexts that themselves are the backdrop to the issues discussed in this book. Increased employment opportunities, together with enhanced female education levels and changes in aspirations, *have* increased the range of alternatives to domesticity for women. Men's employment prospects have also changed and become

---

[3] Here there are echoes of a classic study of parenting that described systematic class-related behaviours amongst parents of young children, from dummy use to discipline. See Newson and Newson 1968.

more unstable. An increasing number of men will find themselves in partnerships with women of equal, or even superior, employment status. As Charles *et al.* (2004) have argued: 'The more equal the sexes are in employment matters, the greater the constraints placed upon occupational choices of each partner on the other.' In previous generations, even when both partners were in employment, the woman was characteristically occupationally weaker. However, the greater the equality in occupational power, the greater the need for negotiation between partners over work–life articulation.[4] In criticising the thesis of increasing 'individuation' in relation to the family, therefore, the aim is not to reject it completely.

Rather, the aim is to emphasise the patterns of continuity within change. Family relationships still remain embedded in kinship networks both of choice and obligation (Charles et al 2004; Finch 1989; Finch and Mason 1993). With the increasing employment of mothers, so family behaviours have also changed. Nevertheless, broad class contrasts are discernible in family behaviours in relation to the manner in which employment and family life are articulated. For example, there are class variations in the nature and extent of mothers' employment, in that more educated women are more likely to be in employment. In the next section, therefore, we return again to the issues already discussed (in relation to the British case) in Chapter 2 – that is, the factors that shape women's participation in paid employment, particularly when their children are young.

Mothers' 'choices' to work for pay

The rhetoric of 'individualisation' has been drawn upon extensively in recent discussions of women's employment and family behaviour. One strand of argument has suggested that mothers in paid employment are prioritising their own needs over those of their families (Dench 1999). In a similar vein, demographers have attributed fertility decline to the increasing desire amongst women for individual autonomy (Sporton 1993). As we have seen, Beck has argued that the growth of individualisation amongst women is the major reason why the family has become a 'zombie category', and Hakim has drawn extensively on the literature of

---

[4] The (small-scale) survey carried out by Charles and her colleagues suggests that in 32 per cent of households, the women's employment status was higher than that of her partner. However, Charles' survey was carried out in an area (Swansea, Wales) that had suffered particularly acutely from deindustrialisation and the loss of 'breadwinner' jobs in the 1980s. Aggregate level data indicate that, even in professional and managerial couples, the man's job is usually given priority. See Blossfeld and Drobnic 2001.

individualisation in developing what she describes as 'preference theory' (Hakim 2000, 2003a, 2004).

As described in Chapter 2, Hakim argues that the characteristic patterning of women's employment as revealed by aggregate level statistics – a tendency to part-time and flexible working, and overrepresentation in lower-level occupations – is an outcome of the fact that there are three different 'types' of women (or 'preference groupings'). 'Home centred' women give priority to their families, and either withdraw from the labour market altogether or work only intermittently when they have children. 'Work centred' women, in contrast, give priority to their employment and are often not married and/or childless. A further category of 'adaptives'[5] – by far the largest category – shift the emphasis of their 'preferences' over their work/family life cycles. These work/family preference categories are also found amongst men, although in different proportions, as fewer men are 'home centred' or 'adaptive'. This difference in the relative size of male and female preference categories is largely due to differences in testosterone levels between men and women, which makes men (on average) more aggressive and competitive than women in the world of employment (Hakim 2000).

Hakim identifies 'preference' categories via an analysis of longitudinal data which demonstrated that young women expressing a preference for a 'homemaking career' in their teens are more likely to be homemakers in their thirties. She also argues that the case of Britain represents a particularly favourable 'test case' for the application of preference theory. In Britain, women have secured equal opportunities, and the flexible, deregulated British labour market (a consequence of neo-liberal economic policies), allows women to exercise their 'choices' freely – particularly in respect of part-time work. Although Hakim's argument might justifiably be described as voluntarist with its emphasis on the overwhelming significance of individual 'choices', some allowance is made for the impact of structural constraints and other factors. The British case is represented as somewhat unusual in having achieved a 'new scenario for women', and in Britain: 'Whatever their ambitions and lifeplans, women can now choose occupations far more freely than in the past' (Hakim 2003a. A similar argument would presumably apply to the US). However, these opportunities are more restricted in other countries (such as Spain, the major focus of Hakim's comparative work), particularly in respect of opportunities for part-time employment.

---

[5] Hakim originally identified this group as 'drifters', but they have undergone a change of name (and assumed considerably more importance) as she has developed her argument.

Structural constraints, however, are inexorably becoming less important, and Hakim states that as more 'good' part-time work becomes
available 'secondary earners who are currently forced to choose full-time
jobs . . . will switch to part-time or temporary jobs instead' (2003a: 262).
Thus 'the only cleavages that will matter within the workforce in the
twenty-first century will be the continuing differences between primary
and secondary earners . . . Sex and gender will cease to be important
factors and are already being replaced by lifestyle preferences as the only
important differentiating characteristic in labour supply' (*ibid.*: 261).
Moreover, Hakim claims that the three lifestyle preference groups she
identifies 'cut across social class, education, and ability differences'
(*ibid.*: 247). Hakim's rejection of the impact of social class on women's
decision-making extends to the issue of teenage motherhood. For
example, she argues that the decision to complete a teenage pregnancy
'reflects a real choice in most cases' (Hakim 2000: 49), as teenage girls
derive pleasure from the ownership of a child, together with priority
access to public sector housing and an independent social welfare
income. However, as we have seen in the discussion of the research of
Lee *et al.* (2004) above, it has been demonstrated that both material and
cultural *class* processes are the most important factors that determine
whether or not a teenage pregnancy is continued.

In Chapter 2, it has been demonstrated that, despite Hakim's insistence
on the primacy of women's individual choices, in Britain, both attitudes to
family life, as well as characteristic combinations of men's and women's
employment within households, show systematic variations by social
class. In this chapter, we will extend our comparative analysis in order
to explore both variations in household employment patterns, as well as
the impact of structural and attitudinal factors on women's employment,
in the six countries that have been previously examined. Using a version
of the household work arrangement categories devised by Moen (see
Chapter 4, p. 101 and Chapter 6, p. 157), we can immediately see the
impact of national working time and labour market regimes on couple
working arrangements in the different countries.[6]

As can be seen from Table 7.1, the largest category (31 per cent) of
couple working arrangements is the 'dual moderates', where both work
full time, but neither works more than 35–40 hours a week. However,

---

[6] It should be remembered that although the ISSP samples are nationally representative,
Table 7.1 should not be read as constituting a nationally descriptive summary, and there
will be variations between the data reported here and aggregate national data. In
particular, only a portion of ISSP respondents – i.e., respondents in couple households
where at least one of the partners is in employment – are included.

Table 7.1. *Couples' work arrangements by country: ISSP surveys (percentage by column)*

Couples' work arrangements[a]	Britain	Finland	France	Norway	USA	Portugal	Total
High commitment	12	7	6	7	16	17	11
Dual moderates	16	55	36	32	14	34	31
Neotraditionalists	32	13	22	25	18	12	22
Alternate commitments	19	20	22	28	20	10	21
Traditionalists	20	6	14	7	32	28	16
Total N	817	401	643	839	299	412	3566

[a]'high commitment': both partners work more than 40 hours a week.
'dual moderates': both partners work full time, but neither works more than 35–40 hours a week.
'neotraditionalists': man works 40 hours a week and the woman works shorter hours, characteristically part time.
'alternate commitments': couples who both work under 40 hours a week but one works less than 35 hours per week.
'traditionalists' man works full time, woman does not work.

there is considerable variation, reflecting differences in national working-time regimes (see Chapter 4, p. 94), around this average. In Finland, where working hours are the shortest of the six countries studied, over a half of the relevant respondents reported living in dual moderate households. Conversely, the proportion of neotraditional households is low in Finland, as it is in Portugal, due to the relative lack of availability of part-time work in these countries. Respondents in Britain, with the second highest level of part-time work amongst women in Europe, report the highest level of neotraditional households. Variations in national levels of women's employment are clearly reflected in the low proportion of traditional households in Finland and Norway, where employment levels amongst women are high.[7]

National or country-specific factors, therefore, clearly have an important impact on couples' working time arrangements and thus women's employment 'choices'. Hakim explicitly recognises this fact, and has, as we have seen, argued that Britain, with its wide availability of part-time work, and lack of labour market regulation, is an important 'test case' for

---

[7] Moen's classification included a further category of 'crossover' couple arrangements, in which the woman took the 'breadwinner' role and worked long hours. As this category was (a) very small and (b) could not reasonably be grouped with any of the other categories, it has been omitted from further analyses.

'preference theory' (presumably a similar argument might be developed for the US).[8] Table 7.1 suggests that structural factors are clearly important in shaping women's employment 'choices', but clearly, attitudes and preferences will also play a part, as well as other proximate factors such as age and the presence of children in the household, as well as (as was argued for the case of Britain in Chapter 4), social class. In order to explore further the relative impact of 'attitudinal' and 'structural' factors, a scale was constructed that measured general attitudes to women's employment (AWE), particularly mothers. This included the following items:

> A working mother can establish just as warm and secure a relationship with her children as a mother who does not work.
> A pre-school child is likely to suffer if his or her mother works.
> All in all, family life suffers when the woman has a full-time job.
> Do you think that women should work outside the home full-time, part-time, or not at all when there is a child under school age.
> Do you think that women should work outside the home full-time, part-time or not at all after the youngest child starts school.

Sores ranged from 5 to 25, with lower scores indicating less conservative attitudes towards women's employment.[9] As can be seen from Table 7.2, for the pooled sample, attitudes to women's employment do appear to have a considerable impact on couples' working arrangements, in that respondents in traditionalist (and to a lesser extent, neotraditionalist) households expressed considerably more conservative attitudes towards mothers' employment than respondents in other categories.

Tables 7.1 and 7.2 demonstrate that, as might be anticipated, *both* structural *and* attitudinal factors shape women's employment decisions. This intertwining is further demonstrated in a multinomial regression on couples' work arrangements, with traditional, 'male breadwinner' households as the reference category (Appendix Table 7.6, p. 188). The regression incorporates two attitudinal variables, the attitudes to women's employment scale (AWE), together with a more general measure of gender role attitudes. Both of these variables are significantly related to couples' working arrangements. However, it also demonstrates

---

[8] In the 'traditional' classification, 'full-time' hours have been set at 35, but the large majority (60 per cent) of men in category 5 work well over 40 hours a week (Table 7.1).
[9] Factor analysis showed 1 factor with an Eigen value of 2.632, explaining 53 per cent of the variance. A reliability analysis recorded a Cronbach's alpha of .77.

Table 7.2. *Attitudes to women's employment (AWE) score by couples' work arrangements (ISSP pooled sample, men and women)*

	N	Mean	S.D.
High commitment	291	11.75	3.80
Dual moderates	886	11.50	3.85
Neotraditionalists	633	12.37	3.56
Alternate commitments	611	12.25	3.70
Traditionalists	474	14.10	3.81
Total	2895	12.30	3.84

ANOVA $F = 38.99$; $p < .001$. *Post hoc* tests showed that traditionalists had significantly more traditional attitudes towards women's employment than all other groups; neotraditionalists had significantly more traditional attitudes than dual moderates.

that a range of 'structural' factors are also highly relevant, including class, education, and in particular, whether or not there is a child in the household.

Disentangling the relative impact of 'structural' and 'attitudinal' factors on the employment choices of women and families is clearly a complex problem that is likely to be impossible to conclusively resolve in either direction, given the extent of multiple cross-country variation in both structural and attitudinal factors. However, one analytical strategy that bypasses this complexity is to take a particular country as an example of a 'critical case' for the test of a theory (in this case, Hakim's 'preference theory'), and a closer examination of the case of Norway proved to be of interest.

Hakim has argued that (2003: 123) 'Research on the decision to return to work or not, and attitudes towards childcare show that women's choices are determined *first* by a woman's values, and only *second* by practical issues such as the availability and cost of childcare.' As we have seen, she has claimed that Britain stands out as a country where women can exercise 'choice', given the extensive opportunities for part-time work in Britain. With this kind of assertion in mind, the findings for one of the countries included in the data set, Norway, were examined separately. In some contrast to Finland (the other Nordic example in the comparative data set), there are good part-time employment opportunities available for women in Norway (in 2002, 43 per cent of employed Norwegian women were classified as part-time workers). Moreover, as a Scandinavian welfare state, Norway is also characterised by a high level of childcare provision as well as general supports for families such as extensive maternity and paternity leaves

Table 7.3. *Mean scores on attitudes to women's employment scale by couples' work arrangements: Norwegian women (ISSP survey)*

	N	Mean	Std. Deviation
High commitments	37	10.5946	3.04101
Dual moderates	126	11.1984	3.47337
Neotraditionalists	83	11.5181	3.70682
Alternate commitments	114	12.2864	3.37502
Traditionalists	27	10.5185	3.66239
Total	387	11.1499	3.46609

ANOVA F = 33.727, n.s.

(Ellingsaeter 2003; Korpi 2000). In short, it might persuasively be argued that in Norway parents are able to make even more unfettered 'choices' relating to parental working arrangements than in Britain. If the assumptions of preference theory are correct, we might reasonably expect that attitudes and preferences will play an important role in making these 'choices' in Norway, given the relative absence of external constraints.

However, when the analysis in Table 7.3 was repeated for Norwegian women, it was found there was no relationship between attitudes to women's employment and couple work arrangements.[10] This suggests that in Norway, a country in which there is extensive capacity to 'choose' in deciding on arrangements relating to employment and family life, individual attitudes do not appear to play a substantial part in the choices that are made.

An exhaustive evaluation of 'preference theory', which would require longitudinal data, has not been attempted here (see McRae 2003). However, to the extent that preference theory suggests the *major* and determining role of attitudinal factors in shaping women's employment decisions, the ISSP data suggest otherwise. It is not disputed that preferences or attitudes will shape individual behaviour, or that particular sets of attitudes to work and family may be found (albeit to varying extents) across a range of social positions and education levels. However, it would seem unwise to assume that women's employment behaviours may be *primarily* accounted for by the hypothesised existence of different 'types' of women, as 'preference theory' suggests.

[10] There was also no relationship between couple work arrangements and attitudes to women's employment when men were included. Couple arrangements in Norway were also evaluated against gender role attitudes, and again, there was no association.

What shapes attitudes to women's employment?

Women's employment choices, therefore, are determined by a complex range of factors in which individual attitudes will play an important, although not determining, part. There remains, however, the question of what factors shape attitudes to women's employment itself. As might have been anticipated given the extent of cross-country variation in gender role attitudes, attitudes to mothers' employment varied considerably by country. Portuguese respondents were the most conservative (mean AWE score 14.2). Interestingly, the US, Finland and Norway all scored significantly lower on AWE as compared to the other three countries with mean scores under 12, Britain and France having similar scores of around 12.6. A regression on the attitudes to women's employment scale on the pooled sample indicated that men were significantly more conservative in their attitudes than women, and that older respondents were more conservative than younger respondents. Respondents with a child in the household were more conservative than those without, and managers and professionals, and full-time employees, were less conservative than non-professional and part-time or non-employed respondents. These findings include male respondents – given that decisions relating to the employment of mothers are likely to be an outcome of discussions between both parents, men's attitudes will be highly relevant. Nevertheless, it is likely that the mothers' attitudes will weigh the heavier in these discussions. A separate analysis, therefore, was carried out for all female respondents with a child (under 16) in the household. This analysis has the added advantage of including non-partnered women, whereas our discussion so far has focused on couple work arrangements.[11]

In Britain, Finland, France and Norway, non-partnered women with a child living with them were less likely to be in employment than partnered women, and for the pooled sample, 33 per cent of partnered women, but 44 per cent of non-partnered women, were not in employment. However, in the US and Portugal, the proportion of partnered and non-partnered women not in employment was very similar (43 per cent partnered, 39 per cent non-partnered in the US, and 41 per cent for both categories of women in Portugal). In fact, for the pooled sample, the proportions of partnered and non-partnered mothers in full-time employment were very similar at around 45 per cent, as partnered mothers were more likely to be in part-time employment (20 per cent *vs.* 12 per cent pooled sample). As

---

[11] Limiting the analysis to women with a child in the household also introduces a *de facto* control for age, which is a significant determinant of attitudes to women's employment.

far as attitudes to women's employment are concerned, it was found that mothers in employment had more liberal attitudes than mothers who were not, and that managerial and professional women were more liberal than women in other occupational class groupings. Single mothers were more liberal in their attitudes than partnered mothers – despite the fact that they were less likely to be in employment. In fact, non-employed partnered mothers held the most conservative attitudes, with a mean AWE score of 13.7, whereas similar non-partnered mothers scored 12.0.[12] Although, as argued previously (see Chapter 2, p. 52), it is impossible to resolve conclusively the 'chicken and egg' question of whether behaviour determines attitudes or vice versa, these findings suggest that 'structural' factors significantly shape attitudes.

A multiple regression on attitudes to women's employment (AWE, see Appendix Table 7.7, p. 188) for mothers with child(ren) at home demonstrates the impact of a number of structural factors on attitudes to mothers' employment. Mothers (with a child at home) in employment themselves are more liberal than mothers who are not, single mothers are more liberal than mothers living with partners, managerial and professional mothers are more liberal than mothers in other occupational categories, and there are also significant country differences. In summary, age, sex and personal circumstances (whether in employment or not, whether or not there is a child in the household, and for women, whether or not a partner is present) all affect attitudes to the employment of mothers, as might have been anticipated. There are also systematic and significant occupational class differences, in that the managerial and professional grouping has a more liberal attitude to mothers' employment. It has been argued previously in this chapter that, contrary to the broad thrust of 'individuation' theory, class differences in family practices, and the characteristic manner in which work–life articulation is achieved, remain important. In the next section, therefore, we will examine in more detail the relationships between occupational class, attitudes, and patterns of work–life articulation and mothers' employment.

Occupational class, attitudes and women's work arrangements

It is a well-established fact that the employment rate amongst mothers with a higher level of education is much greater than amongst mothers with only a low level of education. For example, amongst the

---

[12] This also suggests that women with greater material supports – in this case, the presence of a partner – are able to exercise their 'choices'. Thus a parallel argument may be developed as for managerial and professional women in Britain. See Chapter 2 p. 57.

countries we are examining in this chapter, in 1999, in Norway, 83 per cent of mothers of a child under six with a high level of education were in paid employment, as compared to only 46 per cent of mothers with a low level of education. The comparable figures for Portugal are 93 per cent and 64 per cent, for the UK 70 per cent and 32 per cent, and for France, 72 per cent and 29 per cent (OECD 2001, Table 4.1). This pattern was also found in the ISSP samples. Amongst mothers with a child under 16 in the household, for the pooled sample only 31 per cent of those with above higher secondary education were not in employment, as compared to 44 per cent of mothers with below higher secondary education (p < .001). Not surprisingly, educational level is significantly associated with occupational class, and for the same group of women with a child in the household, 92 per cent of the professional and managerial group was educated to the higher level, as compared to 49 per cent of the intermediate/manual grouping.

Amongst women with children, there were also significant variations by occupational class in the level and extent of employment: 64 per cent of professional and managerial mothers worked full time, as compared to 47 per cent of intermediate/manual mothers (p < .001). Intermediate/manual mothers were more likely to work part time (24 per cent), or not to be in employment (2 per cent). Similarly, only 22 per cent of all professional/managerial women reported that they had stayed at home when their children were under school age, as compared to 38 per cent of intermediate/manual women. These differences in the employment patterns of individual women were reflected in couple working arrangements. Of all respondents with a child in the household, 57 per cent of professional/managerial respondents were in full-time, dual-earner households, as compared to 48 per cent of intermediate/manual respondents, who were more likely to be in 'neotraditional' (man full time, woman part time) or 'traditional' (man full time, woman not working) households (p < .001).[13] As has been argued in Chapter 2, these broad class differences in gendered employment patterns within couple households will contribute to the deepening of material class inequalities. Women in lower educational and occupational categories are less likely than women in professional and managerial occupations to be in full-time employment when their children are young, therefore their material contribution to the household (which would in any case have been lower

---

[13] These broad class differences, however, are cross-cut by the national labour market specificities that were so visible in Table 7.1 above, and 'class' variations in couple household employment patterns were statistically significant only in Britain, Norway and Portugal.

Table 7.4. *Occupational class variations in gender role and family attitudes: ISSP pooled sample*

	Professional/ managerial	Intermediate/ manual	Total
% Agreeing/strongly agreeing that 'A man's job is to earn money, a woman's job is to look after the home and family'	9	21	16
% Agreeing/strongly agreeing that 'Watching children grow up is life's greatest joy'	78	86	83
Mean AWE score	11.6	12.7	12.2

All differences sig. at p < .001.

than that of professional and managerial women) will be further reduced (see also Blossfeld and Drobnic 2001).

Besides these differences in rates of employment between the different class groupings, there were also significant differences in attitudes to gender roles, family life and mother's employment. Table 7.4 summarises, for the pooled sample, these occupational class variations.[14]

These occupational class differences in attitudes were found in all six countries, although they varied in their size.[15] It might be argued, therefore, that the lower levels of employment amongst intermediate and manual mothers are a consequence of a greater level of 'family'-orientedness amongst intermediate and manual respondents.

As we have already seen in Chapter 2, it is not difficult to construct an argument as to why individuals and families in lower-level employment might seem to place a higher value on family life, and have a greater traditionalism in gender roles, as compared to managers and professionals. Most obviously, managerial and professional occupations tend to be

[14] Note that this table does not include controls for age, sex, employment status or child in household, all of which have been demonstrated to have an impact on these attitudinal variables.

[15] In Table 7.4 this occupational class variable has been constructed from the ISCO (International Standard Classification of Occupations) 88 occupational classification (used in the ISSP data sets) to generate three occupational class categories: professional/managerial, intermediate, and routine and manual. It correlates highly with the three-category version of the NS-SEC (see Chapter 2, note 6). As with the three-category version of the NS-SEC, women are significantly overrepresented in the 'intermediate' grouping, and men are overrepresented in the 'routine and manual' grouping. In order to achieve a better gender balance within 'class' groupings, therefore, the three-category scheme has been dichotomised and the 'intermediate' and 'routine and manual' categories aggregated.

associated with higher levels of job satisfaction, (as well as a higher level of material reward), and this was true of the ISSP samples: 84 per cent of managerial and professional respondents said that they were 'fairly' satisfied with their jobs – or better – as compared to 75 per cent of intermediate/manual respondents.[16] Although the extent of class difference in job satisfaction varied, a similar association was found in all six countries. A wide range of quantitative and qualitative evidence has documented class differences in attitudes to and experiences of employment. For example, the Working in Britain survey found that whereas only 21 per cent of higher professional and managerial employees thought of their job as 'just a means to earn a living', this was true of 58 per cent of skilled manual, and 54 per cent of semi and unskilled manual employees (Taylor 2002b: 14).

Qualitative research has also revealed substantial differences between different occupational classes in their experiences of work. For example, Gorman's study (see also Rubin 1994) found that amongst working-class interviewees (although by no means all of them) work provided little by way of satisfaction or sense of accomplishment:

(I) just go along doing what I'm doing. I've got no regrets. I'm doing all right. I've got to stick with (the railroad), I don't want to, but I've got to, nothing else to do. (male truck driver), (Gorman 2000: 709)

None of Gorman's professional or managerial respondents expressed these kinds of views, rather, they saw their working lives as characterised by success and goals achieved:

Well, I've reached my occupational goal; I'm a partner in a fairly good law firm, I guess I'll continue to practise law and improve my standing in the law firm, improve my abilities as an attorney. (male lawyer, Gorman 2000: 710)

Similarly, in Britain the JRF research also revealed accounts of frustrated ambitions and lack of job satisfaction amongst unskilled workers, particularly amongst the Shopwell employees. James, whom we have already discussed in Chapter 2, said of his early career 'ambitions':

JAMES (Shopwell, aged 39): I got thrown into bakery really . . . I'm trying to get out of bakery now . . . I was just left to get on with it, with what I wanted. I started work part time at 14 for the money. I got offered a job when I left school. I knew that I had a job to go to, so I never tried at school. I earned twice what the others at school were earning. Now though it's turned round and I'm on low pay.

---

[16] However, for intermediate/manual respondents, there was no association between job satisfaction and 'familial' attitudes.

GILLIAN (Shopwell, aged 38): They pushed me into kids and marriage. I didn't have much ambition. I just wish I could live again. Things are wonderful now, women have opportunities that I never had at the age of 16. I never dreamt of teaching at 16. I want to contribute to society now, not just to have a job. I wish I'd realised sooner but I've still got 20 years to work once I've qualified [Gillian hopes to retrain as a primary school teacher].

A classic study of working-class youths (Willis 1977) has documented how their rejection of school might be seen as a 'rational' response to the objective lack of employment opportunities they will face in the labour market. However, in relation to domestic and family life, McDowell's (2003: ch. 8) interviews with low-achieving young men found that 22 out of the 24 interviewed (at age 16–17) hoped to be in a stable relationship with a woman five years after the interview. That is, they retained aspirations for conventional domesticity despite their very poor employment opportunities and lack of career prospects. As we have seen above in the case of research on teenage pregnancy, it was found that for many young women with limited career and life prospects, the status of pregnancy and motherhood, even at a very young age, appeared to be a least worst alternative. In short, if employment apparently offers but little by way of personal and life satisfaction, it is not difficult to imagine that positive feelings become directed towards family life, as Hochschild has argued:

I may be subordinate here, but I express myself fully at home. For factory hands, and especially for the women among them, family photos sometimes meant: I may not be the boss here, but I have another life where I am. (Hochschild 1997: 88)

In summary: the ISSP data shows that, in comparison with managerial and professional employees, women in the intermediate and manual class categories are less likely to be in employment when they are mothers, or to have been in employment when their children were under school age. Intermediate and manual respondents have more conservative gender role attitudes, and are more likely to think that children and family life will suffer if the mother works. They are less likely to be satisfied with their jobs, a finding that is in line with a wide range of quantitative and qualitative research that has emphasised the more negative aspects of lower-level employment and its impact on individual employees. Thus for lower-level employees, it is not difficult to see that family life might become a 'haven in a heartless world'. On this interpretation, the lower levels of employment of intermediate and manual women might possibly be represented as an expression of the distribution of 'choices' between different classes, reflecting different class 'cultures of family'.

Although this explanation might seem superficially attractive, it has many pitfalls. It has been argued that both economic and normative, material and cultural, factors have to be taken into account in developing an understanding of the processes of class reproduction. However, it has also been argued that considerable caution needs to be exercised in developing arguments in which 'choice' is the major independent variable, as we have seen in the critique of Hakim's explanation of women's employment patterns. Past debates have also emphasised the dangers of 'culture of poverty' arguments, that effectively 'blame the victims' for their low aspirations and stunted lives (Walker 1990). The most recent example of this *genre* emerged in debates around the supposed emergence of an 'underclass' (in Britain and the US), described as feckless, work-shy and only too willing to live on state benefits (Murray 1990). Critics of 'underclass' theorists have made two major arguments. First, that the circumstances of the very poor were in large part a consequence of major structural changes that had removed both opportunities for employment as well as the possibility of upward mobility (Wilson 1987). Second, a range of empirical evidence has demonstrated that, contrary to the arguments of the 'underclass' theorists, the poor and unemployed are not less committed to the idea of work as employment than other class groupings (e.g., Marshall *et al.* 1996).

In respect of class differences in mother's employment behaviour, therefore, it would be unwise to fall back on attitudinal or 'cultural' explanations. An obvious point that has already been made is that for women as well as men, professional and managerial employment generates considerably more by way of material returns. This point may be linked to a further argument, that is, the relative cost of non-family care, particularly for children. In Britain and the US, childcare services are provided largely by the market. In the case of the US, Williams (2000) has persuasively argued that the cost of 'good' childcare services, and the low quality of less expensive childcare provision, means that for many working-class families, good quality childcare can only be assured if it is provided by the mother (that is, she stays at home). As Gornick and Meyers (2003: 195) have argued, 'The care received by American children in [the] minimally regulated system is often of mediocre to poor quality.' In the case of Britain, the research of Paull *et al.* (2002: 227) has shown that families with pre-school children spend 13 per cent of net family income on childcare, and that the rate of mothers' employment is higher when childcare costs are lower. Many employed mothers do not use formal care, relying on informal arrangements or 'shift parenting' (La Valle *et al.* 2002). Mothers with higher earnings, and families with higher incomes, have a greater preference for (more expensive) individual childcare (nannies and au pairs) – the point may reasonably be raised as to whether this 'preference' is in reality more a reflection of economic advantage.

There are a number of persuasive arguments, therefore, as to why mothers in less advantaged material circumstances might opt for family rather than non-family care – particularly when childcare is relatively expensive, or cheaper alternatives are seen as unsatisfactory. It should not be forgotten, however, that at the aggregate level, there is no simple or straightforward relationship between mothers' employment and the availability of subsidised childcare. For example, in Norway, where state-sponsored childcare is widely available, in 1999 73 per cent of mothers with a child under 6 were in employment. However, in Portugal, with a lower level of provision of subsidised childcare, 71 per cent of similar mothers were in paid work (OECD 2001, Table 4.1). In different countries, a similar-seeming phenomenon may have a different causal explanation (Pickvance 1995). In the case of Portugal, (which has one of the lowest levels of wages in Europe) the high level of mothers' employment is almost certainly a reflection of family need rather than the level of availability of childcare facilities.

Nevertheless, it is not being argued here that class variations in mothers' employment may be wholly explained by material class inequalities, as attitudes and preferences will also shape behaviours. Some insights into the relationships between class, attitudes and mothers' employment can be gained from a comparison of the attitudes of mothers in different class groupings who did, and did not, work when their children were young.[17] Again, as with the ISSP findings described in regression analyses (Appendix Table 7.6, p. 188), a similar pattern of variation between AWE scores and mothers' class and employment patterns was discernible in all countries, although the individual country numbers were too small for statistical tests of significance.

What is immediately striking about Table 7.5 is that the attitudes of stay-at-home mothers do not vary at all by class (although the *proportions* staying at home show substantial variation).[18] As might have been anticipated, these stay-at-home women are the most conservative in their attitudes to mothers' employment. This consistency of attitudes

---

[17] As the patterns of women's employment have changed, age will have a considerable impact on whether a woman worked or not. However, controls for age (including only women under 50) did not have a significant impact on the mean scores. In order to maintain numbers for analysis, no controls for age have been added to Table 7.7.

[18] As this table includes women only, the three-category version of the ISCO 88 occupational class classification has been used. See note 15 above.

Table 7.5. *Mean AWE scores by class and whether or not a woman was employed when her child(ren) were under school age (ISSP pooled sample)*

	Professional/ managerial		Intermediate		Routine and manual	
	N	Mean	N	Mean	N	Mean
When child was under school age mother:						
Worked full time	330	9.7	239	11.0	132	12.1
Worked part time	189	10.9	232	11.7	73	12.4
Stayed at home	98	13.8	211	13.8	73	13.9
Total	1578	11.67				

across classes may be used in support of arguments to the effect that, for a minority of women, an orientation towards domesticity cuts across class boundaries, a finding that gives some partial support to Hakim's thesis. Similarly, Duncan *et al.*'s (2003) qualitative study, discussed in Chapter 2 (p. 50), also found that strong 'primarily mother' orientations cut across class boundaries. However, there are significant differences in attitudes by class amongst women who did work for pay when their children were below school age (and it is also of interest that there is a consistent gradient of attitudes by employment status within each occupational class). Full-time professional and managerial women who were in employment when their children were young express by far the most 'liberal' attitudes to women's employment (indeed *post hoc* tests showed that the mean scores of these women were significantly different from all other groups). In other words, intermediate, and to a greater extent routine and manual women have more conservative attitudes to mothers' employment even if they themselves have been in paid work when their children were young.

The more 'positive' attitude to paid work for mothers expressed by managerial and professional women might be a reflection of the fact that they are likely to have greater possibilities of both material reward and self-realisation from their jobs – or it may even reflect the fact that they have been able to afford better childcare. Such interpretations can only be speculative and it would be best not to push them too far. However, one conclusion that might be reasonably drawn from Table 7.5 is that, as indicated by the association between expressed attitudes and actual behaviour, professional and managerial women seem to have achieved a closer match – that is, they have been better able to realise their 'preferences'.

Discussion and conclusions

In this chapter, we have begun to explore how changes in the employment of mothers and thus in the nature of work-life articulation are having an impact on established patterns of class inequalities. It has been argued that although influential social theorists have argued that both 'class' and 'the family' are redundant, 'zombie' concepts in societies characterised by increasing 'individuation', they nevertheless remain important. Taking the case of the reproduction of educational advantage as an example, it has been shown that both material and cultural inequalities remain central to the processes of the reproduction of class inequalities. Via a critique of Hakim's 'preference theory', it has been shown that theories of individuation and 'choice' in respect of women's employment have the effect of systematically removing from critical examination the embedded practices and institutions that reproduce inequalities. If we return again to the example of teenage parenthood, if the decision to become a mother is seen as entirely the outcome of 'choice', as Hakim (2000: 49) argues, then the material and cultural deprivations that result in some young women 'choosing' motherhood may be safely ignored.

Rates of employment, particularly amongst mothers, are lower amongst less well-educated women in less advantaged occupational groupings. Such women (and similar men) are also more likely to hold more conservative or traditional views relating to women's employment and the necessity for maternal care where children are concerned. It might be suggested, therefore, that the broad class differences in mothers' employment patterns are a reflection of this attitudinal conservatism. That is, working-class parents are more likely to 'choose' a traditional work–life articulation option that will contribute to the widening of material differences between occupational class groupings.

However, this kind of argument, as with more general 'culturalist' explanations of inequality, may be seen as effectively blaming those in the lower reaches of the occupational order for their poverty of aspirations. An orthodox materialist response has been to suggest that 'culture' itself has a material base – as in, for example, Marxist theories of 'false consciousness'. Such accounts are too simplistic. Nevertheless, it is important to explore the manner in which both material deprivations and inequalities as well as associated patterns of beliefs, learned behaviours, and norms combine to reproduce broad patterns of inequality. Rather than reject out of hand these beliefs, behaviours, and norms, we have to systematically address the nature of the circumstances in which they are generated. For many women, poorly paid work opportunities will be seen as an unattractive alternative to domesticity, and the child-care options available on a limited budget not to be worth the perceived negative effects on children.

In the ISSP data, considerable differences between countries were found in couple working arrangements, reflecting the variations in working time regimes and labour market policies that have been discussed in previous chapters. These national differences in couple work arrangements meant that although there was a general tendency for less well-educated mothers to be in employment in all countries, there was considerable variation across countries and not all country differences were statistically significant. However, class had a similar association with attitudes to the family and mothers' employment in all countries, in that respondents not in the professional and managerial category expressed more traditional attitudes to gender roles, were more likely to say that children were 'life's greatest joy', and more likely to have conservative attitudes to mothers' employment. This relative consistency of class variation in family behaviour and attitudes across very different countries echoes previous research that has demonstrated other cross-national class continuities, most notably the persistence of class variations in relative chances of social mobility (Erikson and Goldthorpe 1992).

Does the persistence of class differences mean that in respect of class inequalities, government policies have little to offer? This conclusion would indeed be a depressing one but fortunately this is not the case. Most obviously, policies in respect of taxation and benefits have a considerable impact on the extent of inequalities of income and wealth, as cross-national comparisons demonstrate (Hills 2004). As we have seen in the discussion of work–life conflict in Chapter 5, government policies in respect of dual-earner families can have a measurable impact on conflict, and government policies in respect of employment can affect the quality of working life (Gallie 2003). In short, governments have the capacity to improve the lives of all their citizens, even if class-related inequalities persist.

In respect of improving the quality of work–life articulation, however, it should be emphasised that some national strategies are more likely to deepen class inequalities than others. 'Full employment' is a goal that is being pursued by many governments as a strategy of economic regeneration (Gardiner 2000). However, individual self-sufficiency implies full-time work (that is, an 'ideal worker' or 'full-commodification' model of women's employment. See Williams 2000). The US has been described as an 'integrated free market model' of employment, in which there is a dual labour market consisting of 'good' jobs with a high market value and 'bad' jobs with low market value (Gardiner 2000: 680). Countries such as Britain and the US have high levels of employment, but levels of pay in some full-time jobs (in organisations such as Shopwell, for example), are not sufficient for individual self-sufficiency, let alone a family with only a single earner. Women's caring responsibilities, buttressed by the ideology of domesticity, mean that even with rising levels of education and qualification amongst women, only a minority will achieve individual self-sufficiency in the market. Thus women in part-time and low-paid jobs will continue to experience many of the problems of dependency.

This persisting gender inequality will be cross-cut by class inequality, particularly in the absence of freely available, low-cost childcare. Women in professional and managerial employment, who are likely to be in partnerships with similar men, are more likely to be in employment when their children are young (and as we have seen, are less likely to believe that their employment will damage their children or family life). As discussed in Chapter 4, low wages in free market economies will generate employment amongst women, including mothers. Two-income, low-wage families may just avoid poverty, but at the national level, material class inequalities will deepen. In conclusion, therefore, it is difficult not to be somewhat pessimistic about the consequences of the rise of the dual-earner family for both class and gender inequality in integrated free market economies. Some on the left have seen contemporary strains within the family as a political rallying-point: 'If the Left were to organise around domestic class issues, we might well have a huge, impassioned constituency' (Fraad 2003: 62). However, empirical research suggests otherwise. As Becker and Moen (1999) have demonstrated, many dual-earner families 'scale back' in order to accommodate the demands of family life. However, such solutions are privatised, that is, men and women 'take for granted that the solutions to work–family problems must be provided by individuals and families' (Becker and Moen 1999: 1004). Becker and Moen continue:

Rather than challenging established social hierarchies, privatisation is rooted in them. Women reduce their work commitment when they bear and rear children . . . Privatisation is rooted in other forms of social hierarchy, as well. It is a good fit with the interests of businesses because it places the costs of adapting to social change on families instead of employers. (*Ibid.*: 1005)

For as long as the family remains, in essence, a 'private' sphere as far as policy-makers are concerned, this is likely to continue to be the case.

Appendix

Table 7.6. *Multinomial regression on couples' employment strategies*

	High commitments Exp (B)	Dual moderates Exp (B)	Neotraditionals Exp (B)	Alternate commitments Exp (B)
AWE	.871***	.883***	.950*	.938**
GRA:				
Agree	.565*	.406***	.442***	.508**
Neither	.381***	.605*	.527**	.782
Britain	.404**	.304***	1.711*	1.492
Finland	.402*	2.465*	1.440	3.598**
France	.495*	1.567	2.618**	4.598***
Norway	.570	1.483	2.910***	6.027***
USA	.283***	.109***	.489*	.850
Professional	2.008***	.819	.998	.818
Child in household	.379***	.385***	.518***	.548***
Lower education	.689	.508**	.472***	.548**

Reference category = traditionalists.
Nagelkerke r^2 = .241.

Table 7.7. *Multiple regression on attitudes to women's employment (AWE). Mothers with a child in the household only, pooled sample*

	B	Beta	t-value
Partnered/non-partnered	.961	.101	3.725***
Occupational class (2-cat.)[b]	−.929	−.118	−4.298***
Employed f-t[a]	−2.191	−.285	−8.092***
Employed p-t[b]	−1.131	−.121	−3.597***
Finland[c]	−.462	−.038	−1.209
France[c]	−.025	−.003	.938
Norway[c]	−1.363	−.145	−4.415***
USA[c]	−.523	−.050	−1.572
Portugal[c]	2.067	.145	4.790***

Adjusted R^2 = .121.
[a]managerial and professional *vs.* intermediate and routine and manual.
[b]Reference category = not in employment.
[c]Reference category = Britain.

Conclusions

The major aim of this book has been to examine the changes in the manner of the articulation of employment and the family in Western societies, together with its consequences. Many factors have contributed to these changes, but one of the most important has been the securing, by women in Western-influenced societies, of the recognition of their right to equality with men. Furthermore, the employment of women, particularly mothers, is now recognised as a 'fact of modern life'.[1]

Conceptualising change and development in gendered work

As many other commentators have emphasised, the 'separate spheres' of public and private, of employment and family, are not in reality separate but are, rather, interdependent (Marshall 1994). Feminists have long argued that the labour of caring is necessary to human functioning and should therefore be regarded as essential 'work' for human societies, and paid employees would not be able to function as such were it not for the 'work' carried out within their households. One useful way in which this interdependence between market and family work can be grasped is via Glucksmann's conceptual device of the 'total social organisation of labour' (TSOL), which we have drawn upon in earlier chapters of this book. This is: 'the manner by which all the labour in a particular society is divided up between and allocated to different structures, institutions, and activities . . . the social division of all of the labour undertaken in a given society between institutional spheres' (1995: 67). Besides emphasising this interdependence between market work and family work, this book has also stressed that both the formal as well as the domestic economies are embedded in changing and developing cultural and political contexts. These contexts are characterised by substantial

---

[1] See, for example, the 2005 pre-budget statement of the British chancellor of the exchequer.

cross-national variation, and both shape and are shaped by the prevailing arrangements of market and family work in the national societies in question.

Glucksmann uses the TSOL concept to describe historic changes in the boundaries between market and domestic economies. In the early stages of capitalist development, the household continued to generate a considerable amount of domestic production, largely carried out by women. However:

> The advent of mass production for consumption . . . redrew the boundary and resulted in a transformation of the relation between the two spheres. The shift to production for consumption pulled the household economy much more fully into the orbit of the market economy . . . leading to . . . less insulation and a greater integration between them. At the same time, the possibility of domestic tasks being undertaken on the basis of purchased commodities . . . and on a less labour-intensive basis . . . resulted in a long-term shift of labour out of the household economy and into the wage economy. (1995: 71)

Glucksmann is here addressing herself to a universal trend within capitalist societies, but the socio-historical research in the context of which her theories were developed was carried out in a single country – Britain. In practice, there has been considerable variation both in the timing and extent of the shift of (women's) labour out of the household economy, and in the manner in which the TSOL has been divided up amongst different (national) institutional spheres. Later industrialisation, as in some of the Scandinavian countries, led to a later historical shift of labour out of the household economy. In some countries, most notably in eastern Europe, women were drafted into paid labour as a national duty (Einhorn 1993) and much of the labour of care was provided by the state. Moreover, Pfau-Effinger (2004) has argued that the emergence of the housewife model of the male breadwinner family was crucially dependent not on industrialisation as such, but on the extent of the development and influence of the urban bourgeoisie. In some societies, therefore, such as the Netherlands, the housewife model was established even before industrialisation, whilst in others, including Finland, it was never the norm. Thus as Esping-Andersen and others have argued, national 'path dependency' is likely to have a discernible impact on the nature of the TSOL.

Nevertheless, in many societies, the contemporary increase in the level of women's employment, particularly that of mothers, might be seen as a continuation or intensification of the trends that Glucksmann describes as beginning in Britain during the period between the two world wars. Glucksmann's TSOL concept focuses on the matrix composed of household labour and the market *economy*. However, it has been emphasised in this book that this matrix is embedded in a changing cultural and political context. As many have argued (e.g., Bottero and Irwin 2003, Granovetter and Swedberg 1992), there exists in practice a mutuality of value and material social relations. That is, social relations – including economic relations – are 'embedded' in social and cultural values, and vice versa (Polanyi 1957). As a consequence, 'altered choices and values can still be seen as integral to the social order – even whilst more people are more the agents of their own lives and even whilst that order is undergoing transition' (Bottero and Irwin 2003: 476). In laying this emphasis on the mutuality of values and material social relations, it is not intended to suggest that they cannot be distinguished for the purposes of social science investigation, as some postmodern theorists have argued (e.g., Butler 1998; Du Gay and Pryke 2002). As Fraser has argued, in her critique of Butler, the distinction that she (Fraser) draws between the economic and the cultural 'is not an ontological distinction but a social-theoretical distinction' (Fraser 1998; 138). An 'analytical dualism', therefore, that facilitates the separate social science explor-ation of the 'economic' and the 'cultural', has been a feature of this book. Following from this analytical dualism, the characterisation and in-vestigations of transformations in the TSOL have been explored in parallel with transformations in political and cultural values.

The movement of women into paid employment has been both cause and effect of the increasing marketisation of the work of care. Care replacement is needed for the unpaid caring once carried out by women in the home, and much of the paid employment which women have taken up in recent years has been in caring jobs of all kinds. 'Caring' has a dual meaning, in that it encompasses both caring activities, such as shopping and cleaning, as well as feelings of concern, affection and love. Although 'It matters little to most people . . . who vacuums their floors or cleans their toilets' (Folbre and Nelson 2000: 129), it does matter who reads a bedtime story to a child, or shares in the activities of day-to-day life. Caring is active and passive, incorporating both 'caring for' in a physical sense as well as 'caring about' (Land 2002). Caring, in short, conflates labour and love. It has been argued, therefore, that these unique and particular aspects of caring work mean that it is impossible to commodify in any usually understood sense of the term. These kinds of arguments cannot be rejected out of hand. Despite the emergence of a wide range of caring occupations – which would include psychotherap-ists and 'life coaches' as well as health workers, educators and direct care workers – there will remain a kernel of care that can be provided (and exchanged) only by those bound together by the ties of kinship, affection, or both (but both men and women share these 'care' capacities for concern, affection and love). To emphasise the dual nature of care, therefore, does not mean that care cannot be commodified. Indeed, it is arguable as to whether that aspect of care more usually called love may usefully be described as 'work' in an economic sense.

As Glucksmann (1995: 70) argues, 'the activity of caring . . . includes both economic and non-economic aspects without structural demarcation'. Although the economic dimension of paid work is more immediately apparent, a parallel argument might be made as to the non-economic aspects of paid employment. Many if not most jobs include opportunities for socialising, other jobs allow for the expression of creativity, and so on. Recent developments, including the 'high-commitment' management techniques discussed in this book, seek to encourage a love of, and identification with, the employing organisation on the part of the employee. Both paid employment and unpaid care, therefore, have a dual nature in that they incorporate both economic and non-economic aspects of human behaviour and involvement. Indeed, it may be suggested that when Sennett writes of the 'corrosion of character' in modern organisations, one of the processes he is describing is the erosion of 'caring about' other people in modern workplaces. It is important to recognise that caring is gender *coded* (Fraser 1994), and that this has consequences for marketised care work. First, the identification of women with caring activity has been carried over into the marketplace and women are a majority of paid carers. Second, because caring has been seen as 'natural' to women, requiring few skills, care work is often poorly paid. Moreover, because individualised caring has been such a key process in female identity formation, women who apparently choose not to care are likely to be stigmatised. Nevertheless, the dual nature of care work does not mean that it *cannot* be commodified in respect of those aspects that are necessary for human survival, and women's entry into paid employment has been accompanied by a global increase in paid domestic and care work of all kinds, although, as we shall see, its configuration within the TSOL will vary from country to country.

In previous work (Crompton 1999: 205) an initial attempt was made to capture national variations in the TSOL, which were arranged along a putative continuum of transformations in gender relations, from 'more' to 'less' traditional. To some extent, the categories in Figure 8.1 are paralleled by the 'Moen categories' that have been freely drawn upon in the analysis of the ISSP data (see, for example, Chapter 4, p. 102). For example, Moen's 'neotraditionalists' correspond to the 'male bread-winner/female part-time carer' category in Figure 8.1. It is important to recognise, therefore, that within national boundaries, a multiplicity of

GENDER RELATIONS

traditional   `------------------------------------------------------------------▶`   less
                                                                                            traditional

Male breadwinner/ female carer	Male breadwinner/ female part-time earner	Dual earner/state carer	Dual earner/dual carer
		Dual earner/ marketised carer	

Figure 8.1. Gender relations and household arrangements.

employment and caring combinations will be found amongst families and households. Nevertheless, particular national contexts will be likely to generate a predominance of particular employment and caring combinations. As we have seen in Chapters 4 and 7, for example, the proportion of 'neotraditional' families in Britain is high given that many British women work part time. In the original formulation of Figure 8.1, it was suggested that 'the male-breadwinner/female carer model is most likely to reproduce the normative conditions of female subordination (or traditional gender cultures). At the other pole . . . the dual-earner dual-carer model is most likely to generate less traditional gender relations' (Crompton 1999: 205).

In 1999, it was suggested that 'Women's full-time work in combination with substitute care . . . is more likely to result in less traditional gender relations and greater gender equality' (*ibid.*: 206) – although this statement was qualified by the example of Eastern Europe, where gender relations remained highly traditional despite state provision of substitute childcare. However, it will be argued that although in some circumstances the dual-earner/marketised carer category may result in less traditional gender relations, the particular manner in which substitute care (or marketised caring and domestic work) is provided can perpetuate traditionalism in gender relations, as well as increase class inequality.

The complexities of marketised care, domestic work and workers

In households in which all adults work full time, some kind of assistance with caring responsibilities and domestic work (or reproductive labour, Anderson 2000) is likely to be needed, particularly if working hours are

Service employees		Directly employed household workers	
State facilitated services	Profit-making services	Live in	Live out

Figure 8.2. Gender relations and household arrangements.

long. The career banker described in Chapter 3 (p. 74) bought nursery care for her child, and help with ironing and household work, but nevertheless the thought of a second child still 'filled her with cold horror'. One absence from this book (largely because it was not covered by the data sources drawn upon) has been any systematic exploration of paid care and domestic service work and workers – that is, the suppliers of marketised care.[2] However, the characteristic manner in which paid reproductive work is organised and accessed is subject to considerable cross-national variation, and may serve to reinforce and reproduce class and gender inequalities as well as to erode them. For there is considerable variation in the ways in which marketised care and household work is supplied. These variations are summarised in Figure 8.2.

Marketised care and household work is largely carried out by women, thus reproducing gender stereotypes and hierarchies. Class, as well as racial, hierarchies are also reflected in marketised reproductive work in that these services are largely provided by working-class women (see Chapter 2, p. 55), as well as ethnic minority and immigrant workers (Nakano Glenn 1992). Nevertheless, although in general the growth of marketised reproductive work has been moulded to the contours of gender, class and racial inequality, particular categories of reproductive work will have different consequences for employees, employers, and the nature of the gender relations in which they are embedded.

State-facilitated reproductive work will include employees in establishments providing daycare for children, eldercare homes and other residential services, day centres, home helps and so on. The employment conditions of these workers will be the same as those prevailing in the wider society, and will reflect the value that is given to this kind of work. For example, childcare workers in the Scandinavian countries are well qualified, and paid accordingly. In 1999 (Crompton 1999: 206) it was argued that state-facilitated reproductive services, in combination with

---

[2] Indeed, as our focus has been on changes in those parts of the world that might be described as being influenced by Western political, economic and social arrangements, the gender, family and employment arrangements that characterise most of the population of the globe (see Therborn 2004) have not been systematically investigated.

'state feminist' policies directed at the household (as in the Scandinavian countries), are likely to be associated with an increase in gender equality. Such policies are unlikely to be associated with an increase in class inequality. The evidence reviewed in this book would serve to support this earlier argument.

Profit-making reproductive employment includes commercial domestic cleaning services (where the buyer contracts with the employers of the cleaners), privately owned nurseries and eldercare homes, etc. Reproductive workers employed by private firms are entitled to the same rights in employment (pensions, holidays, overtime payments etc.) as those that prevail in the wider society, although their wages will reflect the relative status of this work. For example, as Hochschild (2000: 144) notes, in the US, dog catchers and traffic meter collectors are better paid than childcare workers. As we have seen in previous chapters, the cost and quality of privatised reproductive services such as childcare can be a disincentive to their purchase, particularly for the poorly paid, and both class and gender inequalities may be therefore reproduced. The employment conditions of reproductive service workers may not be particularly favourable (Ehrenreich 2003), but as Nakano Glenn (1992: 22–3) has noted: 'service workers, especially those who have worked as domestics, are convinced that "public jobs" are preferable to domestic service. They appreciate not being personally subordinate to an individual employer . . . Relations with supervisors and clients are hierarchical, but they are embedded in an impersonal structure governed by . . . explicit contractual obligations and limits.'

With considerable oversimplification, the proportion of household reproductive workers (or servants) is likely to be greater in societies characterised by moderate to high inequality, where educational levels are relatively low and/or there is a relative scarcity of 'good' (i.e., well-paid) jobs for women. For example, in Brazil, 20 per cent of urban women are domestic servants (2001 figure), in Chile, 16 per cent (2000), and in Paraguay 21 per cent (2000).[3] In Europe and the US, the numbers of domestic servants declined sharply during the twentieth century, and it was assumed that this occupational category would simply disappear. However, it has been suggested that the numbers of domestic helpers in Europe are now 'very similar to what they were a century ago' (Lutz 2002: 91). Actual numbers of domestic servants are very difficult to establish, as many are now immigrant workers, often undocumented and informally employed. This is in some contrast to past practices, in which domestic servants were usually young women

[3] Thanks to Irma Arriagada for this information.

recruited from poor rural areas. Historically, in Europe and the US the presence of household domestic workers was a measure of the prestige of bourgeois families, whose women did not go 'out to work'. Although family status persists as a rationale for the employment of domestic servants (in some countries more than others), in these days, household domestic workers are more likely to be employed in order to facilitate women's employment.

There are considerable cross-national variations in the extent to which marketised reproductive work is predominantly purchased via state or commercial service employment, or by the hiring of domestic servants. In Saudi Arabia and the Gulf states, the hiring of domestic servants (immigrants from Indonesia, Sri Lanka, Thailand, the Philippines and India) by the urban elite is ubiquitous. In countries like Taiwan, where eldercare is by custom provided by the daughter-in-law, the hiring of migrant domestics serves to maintain patriarchal traditions of filial piety (Lan 2000). In southern Europe, what were once countries of out-migration (Italy, Spain, Greece and Cyprus) have become receivers of migrants, particularly women (Anthias and Lazaridis 2000: 2). The maid industry in southern Europe has expanded enormously in recent years. Southern European families remain firmly patriarchal (Lazaridis 2000: 57), and there is little or no state provision for the very young, the very old and those with special needs. With an ageing population, the gaps created by the increase in full-time employment amongst local women in these countries have been filled by migrant women, and employing a domestic worker is not only regarded as socially acceptable, but as a status symbol (Anderson and Phizacklea cited in Lazaridis 2000: 59). In countries in which dual-earner households access marketised reproductive work largely via the hiring of domestic servants, the dual earner/marketised carer category (Figure 8.1) may (*contra* the argument developed in Crompton 1999) easily co-exist with enduring traditionalism in gender relations.

The phenomenon of changing patterns of migration, in which women are playing an increasingly important role as maids (and sex workers) has recently achieved a high profile (Ehrenreich and Hochschild 2003). Hochschild (2000: 131) describes 'global care chains', in which emotional 'surplus value' is shifted between women within countries and around the world as when, for example, an older daughter in the Philippines cares for her younger siblings whilst her mother cares for the children of a migrant worker who cares for the children or relatives of a family overseas (see also Perrenas 2000). There are numerous examples of gross exploitation and ill-treatment within these 'global care chains', particularly amongst undocumented workers (Anderson 2000). Because a large proportion of this new feminised migration is undocumented, it is impossible to be precise as to the numbers, and thus the proportions of households, involved. Countries with large informal economies (it is estimated that the informal sector accounts for over 35 per cent of GDP in Greece and 25 per cent in Italy: Iosefides cited in Anthias and Lazaridis 2000: 4), and loose or ineffective labour market controls will more easily absorb undocumented migrants. State regulation of migration, and migrant workers, is crucial in determining the status of these workers (Anderson 2000). As noted above, migrant domestic workers seem to be particularly concentrated in the countries of southern Europe, and live-in domestic work is far less common in northern European countries (Anderson 2000: 69). By no means all domestic servants are migrants (undocumented or otherwise), but the prevalence of informal arrangements and payments amongst directly employed household servants and their employers makes reliable estimates of the extent of these services, and thus realistic cross-national comparisons, very difficult to achieve (Cox and Watt 2002; Gregson and Lowe 1994).

Some indication of the extent of private household services is given by International Labor Organisation (ILO) data. The International Standard Classification of Occupations (ISCO)-88 classification includes category 913: 'domestic and related helpers, cleaners and launderers'.[4] Amongst the countries reviewed in this book, in 2000, 6 per cent of female employees in Finland, 5 per cent in Britain, and 8 per cent in France, fell into this category. In Portugal, ISCO-88 913 was the largest single category of female employment, at 12 per cent (ISCO-88 was not used to classify US data, and detailed breakdowns were not available for Norway). In countries where household domestic help is relatively cheap, its availability will do much to ease the lot of middle- and upperclass women. Thus in Portugal, where middle- and upper-class women have ready access to domestic help, the mean level of work–life conflict amongst professional and managerial women (7.61) is lower than average (8.47), and considerably lower than that of routine and manual women (9.32). However, in Britain, where household domestic help is less readily available, the level of work–life conflict amongst managerial and professional women is high (8.29) compared to the average (7.99) (Lyonette and Crompton 2005). This kind of evidence suggests that ready access to household domestic workers can exacerbate class inequalities in employment and family life. Furthermore, the presence of extensive household domestic assistance is likely to perpetuate

[4] This data excludes agricultural workers. See www.laborsta.ilo.org; segregat data.

traditionalism in gender relations, as there will be little pressure on men to carry out more domestic work.

In summary, dual earning in combination with marketised care (Figure 8.1) can have a range of rather different outcomes in respect of both class inequalities and gender relations. Service employees (the left-hand column of Figure 8.2) cannot be 'forced' to work extra hours without overtime payment, and they will be entitled to statutory employment protections, pay and benefits. In particular, good quality state provision can be supportive of gender equality within the household, giving rise to circumstances approaching the dual-earner/dual-carer model. Where market-organised, profit-making services are the norm they may be too expensive for many households, and as we have seen, it will usually be the women in these households who 'downsize' by temporarily giving up work or working shorter hours. That is, bought-in commercial reproductive services do not usually cover the totality of reproductive work – for example, daycare for children does not include bathing or clothes washing. As was demonstrated in Chapter 6, women will usually find themselves carrying out most of the reproductive 'top-up'. Domestic servants (the right-hand column of Figure 8.2), particularly live-in domestic servants, provide more extensive reproductive supports. However, there are many tensions in the employer–employee relationship, as well as opportunities for exploitation, particularly in the case of migrant domestic workers. From the perspective of the arguments being developed here, however, a significant feature of the employment of household domestic workers, particularly if they live in, is that their presence is likely to preserve, rather than undermine, traditionalism in gender relations, even if the woman is in full-time work.

We have touched only very briefly on the complexity of the outcomes of different varieties of dual-earner/marketised carer arrangements in different countries. This complexity suggests that we should be somewhat critical of more 'epochal' versions of globalisation theories. Nation states still have an enormous impact on the lives (and life chances) of their citizens as well as their (documented and undocumented) migrant workers.

Changes in the world of 'work'

Here we will examine two interrelated themes. The first theme has a focus on the apparently increasingly flexibilised and insecure nature of paid work in contemporary societies, the second focuses on changes in the management of workers as employees. As far as the first theme is concerned, the 'neoliberal free-market utopia' (Beck 2000: 1) is seen as having brought about the 'Brazilianization' of the West, in which those who depend on a wage or salary in full-time work represent only a minority of the active population; the disappearance of 'jobs for life'; and a marked increase in short-term and flexible employment (*ibid.*). Closely related to these kinds of arguments, Sennett (1998) has identified the 'corrosion of character' that takes place when stable, socially embedded forms of employment are undermined, and individuals as a consequence lose any requirement to, or sense of, caring about each other.[5] More measured evaluations have cast some doubt upon these extremely pessimistic scenarios (Nolan 2003), but nevertheless, in neoliberal economies wage inequalities have grown rapidly, and considerable numbers of the 'new' jobs created are flexible, often part time and/or short term (Burchell *et al.* 2002; Purcell *et al.* 1999). The relative decline of 'good' breadwinner jobs has been one of the factors drawing women, particularly working-class women, into paid employment, and many less-well-off households will be supported by more than one 'component' wage (Siltanen 1986).

Such households, in Britain at any rate, will be likely to manage the articulation between employment and family life through a combination of help from kin and friends, and the scaling back of women's employment where necessary. However, although many 'new' jobs are of the flexible, low-paid variety (as discussed in the case of Shopwell in Chapter 3), and are characterised by relatively short hours working, these conditions by no means apply to all employees. For the purpose of our discussion here, however, a crucial question to be raised lies in the nature of the individual qualities and behaviours required to move beyond these lower-level jobs. Here, changes and developments in the manner in which employees and the labour contract are managed come more sharply into focus.

Discussions of recent changes in the management of employees have also drawn upon theoretical ideas of individuation and 'identity'. Changes in both labour markets and the way in which employees are managed, it is argued, 'force' the individual to develop an 'enterprising self' in which they engage in a constant process of identity construction and reconstruction (Du Gay 1996; McDowell 1997; Rose 1989). In particular, as described in Chapters 3 and 4, 'high-commitment' managerial techniques, together with focused attempts to build positive organisational 'cultures of excellence', have become influential. It

---

[5] As Wajcman (1996) has argued, the impact on women is different from that on men given that 'feminine' identity remains bound up with motherhood and domesticity.

is increasingly argued that the conditions of contemporary work – particularly service work – have been transformed so as to require the employees to craft their very identities in the service of their employers. We do not need 'hands' in today's organisations, it is argued, but 'hearts and minds' instead (Thompson and Warhurst 1998). Organisations seek to develop 'cultures of excellence' that work to establish 'that ensemble of norms and techniques of conduct that enables the self-actualising capacities of individuals to become aligned with the goals and objectives of the organisation for which they work' (Du Gay and Pryke 2002: 1). As Du Gay (1996: 72) has argued, such projects of 'excellence' mesh positively with neoliberal ideas as they seek to establish a connection between the self-fulfilling desires of individuals and the achievement of organisational objectives. The person becomes a neoliberal 'entrepreneur of the self', autonomous, responsible, free and choice-making, and through these individual actions organisational goals are achieved.

As we have seen in Chapters 3 and 4, 'self-entrepreneurship' is manifest in a number of the management techniques reviewed at Shopwell and Cellbank. The setting of individual targets at Cellbank enforced entrepreneurship on even lower-level staff by making remuneration dependent on product sales. Indeed, rather than focusing on the cultural or affective impacts of high-commitment management techniques in isolation, it should also be emphasised that a culture of entrepreneurship is not just a matter of changing hearts and minds, but has material consequences for the nature of workers' jobs. The responsibility for staffing had been pushed to the very bottom of the organisational hierarchy in Shopwell and Cellbank, first-line Shopwell managers took the personal responsibility of covering for absent colleagues, and Cellbank managers were in a similar position. This top-down entrepreneurship emerged as being in direct conflict with other company policies that ostensibly attempted to enable employees to better accommodate their family lives, as is demonstrated by this statement from a manager at Cellbank:

VICKY: What we [i.e. her management] are interested in is sales, and if you don't get the sales then you're in trouble. Customer service: yes, they don't want queues but they don't give you adequate members of staff. Like today, that shouldn't be like that [i.e., long queues]. They took a cashier away from me because they said that we were running over . . . If anybody goes off sick then you're in serious trouble. It's all very demoralising for the staff. You are not allowed to talk about being short-staffed. You can't say those words. We have 'staff challenges' in the management meetings, or something like that. But if you talk about being short-staffed you have to stop it . . . I would be shot down in flames . ... He [her manager] totally accepts that people have to have them [carer's days] but we still have to achieve the same level of results. You can't say I didn't achieve that, or I had a queue out the door, I'm sorry, because so and so had a carer's day. That's not acceptable. You have to still achieve the same level [of output] . . . it's down to us to manage that, at my level. It doesn't go any further up.

For many lower-level Cellbank and Shopwell employees, attempts at building a culture of entrepreneurship (the Cellbank term was 'bigger behaviours', in Shopwell 'the Shopwell way of working') fell on relatively stony ground – for them it was 'just a job'. However, those who wished to be promoted through the individualised promotion systems that had been introduced in both companies were constrained to embrace the requirements of this culture, at least overtly. Thus it would seem that to move into a better-paid job, in today's organisations, is likely to mean a considerable increase in both work pressures and working hours. Besides the fact that these pressures will make the articulation of employment and family life more problematic, these conditions have obvious implications for gender equality. The persistence of a 'mutated version' (Williams 2000) of the ideology of domesticity, that assigns caring work to women, results in a tendency for women's identities to be split between home and work. Thus, in aggregate, women do not pursue upward organisational mobility to the same extent as men do. As we have seen in Chapter 3, in Britain, managerial and professional women who do wish to pursue promotion report the highest levels of work–life stress.[6]

Market work domestic work and 'choice'

It has been argued that women, men and families still persist as communities of interdependence and need rather than simply as expressions of individual 'choices' giving rise to 'elective relationships' (Beck and Beck-Gernsheim 2000). Whilst being fully cognisant of the significance of identities, cultural difference and social norms for human behaviour it has been argued that the 'cultural turn' in social theory has moved debates too far in one direction. In particular, the cultural turn has deflected sociological attention away from the exploration and explanation of

---

[6] As we have seen, although this finding is valid for Britain, and would probably be true for the USA as well (see Moen 2003, Williams 2000), it would not be wise to assume that this is necessarily a universal cross-national trend. As the example of Portugal has demonstrated, in a country in which professional and managerial women are likely to have extensive assistance with domestic work, levels of work–life stress are lower amongst professional and managerial women than amongst routine and manual women.

the persistence of material inequalities of all kinds. Indeed, what may be described as 'left culturalism' has many resonances with current, and arguably dominant, neoliberal political policies and thinking.

Thus, in previous chapters, criticisms have been made of theories that have emphasised the contemporary, and overwhelming, significance of individualisation and 'choice', particularly for women. Theories of individualisation have been influential in recent analyses of both global trends as well as of specific arenas of social life such as employment relations, as well as the family. Most generally, individual people are described as having been freed from 'historically inscribed roles' (Beck 2002: 202). It has been argued in this book that the extent to which 'historically inscribed roles' have in fact been transcended has been exaggerated in these accounts, particularly in respect of women. In the Western world, female identity remains profoundly shaped by an ideology of domesticity. Despite these criticisms, however, it has not been the intention to argue that women (and men) do not have more life options in contemporary capitalist societies than in the first half of the twentieth century. When women were systematically excluded from family inheritance and educational opportunities, from gaining job-related qualifications, and simply barred from a whole range of occupations, 'Marriage was close to an economic necessity for a young female' (Folbre and Nelson 2000: 134). In Britain, as well as in other European countries, working-class men in mining villages and steel towns were once almost certain to follow their fathers down the pit or into the steel works. Today, women have more choices to make in respect of marriage or partnership, employment and childbearing, and men cannot rely on following their fathers into traditional occupations. Parallel arguments, therefore, for both men and women, may be developed in relation to the increase of 'choice' in respect of residence, occupation, consumption and interpersonal life. It is not the reality of expanding choice that is being contested in this book, but rather, its nature and significance.

Much of the focus of debate around care and women's employment has drawn on ideas of individualisation and 'choice' by raising the question of whether or not women *choose* to specialise in the work of care. In aggregate, men and women continue to vary considerably in respect of their different employment histories, patterns of occupational location, and in the amounts of time they devote to paid and unpaid work. In short, the gendered division of labour persists into the twenty-first century, and even in societies where the equality of women has been largely accepted as legitimate, women as a whole are less materially advantaged than men as a whole. A wide range of evidence also demonstrates that in aggregate, women's attitudes to gender roles and family life are different from those of men in aggregate. For example, in all countries, the ISSP surveys, which have been drawn on extensively in this book, indicate that women are more gender role 'liberal' than men. Women also differ from men across a range of other attitudinal dimensions – for example, they are less likely to be 'extrinsically' oriented towards their employment (Lowe and Krahn 2000). Whether or not these persisting differences between men and women are an expression of 'real' or essential differences between the sexes is not really an issue that concerns us here.[7] Suffice to say that, given a combination of women's capacities for biological reproduction, together with the persistence of long-standing social norms and behaviours that have always differentiated between the sexes, it would be truly amazing if no differences were to be demonstrated.

It is also the case that women (and men) are differentiated in their preferences for different modes of family living, the kinds of relationships they would ideally like to experience, and the amount of time they are prepared to devote and the priority they are prepared to give to paid employment. Some women have very different priorities, and expectations for their lives, than other women. Thus it is not the aim here to attempt to deny either the persistence of sexual differentiation, or the reality of within-sex diversity in attitudes and preferences. The crucial questions, it is being argued here, lie in the *meaning and consequences* given to both sexual differentiation and female heterogeneity. These meanings and consequences will depend, to a considerable extent, on the account that is given of the origins of these differences, as well as their nature.

Thus Hakim, as well as other neoliberal gender essentialists, has suggested that differences between men and women are innate or essential. Hakim has further argued that different groups of women may be identified on the basis of their innate 'preferences' for different employment and family combinations. Hakim argues that differences in levels of testosterone mean that men as a whole are more competitive in the world of work than are women as a whole, and that 'preference groupings' amongst women are individually generated and relatively fixed (Hakim 2004: 106–7).[8] Therefore, 'because most women are eager to raise their own children personally, it is women who are the main propagators, and the main beneficiaries, of the ideology of the sexual

---

[7] For a review of the literature arguing for and against these arguments, see Connell 2002.

[8] This argument might be qualified by the fact that Hakim's largest group, the 'adaptives' or 'drifters', are identified according to their propensity to change.

division of labour . . .' (Hakim 2004: 199). In short, it is *women* who seek to maintain the gendered *status quo*. Given, then, that these inter- and intra-sex differences are naturally occurring, then it is legitimate – indeed Hakim argues urgently necessary – to develop social arrangements and policies that reflect these preferences.

If policies are to be developed on the basis of preference and choice, then it is first important to establish (i) whether stable preference groupings can be identified, and (ii) whether or not preferences *can* be assumed to be innate and individually generated. If preferences can be demonstrated to be shaped by unjust background conditions, differences in power, and/or powerful normative assumptions, then to shape policies on the basis of individual preferences would simply consolidate these injustices and reproduce an unequal social and gender order.

Whether or not consistent and stable preference groupings can be identified amongst women is an empirical issue. An analysis of three surveys of the same group of mothers (McRae 2003) carried out in 1988 (when their babies were born) and again in 1996 and 1999 indicates that 10 per cent had worked full-time and continuously from within a year of the birth, and a rather smaller percentage had not worked at all.[9] There were significant differences in attitudes between these two groupings. Women in continuous full-time employment were significantly more likely than women who had not worked to reject the statements that a man's job was paid employment whereas a woman's job was home and family, and less likely to think that women can't combine a career and children, and that a job is alright but what most women really want is a home and family (McRae 2003: 327). It is not contentious, therefore, that two, relatively small, groups of women may be identified who are 'work centred' and 'family centred' respectively. However, McRae found that the much larger group of women who had worked either continuously part time, or a mix of part time and full time (who might be identified by Hakim as 'adaptives/drifters') were not sharply distinguished in attitude from the two 'extreme' groups. That is, it was not 'preferences' that distinguished the minority from the majority of women. On the basis of this evidence, therefore, it would appear that 'preferences' are not a particularly reliable basis upon which to identify stable groupings of mothers.

Nevertheless, mothers do have preferences and may be accordingly identified. In Chapter 7 (Table 7.5) it was demonstrated for the pooled ISSP sample that a quarter of the mothers interviewed not only had

---

[9] Due to the nature of the sample, stay-at-home mothers were likely to be under-represented.

highly conservative attitudes to women's employment, but had also stayed at home when their children were under school age.[10] These women were drawn from all class groupings, and may reasonably be held to constitute a maternalist minority amongst women – or Hakim's 'home-centred' preference category.[11] However, although such women were found in all classes, the *proportions* of maternalist women varied significantly by class. Only 16 per cent of professional and managerial women were maternalist in thought and deed, as compared to 31 per cent of intermediate, and 26 per cent of routine and manual, women. This kind of evidence relates to the second question that has been raised above – that is, whether preferences are shaped by unjust background conditions and powerful normative assumptions (both between men and women, and amongst different groups of women).

As McCrae (2003: 329) argues, there are social structural/class differences – in other words, unjust background conditions – in mothers' subjective rationalities that not only shaped their preferred employment 'choices', but also constrained the opportunities open to them relative to their goals. Evidence for this argument has also been presented in Chapters 3 and 7 of this book. That prevailing norms do vary by broad social class groupings, and have material consequences, is neither a new nor an original argument. As we have seen in Chapter 2, Davidoff and Hall have argued that in the nineteenth century, the domestic morality of the non-conformist middle classes was crucial in reshaping more general norms relating to the employment of mothers, and, in a similar vein, class-related ideas about ideal family size have been demonstrated to have a considerable impact on decision-making about fertility (Banks 1954; Irwin 2003).

If, as is being argued, unjust background conditions are shaping both the patterning of mothers' wishes in respect of employment as well as their capacities to realise their preferences, then it follows that policies based on preferences alone are likely to contribute to the reproduction of inequality, not only between men and women, but also between differentially advantaged groupings of women. In Chapter 7,

---

[10] This figure is considerably higher than that revealed in McRae's surveys. This would have been expected given that it includes older women, as well as women in a variety of national contexts.

[11] The question of why particular mothers within broad class groupings 'choose' to behave in a non-(economically) 'rational' manner – for example, a highly qualified and employable mother who chooses to mother full time rather than engage in paid work – can only be answered by further research, most likely of a qualitative nature. Duncan (2005) has suggested that the nature of personal relations with partners, as well as other aspects of personal biography, may be crucial here.

it has been argued that class-differentiated strategies in characteristic patterns of work–life articulation will serve to deepen and perpetuate material class inequalities, in that less-well-educated women, in lower-level occupations, are more likely to withdraw from or reduce their labour market participation when they are mothers. It follows, therefore, that universalist supports for dual-earner families are likely to have the greatest relative impact on less-well-off families who might otherwise find it difficult to purchase market-based solutions to their caring requirements. Thus as Korpi (2000) has demonstrated, in countries characterised by both encompassing social policies and dual-earner family supports (as in Finland and Norway), the extent of both class and gender inequality is low. In countries such as Britain and the US, that have targeted/market-oriented or basic security social policies, together with market-oriented family supports, gender inequality is estimated at only a medium level, but class inequality is high.

Comparative analysis and implications for policy

Women's claims to equality have taken centuries to mature, and still fall far short of being realised. Their partial realisation, as expressed in the increase in women's employment, has, it may be argued, changed the boundaries of the debates. Not surprisingly, most of those authors who have historically been concerned with the position and status of 'women' have tended to focus on 'women' in particular. The care of children, and other domestic matters, have been seen as 'women's' issues, particularly by welfare feminists. Increasingly, however, changes in women's employment behaviour mean that the family and care work become 'issues' for men and women alike. As has been briefly outlined in Chapter 1, changes in the labour market behaviour of women, and in the family, are under way across the more developed world. However, despite this universal trend, there is ample evidence of substantial cross-national variation in the manner in which national societies cope with and adapt to this trend.

The comparative evidence presented in this book (Chapters 5 and 6) describes the wide variations in the policies that national governments have developed (or in some cases, not developed) in response to the growing labour force participation of women. Policies to support dual-earner families may be direct, and would include maternity, paternity and family leaves of all kinds, supports for childcare and eldercare, together with tax and benefit concessions in support of these activities. Indirect supports would include policies directed largely at employers. The regulation of working hours is clearly extremely important as far as employment and family articulation is concerned. Other policies directed at employers may include individual statutory rights as well as a more general encouragement to employers to be 'family friendly'. In general, the Scandinavian countries have developed the best national-level supports for dual-earner families, and as Chapter 5 demonstrates, this is reflected in significantly lower levels of work–life conflict in these countries.

Other, more comprehensive, cross-national reviews of policy have come to very similar conclusions relating to the impact of state family-supportive policies. Both welfare regimes (classified according to Esping-Andersen's categorisation), and policies supportive of mothers' employment, have an impact on both the employment rate of mothers as well as the wage penalties associated with discontinuous or part-time working (Stier and Lewin-Epstein 2001: 1757). Employment continuity is highest among countries in which the state provides support for working mothers, and part-time and discontinuous employment is less likely to reduce earnings in the long run (Stier and Lewin-Epstein 2001: 1757). Gornick and Meyers (2003) have constructed a number of indexes of relative policy performance in relation to dual-earner family supports, relating to early childhood education and care, school scheduling, family leave and working time (Gornick and Meyers 2003: 315ff.). In their twelve-country comparative study, the four Scandinavian countries (Denmark, Sweden, Norway and Finland) scored best on these indexes, and the three English-speaking countries (the UK, Canada, and the US) scored least well. Other European countries (Belgium, France, the Netherlands, Luxembourg and Germany) lay between the two extremes (Gornick and Meyers 2003: 258).

Gornick and Meyers assessed the impact of policy by evaluating their policy indicators against a number of different outcomes, including gender inequality in the labour market, child well-being, family economic security and gender equality in the home. They found that mothers in the countries with the strongest early childhood education and care (ECEC) packages were less likely to report sizeable employment effects of having young children, and that, in general, joint weekly work hours were longest amongst dual-earner couples with children in those countries where working hours were unregulated. Perhaps most shocking, policies directed at early childhood education and care in the younger years were shown to have a measurable impact on the mortality rates of children under five, which were highest in the US, Canada and the UK (Gornick and Meyers 2003: 265). Not surprisingly, a combined index (ECEC, school scheduling, family leave and working time) was strongly associated with family poverty, with the three English-speaking countries again performing the worst in this regard (*ibid.*: 266).

Both the evidence reviewed in this book, therefore, as well as a range of other empirical work, suggests that state policies have a positive impact on gender equality, levels of women's employment and child and family well-being. However, as Gornick and Meyers emphasise (2003: 257), correlational findings cannot conclusively demonstrate that the policies in question determine the outcomes they investigate. They cannot rule out reverse causation (for example, the possibility that high levels of female employment create demand for supportive policies), or the influence of other, unmeasured, national characteristics. As discussed in Chapter 1, in seeking to establish explanatory causal direction, approaches to cross-national research may focus on cross-national similarities (if a similar relationship is demonstrated across a variety of national contexts, then this regularity provides supporting evidence for a particular theory or hypothesis) or cross-national differences. Case-oriented studies focusing on national differences aim for theoretical explanation via a close examination of the factors contributing to this variation. Thus in seeking to explain national variation in levels of work–life conflict (Chapter 5), it was suggested that although national policies can and do 'make a difference' (the Scandinavian countries reporting lower levels of work–life conflict when a range of other factors were controlled for), cultural factors shaping the domestic division of labour, that varied from country to country, also played a part. France assumed the status of a 'critical case' in these discussions.

The domestic division of labour

Although gender role attitudes in France are relatively liberal, the division of domestic work is more traditional in France than in Britain, the United States and the two Scandinavian countries. This disjuncture between attitudes and behaviour in France, it was suggested, was making a contribution to the rather higher levels of reported work–life conflict in France than might have been anticipated on the basis of policies alone (France has relatively short working hours, and state supports for working mothers are at the more generous end of the spectrum). It was also the case that respondents in Portugal reported a much more traditional division of domestic work (and much more of it) than respondents in the other five countries.[12] The gendered division

---

[12] Hakim has repeatedly cited Portugal (e.g., Hakim 2004: 131) as a national example that 'proves' her case that national childcare policies do not have an impact on women's

of domestic work, and gender role traditionalism, therefore, would seem to be less susceptible to the impact of policy than are the patternings of material inequalities, work–life conflict, women's employment and family well-being.

In fact, Gornick and Meyers (2003: 263) found that the policies incorporated into their indexes had an inconsistent association with their indicator of gender equality in the home, which was the ratio of fathers' to mothers' hours of childcare giving. The overall association was weak, but it did suggest that fathers' relative contribution to childcare rises with the strengths of family leave, childcare and working time provision within the English-speaking and Nordic clusters. However, as described in Chapter 6, the impact of national policies designed to increase men's (particularly fathers') involvement in domestic work has not been as successful as those who pin their faith on national policy initiatives might have hoped.

As argued in Chapter 6, the gendered allocation of domestic work is an outcome of both material and normative factors. Domesticity is still seen by many as more 'natural' for women, and being a 'good woman' is often associated with a clean house and well-turned-out children (and husbands). Women carried out more domestic work than men in all of the six countries we investigated via the ISSP data sets. The case of Portugal, it may be suggested, is illustrative of the importance that normative factors may assume in particular national contexts. Portuguese respondents were characterised by the highest level of traditionalism in gender role attitudes, and the domestic division of labour in Portugal is by far the most traditional – and most extensive – of the six countries studied. Portugal has a relatively high level of full-time employment amongst women, but the strength of gender role traditionalism in this country would seem to be more important than the impact of the material factors – the hours spent in market work, the resources brought into the household – that have been demonstrated to have an impact on the gendered allocation of domestic work more generally. Furthermore, as we have seen in our earlier discussion of marketised

employment levels (Portugal has only modest levels of national childcare supports, but a high level of women's employment). A closer inspection of the Portuguese case, however, suggests that women in Portugal work on account of material need. The high level of gender traditionalism in Portugal may be explained with reference to both nationally specific and class-related factors. The corporatist dictatorship enshrined gender role traditionalism in law until the 1970s. Portugal also has only a small professional/ managerial class, and gender role attitudes amongst this group are similar to those in other European countries. The numerical preponderance of the lower occupational groups, therefore, who are more gender traditional, makes a further contribution to overall levels of gender traditionalism in Portugal. See Crompton and Lyonette 2004.

reproductive work, the availability of domestic servants in Portugal is likely to contribute to a *de facto* continuing domestic traditionalism amongst those families who employ them.

Notwithstanding the example of Portugal, a range of material factors – including the extent of women's employment (whether full time, part time or not at all), age, the presence of children, and levels of education – all affect gender traditionalism in the domestic division of labour. In general, as women have devoted more of their time to market work, so men's domestic involvement has risen, although this seems to have reached a plateau in the 1990s. Whilst it would not be sensible or realistic to deny that continuing gender role traditionalism, particularly amongst men (who are in aggregate more gender role traditional than women), makes an important contribution to this persisting gendered disparity in domestic tasks, it is nevertheless reasonable to raise the question of how much domestic work may be expected of an employee who works relatively long hours – and such employees are likely to be men. One of the reasons why, despite their greater involvement in domestic work, a majority of women think that their own domestic division of labour is 'fair' is that their partners are likely to be devoting more hours to paid employment. As we have seen in Chapter 3 (p. 74), one of the major reasons given by the JRF interviewees for the unequal sharing of domestic tasks was the long hours worked by male partners. As a senior corporate wife puts it:

> In the really top jobs, they want blood. They want you morning, noon and night. And that's how the world works . . . If one person is going to put in those kind of hours, someone else has got to put in the hours to look after the children.
> (*Observer Weekend*: 17)

However, one of the findings reported in this book (Chapter 6) suggests that women involved in a traditional division of domestic labour, even if they themselves hold traditional views in relation to domestic roles, tend to report lower levels of domestic and personal happiness. Thus it may yet be the case, that as levels of gender role traditionalism continue to fall amongst women (and women's shift towards a less traditional gender perspective has been growing at a faster rate than men's, see Crompton *et al.* 2005), so the pressures on men to take a more equal share of domestic tasks will increase.

State policies – again

States can and do act in a manner that will perpetuate gender role traditionalism as well as a gender traditional division of labour. As we have seen in this book, 'corporatist' welfare states have acted to support and maintain 'breadwinner' wages and channel welfare resources in a manner that supports family caring. Similar outcomes might be expected from 'cash for care' state supports. States have also acted more directly to support gender traditionalism. For example, in Portugal, until the fall of the Salazar regime in 1974, wives were legally subordinate to their husbands and also legally responsible for domestic work (Wall 1997). Nevertheless, it would seem that state policies directed at gender equality in the domestic sphere have not been particularly successful (Gershuny and Sullivan 2003; Gornick and Meyers 2003) – although this does not mean, as has been argued in Chapters 5 and 6, that they have had no impact at all.

It has been suggested above that gender equality in domestic work, whether promulgated by the state or professed at the level of the in-dividual or family, will nevertheless be constrained by the demands of contemporary workplace arrangements (Crompton and Birkelund 2000; Gallie 2002; Williams 2000). States can, of course, have an impact on workplace arrangements via the statutory control of daily or weekly working hours, overtime payments, the structuring of national insur-ance systems, and the granting of individual-level rights such as family-related leave entitlements and other benefits. These kinds of rights are more likely to be honoured in state enterprises rather than in those that are privately owned (Ellingsaeter 1999) and, as a general rule, neoliberal governments will be less likely than social-democratic or corporatist regimes to introduce legislation that interferes with capital-ist managements' 'right to manage'. Although state policies directed at domestic gender equality, therefore, might appear to have only a limited impact on gender equality in the home, this is not necessarily an argument that they should be abandoned.

However, there would be little dispute that government policies have a significant effect on wider patterns of economic and class inequality. As Korpi has demonstrated, at the level of the nation state, gender and class inequality are not necessarily correlated. Nevertheless, there are important interactions between gender and class inequalities. In neolib-eral regimes, where wage inequalities are high (and growing), women may be 'forced' into employment in order to maintain a decent family income. Thus the relevant quantitative measures may reveal a relatively moderate level of gender inequality (Korpi 2000). However, the rela-tive costs of purchased care are higher for poorer families, and less-well-educated women (who are likely to be in poorer families) are more likely to work part time, or withdraw temporarily from employment. Thus practical strategies of work–life articulation within families will increase material inequalities between households. Conversely, generous dual-earner family supports, including reasonably priced non-family care provision, will not only enhance women's employment levels and thus measures of gender equality, but also reduce material inequalities (it is not being suggested that dual-earner family supports are the only policies contributing to the greater material equalities in such countries).

Thus as Gornick and Meyers (2003: 266) argue, 'progress toward the goals of an earner-carer society – greater gender equality, child well-being, and family economic security – has been best achieved in countries that have developed the most supportive packages of (family) leave, working-time policies, ECEC, and school scheduling'. These countries (including Sweden, Denmark, Norway, Luxembourg and Finland) are also to be found in the lower reaches of cross-national comparisons of income inequality (Hills 2004: 29) – earner-carer societies are also more equal societies. Not surprisingly, social spending in countries characterised by high levels of material inequality tends to be relatively low (Hills 2004: 139). Thus the lack of dual-earner family supports in these states is part of a wider reluctance in such countries to invest in the 'common good', and a preference to 'let the market (i.e., employers) decide' as far as the allocation of resources is concerned.

However, organisational (or market) logic requires a 'disembodied worker who exists only for the work . . . the abstract, bodiless worker, who occupies the abstract, gender-neutral job has no sexuality, no emotions, and does not procreate' (Acker 1990: 149, 151). In the absence of more general supports for provisions such as maternity and parental leave, individual employers will have to bear the costs and may well 'lose out' competitively. Mandating employers to assume these costs will be regarded as unfair and, justifiably, be resisted by individual employers (Gornick and Meyers 2003: 141). Thus as Gornick and Meyers argue, as childrearing (and other caring) provides benefits to society as a whole, then the costs should be borne by the wider society, and not simply loaded onto parents, carers, and the organisations that employ them.[13] If spread widely, these costs are not excessive. For example, Gornick and Meyers (2003: 140) estimate that 'Even in the generous Nordic countries, public outlays for leave approximate only three or four dollars a day for each employed woman.'

[13] As Gornick and Meyers (2003: 108–9, following England and Folbre 1999) have noted, although it may be demonstrated, from mainstream economic principles, that children are public goods, most Americans view the bearing and rearing of children as a private concern and think of 'children as-pets'.

Thus as we have seen in Chapter 4, attempts to persuade employers that it is in their 'best interests' to make extensive contributions to the caring and family needs of their employees have not been particularly successful, not least because this will load disproportionate costs onto those employers with larger than average proportions of employees with caring responsibilities. Relatively costless policies, such as flexible working, may be of more benefit to the employer than the worker – although this is not, of course, a reason for not introducing them. However, policies that cost money – paid caring leave, caregiver replacement such as childcare, and eldercare – will not be as easily adopted by employers. Moreover, as we have seen in the example of Vicky above (see also Chapter 4), even when employers do introduce policies such as paid carers' days, the costs of such schemes are effectively bypassed by increasing the level of work intensity amongst the immediate colleagues of workers who take family leave. The 'rational choice' case for employer provision of work–life policies is also likely to be more persuasive the higher the perceived value of an individual employee. As a number of empirical studies have demonstrated (Dex and Smith 2002; Glass and Estes 1999), the cost of such policies means that they are more likely to be offered to higher-level employees, and/or at managerial discretion. These (perfectly reasonable, from an employers' point of view) strategies of policy implementation will further intensify the socioeconomic disparities in work–life arrangements that arise as a consequence of class-associated variations in the manner in which couples determine their gendered distribution of market and caring work.

In any case, as we have seen in Chapters 3 and 4, many 'valued' (i.e., higher level) employees, particularly women, fail to take advantage of work–life policies (such as parental leave, job sharing or part-time working) for fear of damaging their prospects for organisational advancement – or, in some cases, job security. Given this wide range of countervailing factors, therefore, it is perhaps not surprising that empirical research has demonstrated that in countries with only low levels of statutory support for dual-earner families, as well as a lack of regulation of employee work–life entitlements, 'voluntary' employer provision is relatively meagre and does little to make up for the absence of state supports (Evans 2001; OECD 2001). As Gornick and Meyers (2003: ch. 9) argue, therefore, statutory family-related supports of a material kind, together with regulation of employment relationships and individual employee rights, are required in order not only to combat deepening inequalities at the national level, but also to ameliorate the current forced tradeoffs, particularly in neoliberal societies, between the interests of men, women and children.

Concluding discussion

It has been argued that statutory policies that support dual-earner families will reduce class inequalities. Although gender equality is not necessarily coterminous with class equality, nevertheless, gender equality is also more likely to be achieved in societies characterised by statutory dual-earner family supports.

As Hills (2004: 261) argues: 'Policies matter, and we are free to choose between them.' For example, the very rapid rise in material inequalities in Britain since 1979 was a most unusual phenomenon. Between 1979 and the early 1990s, no other country in the Western world experienced as rapid a rise in inequality as Britain, and by the mid 1990s, inequality in Britain was greater than in any other Western country apart from the US. This rise in inequality was a consequence of the neoliberal economic policies introduced by the Conservative government from its election in 1979 onwards (as described in Chapter 2). In a similar vein, Gornick and Meyers (2004: 107) have argued that: 'The results of the American experiment with market-based solutions [to the needs of dual-earner families] have been calamitous for many American parents and children.'

In social policy debates, Britain is usually categorised (along with other English-speaking countries) as a market-oriented or 'liberal' welfare regime (Esping-Andersen 1990; Korpi 2000). Although there are in practice variations within 'liberal' regimes (particularly in relation to gender, see O'Connor *et al.* 1999), the nature of policy outcomes in the English-speaking countries provides substantial empirical grounds for their location in the same category. As we have seen, on all of the policy outcomes evaluated by Gornick and Meyers, the 'Anglo-Saxon' countries (including Britain) performed least well in relation to mothers' employment, weekly working hours, child mortality and family poverty. Other cross-national comparisons tell a similar story. For example, Hills (2004: 57) demonstrates that at the end of the second millennium, 27 per cent of children in Britain (1999 figures), and 30.2 per cent in the United States (2000 figures), were living below 60 per cent of the population income median. Using the same measure, these figures compare unfavourably to 7.5 per cent of children in Norway (2000 figures), and 14.8 per cent (1999 figures) in the Netherlands, who were living in poverty.

Despite these similarities of policy outcomes, as far as welfare-oriented policies are concerned, there is a wide range of evidence available that suggests that, in fact, the attitudes of the British public towards welfare spending and the role of the state are much closer to those to be found in Europe than in the US – that Britain and Europe are, as Hutton (2002: 257) has put it, 'siblings under the skin'. In a direct comparison of attitudes, Davis (1986) found that as compared to the United States, British respondents were more inclined to support government-supported social and economic welfare policies, government intervention in the economy, and increased government spending. In general, British respondents (average 57 per cent) were far more likely to say that it is the government's responsibility to provide jobs, keep prices under control, provide health care for the sick, a decent standard of living for the old and the unemployed, help industry, and reduce income differences between the rich and poor, than were those in the US (average 24 per cent) (Davis 1986: 101–2). In summary, this research found that Britons and Americans have essentially similar relative priorities for welfare state activities, but the British were more enthusiastic about every one of them.

In a further comparison between Britain and Germany, Kaase and Newton (1998) found very similar attitudes concerning state provision, particularly in respect of health care and pensions. In fact, support for an active role for the state in general was higher in Britain than it was in Western Germany (Kaase and Newton 1988: 45), and there was no evidence from either country of support for the 'rolling back of the state'. As Kaase and Newton (1998: 52) conclude: 'Both nations are . . . close . . . to a general EU consensus in respect of attitudes to the scope of government.' In a similar vein, Hills (2004, Hills and Lelkes 1999) has consistently found that British survey respondents endorse increased government spending on health, education and social benefits, even if this means higher taxes, believe that poverty in Britain has increased, and that one major task of government is to combat poverty.[14]

Despite the broad similarity, therefore, in many policies, and policy outcomes, between Britain and the United States, the two countries are in fact very different. There are also major policy differences – most notably, the provision of a publicly funded system of health care in Britain. The New Labour government, in office since 1997, has also made a point of directing resources in order to bring down the level of child poverty in Britain (although as we have seen, recent figures suggest that child poverty in Britain is still the highest in Europe). Resources directed at child poverty by the British government have been highly selective, and targeted on the poorest families. They include the introduction of the Working Families Tax Credit (WFTC), an

[14] There was an unexplained fall in the proportion of respondents believing that poverty had increased after the election of the 'New Labour' government in 1997.

increase in Child Benefit, and the introduction of a Child Tax Credit (CTC) paid to families both in and out of employment (Hills 2004: 212–13). Tax credits have also been introduced for childcare costs. More precisely targeted programmes include Sure Start, a community-based programme aimed at families with children in low-income areas. These include home visits, the provision of day nurseries, and other community facilities. Early years education has been enhanced, and Educational Maintenance Allowances introduced for older children from disadvantaged backgrounds (Hills 2004: 217). These policies have served to bring down the number of children in Britain living in absolute poverty (Hills 2004: 50).[15] They are also more generous than parallel US policies. For example, in Britain, lone mothers are not *compelled* to take up paid employment until a child is 16 years old, whereas in twenty states in the US, full-time participation in paid employment for 'welfare' mothers may be required once children reach the age of 16 weeks (Hills 2004: 211; see also Orloff 1999).

Although improvements have recently been made in Britain, it cannot be emphasised too much that family-related policies *are* highly selective, and in many cases will not cover even the agreed proportion of actual costs. For example, the limit of tax deductible childcare costs (allowed up to 70 per cent of total costs) is £100 (to be raised to 80 per cent of costs and £175) a week, but good market-provided childcare in London costs £250 a week.[16] Nevertheless, there have been positive changes, and the bottom of the income distribution in Britain has been catching up with the middle. As a consequence, poverty rates have begun to fall. However, overall, income inequality in Britain has continued to rise since the election of 'New Labour', as the gap between the top and bottom income deciles continues to widen (Hills 2004: 76).

Thus the British government under 'New Labour', as in the US, has held back from the introduction of universal provisions that would provide statutory rights for dual-earner families. Selectivity in dual-earner supports might help poorer families, but it will do little to change the wider structure of inequality that is in part generated and perpetuated by the characteristic manner in which broad class groupings achieve work–life articulation. Government policy is also characterised by a marked reluctance to interfere with the employers' 'right to

---

[15] Hills (2004: 221) notes that child and family poverty will also have been brought down by the continuing strength of UK economic performance.

[16] At the time of writing, 'New Labour' government proposals also include the extension of maternity and paternity leave, as well as an extension of the Sure Start programme and an increase in nursery places.

manage', and indeed, work–life policies are promoted via strenuous attempts to demonstrate the 'business case' for them. Businesses have met the challenge by facilitating extreme flexibility, particularly for lower-level employees. Such policies are relatively cheap and, particularly in the case of 24 hour establishments, rather convenient for employers. Gornick and Meyers (2003: 263) found a negative association between policies affecting children under the age of six and the prevalence of evening or night-time work among employed parents. The US and the UK had the highest incidence of such work. A minority of employers have also introduced an extended range of work–life benefits such as, for example, enhanced parental and carer's leaves. However, as we have seen, they may not be used by employees for a variety of reasons, including a perceived need to protect individual job or promotion prospects, as well as not to be seen to be a 'burden' on workplace colleagues.

In this book, it has been argued that changing men (or making men 'more like women', that is, individuals who routinely engage in both caring and market work, see Fraser 1994), is a necessary but not a sufficient condition for achieving a true 'balance' between work and family life for men and women in dual-earner societies. Within nation states, the three major players shaping the manner in which this articulation is achieved are: states; families (that is, men and women); and employers (or markets). Attitudes and behaviours within families *are* changing, although our cross-national comparisons indicate that they have changed faster in some societies than in others. Capitalist employers have no obligations to families, they are free to effectively marginalise all employees who have responsibility for family work (predominantly women), and demand long hours and increased effort from employees (predominantly men) who are seen not to have these responsibilities. Recent developments in employer–employee relationships, including the introduction of 'high commitment' management techniques, would appear to be making full-time employment *more* family 'unfriendly', not less. As far as the self-regulating market is concerned, the family, and the 'private sphere' more generally, lies outside of its influence and control. However, one of the arguments of this book is that the self-regulating market is itself an abstraction (or as Polanyi would put it, 'fictive'), as markets are invariably embedded in social relationships, and are regulated in different ways and to varying degrees.

Thus contexts can be changed, and markets and the relationships within them (such as, for example, those between employers and employees) can be re-regulated. The evidence reviewed in this book suggests that controls over working hours would make a major contribution to a reconfiguration of employment and family life. If working hours were shorter, men would be enabled to increase their contribution to the work of caring, and women would be better enabled to avoid the 'mummy track' of part-time work (although the example of France suggests that changes in working hours need to be matched by changes within the family as well). Direct intervention (via statutory rights or other controls) in the employee–employer relationship would be unpopular with employers (and some employees), and would work against the prevailing mood of the times (particularly in Britain and the US). Nevertheless, it is likely to be necessary if contemporary societies are to effectively adapt to what has been one of the most significant social changes in contemporary Western societies – the recognition and legitimacy of women's equal status to that of men.

Appendix A Additional ISSP Family 2002 questions funded via ESRC: R000239727: 'Employment and the Family'

E1. Have you ever had a paid job?

Yes	1	**Answer E2**
No	2	**GO TO E4**

E2a. Have you ever changed your hours or working arrangements to look after any of the following people?

No	1
Yes, for: Children (own/step/foster)	2
Husband/wife/partner	3
Father, mother, grandparent	4
Father-in-law/mother-in-law/grandparent-in-law	5
Grandson/granddaughter	6
Other relative	7
Other non-relative	8

b. Have you ever given up work to look after any of the following people? Please do **not** include any time spent on maternity leave.

No	1
Yes, for: Children (own/step/foster)	2
Husband/wife/partner	3
Father, mother, grandparent	4
Father-in-law/mother-in-law/grandparent-in-law	5
Grandson/granddaughter	6
Other relative	7
Other non-relative	8

E3. How much, if at all, do you think your family responsibilities have got in the way of your progress at work or your job prospects?

A great deal	1
Quite a lot	2
A bit	3
Not very much	4
Not at all	4
Can't say	8

E4. How much do you agree or disagree with the following statements?

PLEASE TICK ONE *CODE* ON *EACH LINE*	Agree strongly	Agree	Neither agree nor disagree	Disagree	Disagree strongly
a. It is important to move up the ladder at work, even if this gets in the way of family life	1	2	3	4	5
b. It is not good if the man stays at home and cares for the children and the woman goes out to work	1	2	3	4	5
c. If a person cannot manage their family responsibilities they should stop trying to hold down a paid job	1	2	3	4	5

CARD

E5a. I'd like you to think about the person at work you go to if you have to take time off – this may be your supervisor, your line manager or someone else. How understanding would this person be if you had to take time off for family or personal reasons?

Very understanding   1
Fairly understanding   2
Not very understanding   3   **ASK b**
Not at all understanding   4
(Varies too much to say)   5
(Doesn't have to ask anyone if takes time off)   6   **GO TO E6**
(Don't know)   8   **ASK b**

IF CODES 1-5, 8 AT E5

E5b. Is this person a man or a woman?

Man	1
Woman	2

CARD

E6. Say you had to take a day off work, with little notice, for family or personal reasons. In general, which of the things on this card would you do to cover the lost time? Which others? CODE ALL THAT APPLY.

Use holiday or flexi hours	1
Put in extra effort within normal working hours	2
Work extra hours afterwards	3
Take unpaid leave	4
None of these	5
(Don't know)	8

E7. And if you took time off work for family or personal reasons would you . . . **READ OUT** . . .

. . . usually lose money as a result,	1
sometimes lose money,	2
or, not usually lose money as a result?	3
(Varies too much to say)	4
(Don't know)	8

CARD

E8. I'd like you to think about how people in your kind of job move up the ladder at your workplace – for example, by getting themselves promoted. Do you agree or disagree that people who want to do this usually have to put in long hours?

Agree strongly	1
Agree	2
Neither agree nor disagree	3
Disagree	4
Disagree strongly	5
(No-one moves up ladder/ gets promoted)	6
(It depends)	7
(Don't know)	8

CARD AGAIN

E9. And do you agree or disagree that people in your kind of job who want to move up the ladder at your workplace have to be prepared to move from one part of the country to another?

Agree strongly	1
Agree	2
Neither agree nor disagree	3
Disagree	4
Disagree strongly	5
(No-one moves up ladder/ gets promoted)	6
(It depends)	7
(Don't know)	8

CARD

E10. Speaking for yourself, how important is it that you move up the career ladder at work?

Very important	1
Fairly important	2
Not very important	3
Not important at all	4
(Don't know)	8

CARD

E11. How much do you agree or disagree that if you take time off work at short notice it makes things difficult for the people you work with?

Agree strongly	1
Agree	2
Neither agree nor disagree	3
Disagree	4
Disagree strongly	5
(Don't know)	8

CARD AGAIN

E12. How much do you agree or disagree that people in your kind of job are expected to work longer hours these days than they used to?

Agree strongly	1
Agree	2
Neither agree nor disagree	3
Disagree	4
Disagree strongly	5
(Don't know)	8

Appendix B Joseph Rowntree Foundation (JRF) interviewees cited

Ref.	Pseudonym	Sex	Age (at int.)	Location	Organisation	Grade	Highest qualification	Children
9	Abigail	F	30	Canterbury	Cellbank	G3	A level or equivalent	yes
1	Adam	M	29	Canterbury	Cellbank	G4+	A level or equivalent	no
57	Alice	F	35	Canterbury	Shopwell	Shopfloor	A level or equivalent	yes
23	Alison	F	57	Canterbury	Cellbank	G1	A level or equivalent	yes
2	Bill	M	33	Canterbury	Cellbank	G3	A level or equivalent	yes
55	Carolynne	F	27	Canterbury	Shopwell	Shopfloor (key worker)	GCSE or equivalent	no
27	Charles	M	39	Canterbury	Council	G6–9 (LA)	Higher ed below degree	yes
50	Craig	M	40	Canterbury	Shopwell	Manager	A level or equivalent	yes
113	Donna	F	30	Sheffield	Shopwell	Shopfloor	Comm quals/apprentice	yes
16	Flora	F	41	Canterbury	Cellbank	G4+	A level or equivalent	yes
118	Gillian	F	38	Sheffield	Shopwell	Shopfloor	GCSE or equivalent	yes
58	Grace	F	41	Canterbury	Shopwell	Manager	GCSE or equivalent	yes
76	Hannah	F	27	Sheffield	Cellbank	G3	A level or equivalent	no
64	Irene	F	51	Canterbury	Shopwell	Shopfloor	No qualifications	yes
34	Isobel	F	32	Canterbury	Council	G3 (LA)	GCSE or equivalent	yes
110	James	M	39	Sheffield	Shopwell	Shopfloor	GCSE or equivalent	yes
37	Joyce	F	41	Canterbury	Council	G6–9 (LA)	Comm. quals./apprentice	yes
66	Jean	F	58	Canterbury	Shopwell	Shopfloor	No qualifications	yes
15	Kerry	F	40	Canterbury	Cellbank	G4+	GCSE or equivalent	yes
62	Laura	F	45	Canterbury	Shopwell	Shopfloor	GCSE or equivalent	no
48	Martin	M	36	Canterbury	Shopwell	Manager	GCSE or equivalent	yes
115	Megan	F	34	Sheffield	Shopwell	Shopfloor	GCSE or equivalent	yes
75	Natalie	F	21	Sheffield	Cellbank	G1	A level or equivalent	no
21	Nerys	F	53	Canterbury	Cellbank	G1	GCSE or equivalent	yes
42	Patsy	F	51	Canterbury	Council	G10+ (LA)	Degree or equivalent	yes
85	Peggy	F	45	Sheffield	Cellbank	G4+	Degree or equivalent	yes

5	Philip	M	42	Canterbury	Cellbank	G3	A level or equivalent	yes
24	Rachel	F	59	Canterbury	Cellbank	G2	GCSE or equivalent	yes
3	Scott	M	34	Canterbury	Cellbank	G3	GCSE or equivalent	yes
87	Shirley	F	47	Sheffield	Cellbank	G3	GCSE or equivalent	no
123	Thea	F	48	Sheffield	Shopwell	Shopfloor (key worker)	GCSE or equivalent	yes
17	Vicky	F	42	Canterbury	Cellbank	G4+	GCSE or equivalent	no
77	Zoe	F	29	Sheffield	Cellbank	G4+	GCSE or equivalent	yes

[a] (For a full listing of interviewees see R. Crompton, J. Dennett and A. Wigfield 2003, *Organisations, Careers and Caring*, Policy Press, Bristol, Appendix 2).

Bibliography

Abercrombie, N. and J. Urry 1983 *Capital, labour and the middle classes*, Allen and Unwin, London

Acker, J. 1973 'Women and stratification: a case of intellectual sexism' in J. Huber (ed.), *Changing women in a changing society*, Chicago

— 1990 'Hierarchies, jobs, bodies: a theory of gendered organisations', *Gender and Society* 4.2: 139–58

Adkins, L. 2002a 'Sexuality and economy: historicisation *vs.* deconstruction', *Australian Feminist Studies* 17, 37: 31–41

— 2002b *Revisions: gender and sexuality in late modernity*, Open University, Buckingham

Anderson, B. 2000 *Doing the dirty work? The global politics of domestic labour*, Zed Books, London

Anderson, M. 1985 'The emergence of the modern life cycle in Britain', *Social History* 10, 1: 69–87

Anthias, F. and G. Lazaridis 2000 *Gender and migration in southern Europe*, Berg: Oxford.

Anttonen, A. 2002 'Universalism and social policy: a Nordic-feminist revaluation', *NORA* 10, 2: 71–80

Appelbaum, E., T. Bailey, P. Berg and A. Kalleberg 2003 'Organisations and the intersection of work and family: a comparative perspective', Center for Women and Work, Rutgers, NJ

Atkinson, J. 1984 'Manpower strategies for flexible organisations', *Personnel Management* 16: 28–31

Badgett, M. V. L. and N. Folbre 1999 'Assigning care: gender norms and economic outcomes', *International Labour Review* 138, 3: 311–26

Bagilhole, B. M. A. R., J. Dainty and R. H. Neale 2000 'Women in the construction industry in the UK: a cultural discord?' *Journal of Women and Minorities in Science and Engineering* 6, 1: 73–86

Bailyn, L. 1993 *Breaking the mold*, The Free Press, New York

Ball, S. 2003 *Class strategies and the education market*, Routledge/Falmer, London

Banks, J. A. 1954 *Prosperity and parenthood*, Routledge and Kegan Paul, London

Barlow, A., S. Duncan and G. James 2002 'New Labour, the rationality mistake and family policy in Britain' in A. Carling, S. Duncan and R. Edwards (eds.), *Analysing families*, Routledge, London

Barrett, M. and M. Mackintosh 1991 *The anti-social family*, Verso, London

Barron, R. D. and G. M. Norris 1976 'Sexual divisions and the dual labour market' in D. L. Barker and S. Allen (eds.), *Feminism and materialism*, Routledge, London

Baudrillard, J. 1993 'Hyperreal America', *Economy and Society*, 22, 2: 243–52

Bauman, Z. 2002 in Beck U. and E. Beck-Gernsheim, *Individualization*, Sage, London

Baxter, J. 2000 'The joys and justice of housework', *Sociology* 43, 4: 609–31

Baxter, J., B. Hewitt and M. Western 2004 'Post-familial families and the domestic division of labour', School of Social Science, University of Queensland

Beck, U. 1992 *Risk society*, Sage, London

  2000 *The brave new world of work*, Polity, Cambridge

Beck, U. and E. Beck-Gernsheim 2002 *Individualization*, Sage, London

Beck, U., A. Giddens and S. Lash 1994 *Reflexive modernisation*, Polity, Cambridge

Becker, G. 1991 *A treatise on the family*, Harvard University Press, Cambridge, MA

Becker, P. E. and P. Moen 1999 'Scaling back: dual-earner couples' work-family strategies', *Journal of Marriage and the Family* 61: 995–1007

Berg, P. A., L. Kalleberg and E. Appelbaum 2003 'Balancing work and family: the role of high-commitment environments', *Industrial Relations* 42, 2: 168–87

Beynon, H. 1973 *Working for Ford*, Allen Lane, London

Bianchi, S. M., M. A. Milkie, L.C. Sayer and J. P. Robinson 2000 'Is anyone doing the housework? Trends in the gender division of household labor', *Social Forces* 79, 1: 191–228

Bishop, K. 2004 'Working time patterns in the UK, France, Denmark and Sweden', *Labour Market Trends* (March): 113–22

Blackburn, R. M., J. Jarman and B. Brooks 2000 'The puzzle of gender segregation and inequality: a cross-national analysis', *European Sociological Review* 16, 2: 119–35

Blau, P. and O. D. Duncan 1967 *The American occupational structure*, John Wiley, New York

Blauner, R. 1964 *Alienation and freedom*, University of Chicago Press, Chicago

Blood, R. and D. Wolfe 1960 *Husbands and wives: the dynamics of married living*, Free Press, Glencoe, IL

Blossfeld, H.-P. and S. Drobnic (eds.) 2001 *Careers of couples in contemporary societies*, Oxford University Press, Oxford

Bock, G. and P. Thane (eds.) 1991 *Maternity and gender policies*, Routledge, London

Bottero, W. and S. Irwin 2003 'Locating difference: class, race and gender, and the shaping of social inequalities', *Sociological Review* 51, 4: 463–83

Bourdieu, P. 1973 *Distinction: a social critique of the judgement of taste*, Routledge, London/New York

  1990 *Reproduction in education, society and culture*, 2nd edn, Sage, London

Bowlby, J. 1965 *Child care and the growth of love*, Penguin, Harmondsworth

Bradley, H. 1989 *Men's work, women's work*, Polity, Cambridge

  1998 *Gender and power in the workplace*, Macmillan, Basingstoke

Brandth, B. and E. Kvande 2001 'Flexible work and flexible fathers', *Work, Employment and Society* 15, 2: 251–67

Brannen, J., P. Moss and A. Mooney 2004 *Working and caring over the twentieth century*, Palgrave Macmillan, Basingstoke

Braverman, H. 1974 *Labor and monopoly capital*, Monthly Review Press, New York

Burchell, B., D. Ladipo and F. Wilkinson (eds.) 2002 *Job insecurity and work intensification*, Routledge, London

Bussemaker J. and L. Kersbergen 1999 'Introduction' in J. Bussemaker (ed.), *Citizenship and welfare state reform in Europe*, Routledge, London

Butler, J. 1998 'Merely cultural', *New Left Review* 227: 33–44

Castells, M. 1997 *The power of identity*, Blackwell, Oxford
    2000 'Materials for an exploratory theory of the network society', *British Journal of Sociology* 51: 14–24

Charles, N., C. Davies and C. Harris 2004 'Continuity and change in work–life balance choices', Paper presented at a conference organised by the Centre for Research on Families and Relationships, University of Edinburgh, July

Cheal, D. 1991 *Family and the state of theory*, Harvester Wheatsheaf, Hemel Hempstead

Clarkberg, M. and S. S. Merola 2003 'Competing clocks: work and leisure' in P. Moen (ed.), *It's about time*, Cornell University Press, Ithaca and London

Cockburn, C. 1983 *Brothers: male dominance and technological change*, Pluto Press, London
    1991 *In the way of women*, Macmillan, Basingstoke

COM 2001 'Employment and social policies: a framework for investing in quality', Brussels 20 June

Connell, R. W. 2002 *Gender*, Blackwell, Oxford

Cox, R. and P. Watt 2002 'Globalisation, polarisation and the informal sector: the case of paid domestic workers in London', *Area* 34, 1: 39–47

Crompton, R. 1993 [1998] *Class and stratification*, Polity, Cambridge
    1989 'Women in banking', *Work, Employment and Society* 3, 2: 141–56
    2001a 'Gender restructuring, employment, and caring', *Social Politics* (Fall): 266–91
    2001b 'Gender, comparative research and biographical matching', *European Societies* 3, 2: 167–90
    2002 'The gendered restructuring of the middle classes' in J. Baxter and M. Western (eds.), *Reconfigurations of class and gender*, Stanford University Press, Stanford, CA

Crompton, R. (ed.) 1999 *Restructuring gender relations and employment*, Oxford University Press, Oxford

Crompton, R. and G. Birkelund 2000 'Employment and caring in British and Norwegian banking: an exploration through individual careers', *Work, Employment and Society* 14, 2: 331–52

Crompton, R. and F. Harris 1998a 'Explaining women's employment patterns: "Orientations to work" revisited', *British Journal of Sociology* 49, 1: 118–36
    1998b 'Gender relations and employment: the impact of occupation', *Work, Employment and Society* 12, 2: 297–315

Crompton, R. and G. Jones 1984 *White-collar proletariat*, Macmillan, London

Crompton, R. and C. Lyonette 2005 'Family, gender and work–life articulation: Britain and Portugal compared', Instituto de Ciencias Sociais, Lisbon

Crompton, R. and N. Le Feuvre 2000 'Gender, family and employment in comparative perspective: the realities and representations of equal opportunities in Britain and France', *Journal of European Social Policy* 10, 4: 334–48

Crompton, R. and K. Sanderson 1986 'Credentials and careers', *Sociology* 20, 1: 25–42.

1990 *Gendered jobs and social change*, Unwin Hyman, London

Crompton, R., M. Brockmann and D. Wiggins 2003a 'A woman's place … employment and family life for men and women' in A. Park, J. Curtice, K. Thomson, L. Jarvis and C. Bromley (eds.), *British Social Attitudes, the 20th Report*, Sage, London

Crompton, R., J. Dennett and A. Wigfield 2003b *Organisations, careers and caring*, Policy Press, Bristol

Crompton, R., D. Gallie and K. Purcell (eds.) 1996 *Changing forms of employment*, Routledge, London

Crompton, R., M. Brockmann and C. Lyonette 2005 'Attitudes, women's employment and the domestic division of labour: a cross-national analysis in two waves', *Work, Employment and Society* 19, 2: 213–33

Crook, S., J. Pakulski and M. Waters 1992 *Postmodernisation: change in advanced society*, Sage, London

Crouch, C. 1999 *Social change in Western Europe*, Oxford University Press, Oxford

Crouch, C. and W. Streeck (eds.) 1997 *Political economy of modern capitalism*, Sage, London

Daniel, W. 1969 'Industrial behaviour and orientations to work', *Journal of Management Studies* 6: 152–69

1971 'Productivity bargaining and orientation to work: a rejoinder to Goldthorpe', *Journal of Management Studies* 8: 329–35

Davidoff, L. and C. Hall 1987 *Family fortunes*, Hutchinson, London

Davidson, M. J. and C. Cooper 1992 *Shattering the glass ceiling*, Chapman, London

Davis, J. A. 1986 'British and American attitudes: similarities and contrasts' in R. Jowell, S. Witherspoon and L. Brook, *British social attitudes, the 1986 Report*, Gower/SCPR, London

Davis, J. A. and Roger Jowell 1989 'Measuring national differences' in R. Jowell, S. Witherspoon and L. Brook *British social attitudes: Special International Report*, Gower, Aldershot

Dench, G. (ed.) 1999 *Rewriting the sexual contract*, Transaction, New Brunswick, NJ

Dench, S., J. Aston, C. Evans, N. Meager, M. Williams and R. Willison 2002 *Key indicators of women's position in Britain*, Department of Trade and Industry, London

Department of Trade and Industry 2000 *Work and parents: competitiveness and choice*, Stationery Office, London

Department of Trade and Industry/HM Treasury (2003) *Balancing work and family life: enhancing choice and support for parents*, Stationery Office, London

Devine, F. 2004 *Class practices: how parents help their children get good jobs*, Cambridge University Press, Cambridge

Dex, S. 1987 *Women's occupational mobility*, Macmillan, Basingstoke

Dex, S. and A. McCulloch 1997 *Flexible employment*, Macmillan, Basingstoke and London

Dex, S. and F. Scheibl 1999 'Business performance and family-friendly policies', *Journal of General Management* 24, 4: 22–37

Dex, S. and L. B. Shaw 1986 *British and American women at work: do equal opportunities policies matter?* Macmillan, Basingstoke

Dex, S. and C. Smith 2002 *The nature and patterns of family-friendly employment policies in Britain*, York Publishing Services, York

Dex, S. and P. Walters 1989 'Women's occupational status in Britain, France and the USA: explaining the difference', *Industrial Relations Journal* 20, 3: 203–12

Doeringer, P. B. and M. J. Piore 1971 *Internal labor markets and manpower analysis*, Heath, Lexington, MA

Doyle, L. 2001 *The surrendered wife: a practical guide for finding intimacy, passion and peace with a man*, Simon and Schuster, New York

Drago, R. and D. Hyatt 2003 'Symposium: the effect of work–family policies on employees and employers', *Industrial Relations* 42, 2: 139–43

Drew, E. 1998 'Re-conceptualising families' in E. Drew, R. Emerek and E. Mahon, *Women, work and the family in Europe*, Routledge, London

Drew, E., R. Emerek and E. Mahon 1998 *Women, work and the family in Europe*, Routledge, London

Du Gay, P. 1996 *Consumption and identity at work*, Sage, London

Du Gay, P. and M. Pryke 2002 *Cultural economy*, Sage, London

Duncan, S. 2003 'Mothers, care and employment: values and theories', CAVA Working Paper No 1, University of Leeds
    2005 'Mothering, class and rationality', *Sociological Review* 53: 2

Duncan, S. and R. Edwards 1999 *Lone mothers, paid work, and gendered moral rationalities*, Macmillan, Houndmills

Duncan, S., R. Edwards, T. Reynolds and P. Alldred 2003 'Motherhood, paid work and partnering', *Work, Employment and Society* 17, 2: 309–30

Eaton, S. C. 2003 'If you can use them: flexibility policies, organizational commitment, and perceived performance', *Industrial Relations*, 42, 2: 145–67

Ehrenreich, B. 2003 'Maid to order' in B. Ehrenreich and A. R. Hochschild, *Global Woman*, Granta Books, London

Einhorn, B. 1993 *Cinderella goes to market*, Verso, London

Ellingsaeter, A.-M. 1999 'Dual breadwinners between state and market' in R. Crompton (ed.), *Restructuring gender relations and employment*, Oxford University Press, Oxford

Ellingsaeter, A. L. 2003 The complexity of family policy reform: the case of Norway, *European Societies* 5, 4: 419–43

Erikson, R. and J. H. Goldthorpe 1992 *The constant flux*, Clarendon Press, Oxford

Esping-Andersen, G. 1990 *The three worlds of welfare capitalism*, Polity, Cambridge
    1999 *Social foundations of postindustrial economies*, Oxford University Press, Oxford
    2000 'Interview on post-industrialism and the future of the welfare state', *Work, Employment and Society* 14, 4: 757–69

2002 (with D. Gallie, A. Hemerijck and J. Myles), *Why we need a new welfare state*, Oxford University Press, Oxford

Evans, J. 2001 *Firms' contribution to the reconciliation between work and family life*, OECD Labour Market and Social Policy Occasional Papers, Paris

Fagan, C. 2001 'Time, money and the gender order: work orientations and working-time preferences in Britain', *Gender, Work and Organization* 8, 3: 239–66

2002 'How many hours? Work-time regimes and preferences in European countries' in G. Crow and S. Heath (eds.), *Social conceptions of time – structure and process in work and everyday life*, Palgrave/Macmillan, London

Fagan, C. and B. Burchell 2002 *Gender, jobs and working conditions in the European Union*, European Foundation for the Improvement of Living and Working Conditions, Dublin

Featherstone, M. 1991 *Consumer culture and postmodernism*, Sage, London

Fein, E. and S. Schneider 2002 *The rules: time-tested secrets for capturing the heart of Mr Right*, Warner Books,

Ferguson, K. E. 1984 *The feminist case against bureaucracy*, Temple University Press, Philadelphia

Finch, J. 1983 *Married to the job*, George Allen and Unwin, London

1989 *Family obligations and social change*, Basil Blackwell, Oxford

Finch, J. and J. Mason 1993 *Negotiating family responsibilities*, Tavistock/Routledge, London

Folbre, N. and J. A. Nelson 2000 'For love or money – or both?' *Journal of Economic Perspectives* 14, 4: 123–40

Forth, J., S. Lissenburgh, C. Callender and N. Millward 1997 *Family friendly working arrangements in Britain*, Research Report No 16, Department for Education and Employment, London

Fraad, H. 2003 'Class transformation in the household: an opportunity and a threat', *Critical Sociology* 29, 1: 47–65

Franco, A. and K. Winqvist 2002 'Women and men reconciling work and family life', *Statistics in focus*, Eurostat

Frank, T. 2000 *One market under God*, Doubleday, New York

Fraser, N. 1994 'After the family wage', *Political Theory* 22: 591–618

1998 'Heterosexism, misrecognition and capitalism: a response to Judith Butler', *New Left Review* 228: 140–9

2000 'Rethinking recognition', *New Left Review* (May/June)

Freedman, M. 1984 'The search for shelters' in K Thompson (ed.), *Work, employment and unemployment*, Open University Press, Milton Keynes

Freeman, R. B. 2000 'The US economic model at Y2K: lodestar for advanced capitalism?' NBER (National Bureau of Economic Research) Working Paper 7757

Friedan, B. 1965 *The feminine mystique*, Penguin, Harmondsworth

Fukuyama, F. 1999 *The great disruption*, Profile Books, London

Gallie, D. 2002 'The quality of working life in welfare strategy' in G. Esping-Andersen *et al.*, *Why we need a new welfare state*, Oxford University Press, Oxford

2003 'The quality of working life: is Scandinavia different?' *European Sociological Review* 19, 1: 61–79

Gardiner, J. 2000 'Rethinking self-sufficiency: employment, families and wel-fare', *Cambridge Journal of Economics* 24: 671–89

Gershuny, J. and O. Sullivan 2003 'Time use, gender and public policy regimes', *Social Politics* 10, 2: 205–28

Gershuny, J., M. Godwin and S. Jones 1994 'The domestic labour revolution: a process of lagged adaptation' in M. Anderson, F. Bechhofer and J. Gershuny (eds.), *The social and political economy of the household*, Oxford University Press, Oxford

Giddens, A. 1982 'Hermeneutics and social theory' in *Profiles and critiques in social theory*, Macmillan, Basingstoke

1991 *Modernity and self identity*, Polity, Cambridge

Gittins, D. 1993 *The family in question*, Macmillan, Basingstoke

Glass, J. L. and S. B. Estes 1999 'The family responsive workplace', *Annual Review of Sociology*, 23: 289–313

Glover, J. 1992 'Studying working women cross-nationally', *Work, Employment and Society*, 6, 3: 489–98

2002 'The "balance model": theorising women's employment behaviour' in A. Carling, S. Duncan and R. Edwards (eds.), *Analysing families*, Routledge, London

Glucksmann, M. 1995 'Why "work"? Gender and the "total social organisation of labour"', *Gender, Work and Organisation* 2, 2: 63–75

2000 *Cottons and casuals: the gendered organisation of labour in time and space*, Sociology Press, Durham

Goldthorpe, J. H. 1972 'Daniel on orientations to work: a final comment', *Journal of Management Studies* 9: 266–73

1980 [1987] *Social mobility and class structure in modern Britain*, Clarendon Press, Oxford

1985 'On economic development and social mobility', *British Journal of Sociology* 36, 4: 549–60

1994 'Current issues in comparative macrosociology', ISO-RAPPORT no. 6, University of Oslo

1996 'Class analysis and the reorientation of class theory: the case of persisting differentials in educational attainment', *British Journal of Sociology* 47, 3: 481–505

Goldthorpe, J. H., D. Lochwood, F. Bechhofer and J. Platt 1968 *The affluent worker: industrial attitudes and behaviour*, Cambridge University Press, Cambridge

Gonyea, J. G. and B. Googins 1996 'The restructuring of work and family in the United States' in S. Lewis and J. Lewis (eds.), *The work–family challenge*, Sage, London

Gonzalez-Lopez, M. J. 2002 'A portrait of Western families' in A. Carling, S. Duncan and R. Edwards, *Analysing families*, Routledge, London

Goode, W. J. (ed.) 1964 *Readings on the family and society*, Prentice-Hall, New York

Goodman, A., P. Johnson and S. Webb 1997 *Inequality in the UK*, Oxford University Press, Oxford

Gorman, T. J. 2000 'Reconsidering worlds of pain: life in the working class(es)', *Sociological Forum* 15, 4: 693–717

Gornick, J. C. and M. K. Meyers 2003 *Families that work*, Russell Sage Foundation, New York

Gottfried, H. 2000 'Compromising positions: emergent neo-Fordisms and embedded gender contracts', *British Journal of Sociology* 51, 2: 235–59

　2003 'Temp(t)ing bodies: shaping gender at work in Japan', *Sociology* 37, 2: 257–76

Granovetter, M. and R. Swedberg (eds.) 1992 *The sociology of economic life*, Westview Press, Boulder, CO

Gray, J. 1992 *Men are from Mars, women are from Venus: how to get what you want from your relationships*, HarperCollins, London

Green, F. 2001 'It's been a hard day's night: the concentration and intensification of work in late twentieth-century Britain', *British Journal of Industrial Relations* 39, 1: 53–80

Gregory, A. and J. Windebank 2000 *Women's work in Britain and France*, Macmillan, Houndmills

Gregson, N. and M. Lowe 1994 *Servicing the middle classes*, Routledge, London

Grimshaw, D., H. Beynon, J. Rubery and K. Ward 2002 'The restructuring of career paths in large service sector organisations: "delayering" upskilling and polarisation', *Sociological Review* 51, 1: 89–115

Grimshaw, D., K. G. Ward, J. Rubery and H. Beynon 2001 'Organisations and the transformation of the internal labour market in the UK', *Work, Employment and Society* 15, 1: 25–54

Haas, L. L. and P. Hwang 1995 'Company culture and men's use of family leave benefits in Sweden', *Family Relations* 44: 28–36

Hakim, C. 1979 *Occupational segregation*, Department of Employment, Research Paper No 9

　1992 'Explaining trends in occupational segregation: the measurement, causes, and consequences of the sexual division of labour', *European Sociological Review* 8, 2: 127–52

　2000 *Work–lifestyle choices in the 21st century*, Oxford University Press, Oxford

　2003a 'Models of the family in modern societies', Ashgate, Aldershot

　2003b 'Public morality versus personal choice', *British Journal of Sociology* 53, 3: 339–46

　2004 *Key issues in women's work*, GlassHouse Press, London

Halford, S., M. Savage and A. Witz 1997 *Gender, careers and organisations*, Macmillan, Basingstoke and London

Halsey, A. H., H. Lauder, P. Brown and A. S. Wells (eds.) 1997 *Education: culture, economy and society*, Oxford University Press, Oxford

Handy, C. B. 1984 *The future of work*, Blackwell, Oxford

　1994 *The empty raincoat*, Hutchinson, London

Hantrais, L. 1990 *Managing professional and family life: a comparative study of British and French women*, Dartmouth, Aldershot

　1993 'Women work and welfare in France' in J. Lewis (ed.), *Women and social policies in Europe*, Edward Elgar, Aldershot

Hartmann, H. 1976 'Capitalism, patriarchy and job segregation by sex' in M. Blaxall and B. M. Reagan (eds.), *Women and the workplace*, Chicago University Press, Chicago

Hernes, H. 1987 *Welfare state and woman power*, Norwegian University Press, Oslo

Hills, J. 2004 *Inequality and the state*, Oxford University Press, Oxford

Hills, J. and O. Lelkes 1999 'Social security, selective universalism and patchwork redistribution' in R. Jowell, J. Curtice, A. Park and K. Thompson, *British Social Attitudes*, 16th Report, Ashgate, Aldershot

Himmelweit, S. and M. Sigala 2003 'Internal and external constraints on mothers' employment', Working Paper no. 27, ESRC Future of Work Programme

Hirdman, Y. 1998 'State policy and gender contracts' in E. Drew, R. Emerek and E. Mahon (eds.), *Women, work and the family in Europe*, Routledge, London

Hirsch, F. and J. H. Goldthorpe (eds.) 1978 *The political economy of inflation*, Martin Robertson, London

Hirst, P. and J. Zeitlin 1997 'Flexible specialisation' in J. R. Hollingsworth and R. Boyer (eds.), *Contemporary capitalism*, Cambridge University Press, Cambridge

Hochschild, A. 1983 *The managed heart*, University of California Press, Los Angeles

1997 *The time bind*, Metropolitan Books, New York

2000 'Global care chains and emotional surplus value' in W. Hutton and A. Giddens (eds.), *On the edge: living with global capitalism*, Jonathan Cape, London

Hojgaard, L. 1997 'Working fathers; caught in the web of the symbolic order of gender', *Acta Sociologica*, 40: 245–61

Hudson, R. and A. M. Williams 1995 *Divided Britain*, John Wiley and Sons, Chichester, England

Humphries, J. 1982 'Class struggle and the persistence of the working-class family' in A. Giddens and D. Held (eds.), *Classes, power and conflict*, Macmillan, Basingstoke

1984 'Protective legislation, the capitalist state and working-class men' in R. Pahl (ed.), *Divisions of labour*, Basil Blackwell, Oxford

Hutton, W. 2002 *The world we're in*, Little, Brown, London

Irwin, S. 2003a 'Interdependencies, values and the reshaping of difference: gender and generation at the birth of twentieth-century modernity', *British Journal of Sociology* 54, 4: 565–84

2003b 'The changing shape of values, care and commitments', Paper prepared for ESPAnet conference, Danish National Institute of Social Research, Copenhagen

Irwin, S. and W. Bottero 2000 'Market returns? Gender and theories of change in employment relations', *British Journal of Sociology* 51, 2: 261–80

Jacobs, J. and K. Gerson 1998 'Who are the overworked Americans?', *Review of Political Economy* 56, 4: 442–59

Jenson, J. 1986 'Gender and reproduction', *Studies in Political Economy* 20: 9–46

Joseph Rowntree Foundation 1995 *Inquiry into income and wealth*, York

Jowell, R. 1998 'How comparative is comparative research?', *American Behavioral Scientist* 42, 3: 168–77

Jowell, R., L. Brook and L. Dowds 1993 *International social attitudes*, Dartmouth, Aldershot

Kaase, M. and K. Newton 1998 'What people expect from the state' in
R. Jowell, J. Curtice, A. Park, L. Brook, K. Thompson and C. Bryson,
British and European social attitudes: how Britain differs, Ashgate, Aldershot

Kanter, R. M. 1977 *Men and women of the corporation*, Basic Books, New York
1990 *When giants learn to dance*, Unwin, London

Kohn, M. L. 1987 'Cross-national research as an analytical strategy', *American
Sociological Review* 52: 713–31

Korpi, W. 2000 'Faces of inequality', *Social Politics* 7, 2: 127–91

Kristol, W 1998 'A Conservative perspective on public policy and the family' in
C. Wolfe (ed.), *The family, civil society, and the state*, Rowman and Littlefield,
Oxford

La Valle, I., S. Arthur, C. Millward, J. Scott with M. Clayden 2002 *Happy
families? Atypical work and its influence on family life*, Final Report, Joseph
Rowntree Foundation, York

Ladipo, D. and F. Wilkinson 2002 'More pressure, less protection' in B. Burchell,
D. Ladipo and F. Wilkinson (eds.), *Job insecurity and work intensification*,
Routledge, London

Lan, P. C. 2003 'Among women: migrant domestics and their Taiwanese employers across generations' in B. Ehrenreich and A. R. Hochschild, *Global
woman*, Granta Books, London

Land, H. 1986 *Women and economic dependency*, Equal Opportunities Commission, Manchester
2002 'Spheres of care in the UK: separate and unequal', *Critical Social Policy*
22, 1: 13–32

Lash, S. 2002 'Introduction' in U. Beck and E. Beck-Gernsheim, *Individualization*, Sage, London

Lash, S. and J. Urry 1994 *Economies of signs and space*, Sage, London

Laslett, P. 1965 *The world we have lost*, Methuen, London

Lazaridis, G. 2000 'Filipino and Albanian women migrant workers in Greece:
multiple layers of oppression' in F. Anthias and G. Lazaridis, *Gender and
migration in southern Europe*, Berg, Oxford

Lee, E., S. Clements, R. Ingham and N. Stone 2004 *A matter of choice? Explaining
national variation in teenage abortion and motherhood*, Joseph Rowntree
Foundation, York

Leira, A. 1992 *Welfare states and working mothers*, Cambridge University Press,
Cambridge
2002 *Working parents and the welfare state*, Cambridge University Press
Cambridge

Lewis, J. 1992 'Gender and the development of welfare regimes', *Journal of
European Social Policy* 2, 3: 159–73
2002 'Gender and welfare state change', *European Societies* 4, 4: 331–57

Lewis, J. and G. Astrom 1992 'Equality, difference and state welfare: labor
market and family policies in Sweden', *Feminist Studies* 18, 1: 59–87

Lewis, S. 1997 'Family friendly employment policies: a route to changing
organisational culture or playing about at the margins?', *Gender Work and
Organisation* 4, 1: 1–23

Lewis, S. and J. Lewis (eds.) 1996 *The work–family challenge*, Sage, London

Lister, R. 2003 *Citizenship: feminist perspectives*, Palgrave Macmillan, Basingstoke

Lockwood, D. 1958 [1989] *The black coated worker*, Allen and Unwin, London; Oxford University Press, Oxford
    1966 'Sources of variation in working-class images of society', *Sociological Review* 14, 3: 244–67
Lowe, G. S. and H. Krahn 2000 'Work aspiration and attitude in a era of labour market restructuring', *Work, Employment and Society* 14, 1: 1–22
Lutz, H. 2002 'At your service madam! The globalisation of domestic service', *Feminist Review* 70: 89–104
MacInnes, J. 1998 *The end of masculinity*, Open University Press, Buckingham
Marshall, B. 1994 *Engendering modernity*, Polity, Cambridge
Marshall, G., R. Roberts and C. Burgoyne 1996 'Social class and underclass in Britain and the United States', *British Journal of Sociology* 47, 1: 22–44
Marshall, G., A. Swift and S. Roberts 1997 *Against the odds?*, Clarendon Press, Oxford
Marshall, J. 1984 *Women managers*, Wiley, Chichester
Marshall, T. H. 1948 [reprinted 1963] 'Citizenship and social class' in *Sociology at the crossroads*, Heinemann, London
Maurice, M., F. Sellier and J. J. Silvestre 1986 *The social foundations of industrial power*, MIT Press, Cambridge, MA
McDowell, L. 1997 *Capital culture: gender and work in the City*, Blackwell, Oxford
    2003 *Redundant masculinities?*, Blackwell, Oxford
McGovern, P., V. Hope-Hailey and P. Stiles 1998 'The managerial career after downsizing', *Work, Employment and Society* 12, 3: 457–77
McRae, S. 2003 'Constraints and choices in mothers' employment careers', *British Journal of Sociology* 53, 3: 317–38
Millar, J. and A. Warman 1996 *Family obligations in Europe*, Family Policy Studies Centre, London
Mincer, J. and S. Polachek 1974 'Family investments in human capital: earnings of women', *Journal of Political Economy* 82: 76–108
Mitchell, W. and E. Green 2002 'I don't know what I'd do without our Mam: motherhood, identity and support networks', *Sociological Review* 50, 1: 1–22
Moen, P. (ed.) 2003 *It's about time: couples and careers*, Cornell University Press, Ithaca and London
Morgan, D. H. J. 1985 *The family, politics and social theory*, Routledge and Kegan Paul, London
Morgan, P. 1999 'Evaluating the effects on children of mothers' employment' in G. Dench (ed.), *Rewriting the sexual contract*, Transaction, New Brunswick, NJ
Murray, C. A. (ed.) 1990 *The emerging British underclass*, IEA Health and Welfare Unit, London
Nakano, Glenn 1992 'From servitude to service work: historical continuities in the racial division of paid reproductive labour', *Signs* 18, 1: 1–43
Newson, J. and E. Newson 1968 *Four years old in an urban community*, Allen and Unwin, London
Nolan, P. 2003 'Reconnecting with history', *Work, Employment and Society* 17, 3: 473–80
Nussbaum, M. C. 2000 *Women and human development*, Cambridge University Press, Cambridge

O'Connor, J. S., A. S. Orloff and S. Shaver 1999 *States, markets, families*, Cambridge University Press, Cambridge

O'Neill J 1999 'Economy, equality and recognition' in Ray and Sayer (eds.) *Culture and Economy after the Cultural Turn*, Sage, London

O'Reilly, J. 1992 'Where do you draw the line?', *Work Employment and Society* 6, 3: 369–96

OECD 2000 *Firms' contribution to the reconciliation between work and family life*, Occasional paper, Directorate for Education, Employment, Labour and Social Affairs, Paris

OECD 2001 'Balancing work and family life: helping parents into paid employment', chapter 4, *Employment Outlook*, Paris

OECD 2002 *Employment Outlook*, Paris

Olsen, F. E. 1983 'The family and the market: a study of ideology and legal reform', *Harvard Law Review* 96, 7: 1497–578

Orloff, A. S. 1999 'Motherhood, work and welfare in the United States, Britain, Canada and Australia' in G. Steinmetz, *State/Culture: state formation after the cultural turn*, Cornell University Press, Ithaca and London

Osterman, P. 1995 'Work–family programs and the employment relationship', *Administrative Science Quarterly* 40: 681–700

Pakulski, J. and M. Waters 1996 'The reshaping and dissolution of social class in advanced society', *Theory and Society* 25: 667–91

Parrenas, R. S. 2000 'Migrant Filipina domestic workers and the international division of reproductive labour', *Gender and Society* 14, 4: 560–80

Parsons, T. 1949 'The social structure of the family' in R. Anshen (ed.), *The family, its function and destiny*, Harper, New York

Pateman, C. 1988 *The sexual contract*, Polity, Cambridge
  1989 'The patriarchal welfare state' in C. Pateman (ed.), *The disorder of women*, Polity, Cambridge

Paull, G., J. Taylor and A. Duncan 2002 *Mothers' employment and childcare use in Britain*, Institute for Fiscal Studies, London

Perrons, D. 1999 'Flexible working patterns and equal opportunities in the European Union', *European Journal of Women's Studies* 6: 391–418

Pfau-Effinger, B. 1999 'The modernization of family and motherhood in Western Europe' in R. Crompton (ed.), *Restructuring gender relations and employment*, Oxford University Press, Oxford
  2004 'Socio-historical paths of the male breadwinner model – an explanation of cross-national differences', *British Journal of Sociology* 55, 3: 37–200

Pickvance, C. 1995 'Comparative analysis, causality and case studies in Urban Studies' in A. Rogers and S. Vertovec (eds.), *The urban context*, Berg, Oxford and Washington, DC

Pinchbeck, I. 1981 *Women workers in the industrial revolution*, Virago, London

Polanyi, K. 1957 *The great transformation*, Beacon Press, Boston

Pollert, A. 1988 'The flexible firm: fixation or fact?', *Work, Employment and Society* 2, 3: 281–316

Procter, I. and M. Padfield 1998 *Young adult women, work, and family: living a contradiction*, Mansell, London and Washington DC

Purcell, K., T. Hogarth and C. Simm 1999 *Whose flexibility?*, Joseph Rowntree Foundation, York

Ragin, C. 1987 *The comparative method*, University of California Press, Berkeley and Los Angeles

Ragin, C. (ed.) 1991 'Introduction' to *Issues and alternatives in comparative social research*, E. J. Brill, Leiden

Rake, K., H. Davies, H. Joshi and R. Alami 2000 *Women's incomes over the lifetime*, Stationery Office, London

Reay, D. 1998 *Class work, mothers' involvement in their children's primary schooling*, UCL Press, London

Reay, D. and H. Lucey 2003 'The limits of "choice"', *Sociology* 37, 1: 121–42

Reskin, B. F. and P. A. Roos 1990 *Job queues, gender queues*, Temple University Press, Philadelphia

Riley, D. 1983 *War in the nursery*, Virago, London

Rose, D. and D. Pevalin 2002 *A researcher's guide to the National Statistics Socio-Economic Classification*, Sage, London

Rose, M. 1985 'Universalism, culturalism and the Aix group', *European Sociological Review* 1, 1: 65–83

Rose, N. 1989 *Governing the soul*, Routledge, London

Rubery, J., M. Smith and C. Fagan 1998 'National working-time regimes and equal opportunities', *Feminist Economics* 4, 1: 71–101

Rubery J., K. Ward, D. Grimshaw and H. Beynon 2003 'Time and the new employment relationship', Manchester School of Management, UMIST, University of Manchester Institute of Science and Technology

Rubin, L. B. 1994 *Families on the faultline*, HarperCollins, New York

Sainsbury, D. (ed.) 1994 *Gendering welfare states*, Sage, London

Saraceno, C. 1997 'Family change, family policies and the restructuring of welfare' in OECD, *Family, market and community: equity and efficiency in social policy*, Paris

Savage, M. 2000 *Class analysis and social transformation*, Open University Press, Buckingham

Savage, M., J. Barlow, A. Dickens and T. Fielding 1992 *Property, bureaucracy, and culture*, Routledge, London

Sayer, A. 2002 'What are you worth?', *Sociological Research Online* 7, 3

Schor, J. 1991 *The overworked American: the unexpected decline of leisure*, Basic Books, New York

Seccombe, W. 1993 *Weathering the storm*, Verso, London and New York

Sennett, R. 1998 *The corrosion of character*, W. W. Norton and Company, New York and London

Sennett, R. and J. Cobb 1973 *The hidden injuries of class*, Vintage Books, New York

Sevenhuijsen, S. 2002 'A third way? Moralities, ethics and families: an approach through the ethic of care' in A. Carling, S. Duncan and R. Edwards (eds.), *Analysing families*, Routledge, London

Showstack Sassoon, A. (ed.) 1987 *Women and the state*, Hutchinson, London

Siltanen, J. 1986 'Domestic responsibilities and the structuring of employment' in R. Crompton and M. Mann (eds.), *Gender and stratification*, Polity, Cambridge

Silva, E. B. and C. Smart (eds.) 1999 *The 'new' family?*, Sage, London

Skeggs, B. 1997 *Formations of class and gender*, Sage, London

Skocpol, T. 1992 *Protecting soldiers and mothers*, Harvard University Press, Cambridge, MA

Smith, V. 1997 'New forms of work organisation', *Annual Review of Sociology* 23: 315–39

Soskice, D. 1999 'Divergent production regimes: coordinated and uncoordinated market economies in the 1980s and 1990s' in H. Kitschelt, P. Lange, G. Marks and J. D. Stephens (eds.), *Continuity and change in contemporary capitalism*, Cambridge University Press, Cambridge

Sporton, D. 1993 'Fertility: the lowest level in the world' in D. Noin and R. Woods (eds.), *The changing population of Europe*, Blackwell, Oxford

Stewart, A., K. Prandy and R. M. Blackburn 1980 *Social stratification and occupations*, Macmillan, London/Basingstoke

Stier, H. and N. Lewin-Epstein 2001 'Welfare regimes, family-supportive policies, and women's employment along the life-course', *American Journal of Sociology* 106, 6: 1731–60

Still, M. C. and D. Strang 2003 'Institutionalising family-friendly policies' in P. Moen (ed.), *It's about time*, Cornell University Press, Ithaca and London

Strange, S. 1997 'The future of global capitalism; or, will divergence persist forever?' in Crouch, C. and W. Streeck (eds.), *Political economy of modern capitalism*, Sage, London

Streeck, W. 1989 'Skills and the limits of neoliberalism', *Work, Employment and Society* 3: 90–104

Sullivan, O. and J. Gershuny 2001 'Cross-national changes in time use', *British Journal of Sociology* 52, 2: 331–47

Sutherland, H., T. Sefton and D. Piachaud 2003 *Poverty in Britain: the impact of government policy since 1997*, Joseph Rowntree Foundation, York

Szreter, S. R. S. 1984 'The genesis of the registrar-general's social classification of occupations', *British Journal of Sociology* 35: 522–46

Taylor, R. 2002a 'The future of work–life balance', Economic and Social Research Council

2002b 'Britain's world of work – myths and realities', Economic and Social Research Council, Swindon

Therborn, G. 2004 *Between sex and power: family in the world, 1900–2000*, Routledge, London

Thompson, P. 2003 'Disconnected capitalism', *Work, Employment and Society* 17, 2: 359–78

Thompson, P. and C. Warhurst (eds.) 1998 *Workplaces of the future*, Macmillan, Basingstoke

Torp, H. and E. Barth 2001 'Actual and preferred working time', Institute for Social Research, Oslo

Valcour, P. M. and R. Batt 2003 'Work–life integration: challenges and organizational responses' in P. Moen (ed.), *It's about time*, Cornell University Press, Ithaca and London

Wajcman, J. 1996 'The domestic basis for the managerial career', *Sociological Review* 44, 4: 609–29

1998 *Managing like a man*, Polity, Cambridge

Wajcman, J. and B. Martin 2001 'My company or my career: managerial achievement and loyalty', *British Journal of Sociology* 52, 4, 559–78

2002 'Narratives of identity in modern management', *Sociology* 36, 4: 985–1002

Walby, S. 1986 *Patriarchy at work*, Polity Press, Cambridge

1990 *Theorizing patriarchy*, Basil Blackwell, Oxford

Walker, A. 1990 'Blaming the victims' in C. A. Murray (ed.), *The emerging British underclass*, IEA Health and Welfare Unit, London

Walkowitz, C. 1980 *Prostitution in Victorian society*, Cambridge University Press, Cambridge

Wall, K., 1997 'Portugal: issues concerning the family' in J. Ditch *et al.*, *Developments in national family policies*, European Observatory on Family Policies, DGV/University of York, pp. 213–49

Warren, T. 2003 'Class and gender-based working time?, *Sociology* 37, 4: 733–52

Weber, M. 1958 'Bureaucracy' in H. Gerth and C. W. Mills (eds.), *From Max Weber*, Routledge, London

West, C. and D. H. Zimmerman 1987 'Doing gender', *Gender and Society* 1: 125–51

Westergaard, J. and H. Resler 1975 *Class in a capitalist society*, Heinemann, London

Wharton, A. S. and M. Blair-Loy 2002 'The "overtime culture" in a global corporation', *Work and Occupations* 29, 1: 32–63

White, M., S. Hill, P. McGovern, C. Mills and D. Smeaton 2003 'High-performance' management practices, working hours and work–life balance', *British Journal of Industrial Relations* 41, 2: 175–95

Williams, J. C. 1991 'Domesticity as the dangerous supplement of Liberalism', *Journal of Women's History* 2, 3: 69–88

2000 *Unbending gender*, Oxford University Press, New York

Willis, P. 1977 *Learning to labour*, Saxon House, Farnborough

Wilson, E. 1977 *Women and the welfare state*, Tavistock, London

Wilson, J. 1987 *The truly disadvantaged*, University of Chicago Press, Chicago

Windebank, J. 2001 'Dual-earner couples in Britain and France', *Work Employment and Society* 15, 2: 269–90

Witz, A. 1992 *Professions and patriarchy*, Routledge, London

Womack, J. P., D. T. Jones and D. Roos 1990 *The machine that changed the world*, Macmillan, New York

Wright, E. O. 1997 *Class counts*, Cambridge University Press, Cambridge

Wrong, D. 1964 'The over-socialized conception of man in modern sociology' in L. Coser and D. Rosenberg (eds.), *Sociological theory*, Collier-Macmillan, London

Yancey Martin, P. 2003. '"Said and done" versus "saying and doing": gendering practices, practicing gender at work', *Gender & Society* 17: 342–66.

Yeandle, S., A. Wigfield, R. Crompton and J. Dennett 2003 *Employers, communities and family-friendly employment policies*, Policy Press, Bristol

Young, M. and P. Willmott 1962 *Family and kinship in East London*, Penguin, Harmondsworth

Zaretsky, E. 1976 *Capitalism, the family and personal life*, Pluto Press, London

Zwieg, M. 2000 *The working class majority*, Cornell University Press, Ithaca and London

Index

Acker, J. 212
Adkins, L. 67
attitudes 20
  and behaviour 52–3, 184
    congruent liberal 154, 159
    congruent traditional 154, 159
  change in 44–5
  gender variations in 203
  inconsistent 154, 159
  to family and gender roles 43–4,
    153, 173
  and happiness 156, 157–8,
    159, 210
  national variations in 144
  to women's employment 173,
    176–7, 205
    mothers' 176
    national variations in 176
    scale 173
  see also couple work arrangements,
    impact of attitudes on, class,
    attitudinal variations in

banking 67–74
Beck, U. 49, 59, 114, 199
  and Beck-Gernsheim, E. 166
Beveridge Report 40
Bottero, W. 60, 164, 165, 191
Bourdieu, P. 166
Brandth, B. 144
Braverman, H. 4
Brazil 195
Britain 26, 92–3, 95, 105, 128,
  133, 135, 170, 190, 197,
  202, 214, 216
  'Employment in Britain' survey 95,
    110, 180
  hours of work 118
bureaucracy 4, 21, 22, 64
  and gender 65–6
  see also careers, bureaucratic

capitalism
  development of 18
  and women 2
care 124, *see also* work, caring
careers 4, 5, 21–3, 62, 75, 76,
  82, 108
  aspirations 77, 80
  bureaucratic 68
  men's 69, 112
  'portfolio' 62
  women's 22–3, 64–7
  working-class 82, 181
  see also promotion
Castells, M. 7, 14, 85
childcare 122, 123, 128, 129, 182, 183,
  184, 187, 213
choice 9, 10, 18, 49, 60, 89, 168,
  182, 201, 202
  women's employment and 13, 78, 123,
    170, 202
citizenship 118–19, 135
class 17–21, 125, 164
  and education 165–6
  and employment 45, 54–5, 64
  and the family 165
  and promotion 68
  and teenage pregnancy 168, 171, 181
  attitudinal variations in 51, 53, 56–7,
    177, 179, 186, 205
  conceptualisation of 164
  consciousness 18, 20, 185
  employment aggregate approach 19, 164
  inequality 42, 178, 197, 206, 211
  mothers' employment and 177, 178, 183
  schemes 45
  'underclass' 182
  see also job satisfaction, class variation in;
    culture of poverty
comparative research 24–5, 208
  case-oriented 25–6
  variable-oriented 24–5

Conservative government 42, 59
Crouch, C. 3, 13
cultural capital 165
culture 10, 18, 20, 21, 22,
    67, 191
  context 191
  'cultural turn' 8, 9, 20, 66, 201
  national 126, 127
  of poverty 182
  organisational 67, 84, 63, 113, 199

Devine, F. 164
Dex, S. 87, 106, 109
discrimination
  in employment 65
  in organisations 64
  see also equal opportunity
division of labour 22, 123
  domestic 37, 74, 126, 140–2, 151,
      208–10
    theories of 140–1
    national variations in 145–7,
        148–9, 152, 160
    index 147
  'male breadwinner' 2–3, 6, 8, 15, 19,
      36, 39, 40, 59, 167
divorce 39, 41
domestic employees/employment
    194–8, 210
  migrant 195, 196, 197, 198
  national variations in 196, 197
Drago, R. 113
Du Gay, P. 63, 86, 200
Duncan, S. 12–13, 50, 51, 184

employment
  change in 62, 63, 199
  mothers' 45, 53, 74–6, 123, 152
  part-time 72, 75, 77, 80, 94, 117, 129,
      130, 171, 172
  relationship 97, 99
  women's 12–13, 15, 19, 39, 41, 42, 44,
      63, 92, 120, 121
  see also class, mothers employment and;
      class and employment; work, service
      sector
equal opportunity 45, 58, 65, 69, 76,
    85, 151
  equal pay 41
Esping-Andersen, G. 15, 92, 119,
    121–4, 128, 136
  feminist critique of 120–1
Europe 94, 104, 121, 135
Evans, J. 91, 105

Fagan, C. 118
family 143
  and caring 135, 136
  changes in 6–7
  dual earner 186, 198, 206, 212, 216
  industrialisation and 32–8
  middle class 33, 165, 205
  'modern' theories of 31–2
  responsibilities 14, 22
  wage 36–7
  working class 34, 167
  see also class and the family;
      individualisation and the family
feminism, feminist 6, 15, 16, 39, 41, 60,
    125, 206
  conservative 142, 157
  state 125, 156; see also
      state, 'woman-friendly'
  see also Esping-Andersen, G., feminist
      critique of
fertility 37–8, 166, 169, 205
Finland 129, 132, 134, 174
  see also Nordic states
flexibility, flexible employment 4–5, 7,
    68, 87, 91, 92, 97, 98, 99, 108,
    198, 213, 217
Fordism 3, 4, 6, 14, 15, 62
France 95, 129, 130, 133, 134, 143, 148,
    149, 153, 155, 208
Fraser, N. 136, 191, 192
Freeman, R. B. 91
Fukuyama, F. 142

Gallie, D. 124, 133
gender
  contract 14, 121
  equality 122, 124, 126–7, 136, 150, 166,
      187, 193, 195, 201, 207, 211,
  essentialism 142, 156, 203
  normative assumptions and 125
  relations 16, 192, 198
  see also equal opportunity; bureaucracy;
      women
Gershuny, J. 144
Giddens, A. 9, 11
globalisation 96, 121, 135, 198
Glover, J. 52
Glucksmann, M. 17, 190, 192
Goldthorpe, J. H. 24
Gornick, J. C. 91, 92, 182, 207–8,
    209, 212
Gottfried, H. 66
Gregory, A. 150
Grimshaw, D. 83

Hakim, C. 11–12, 27, 49, 51, 53, 122,
    170–1, 174, 184, 203
Halford, S. 66, 72, 86
Handy, C. B. 62
Hills, J. 214, 215
Himmelweit, S. 52
Hochschild, A. 109–10, 196
Hojgaard, L. 112
household
    couple work arrangements 101–2,
        156, 171, 178
    determinants of 174
    impact of attitudes on 173, 175
    national variations in 193
    employment variations in 46–7,
    income 47
    working time 94
housework 141, 145
    conflict over 158–9
    see also division of labour, domestic;
        domestic employees
Hyatt, D. 113

identity, identities 8, 14
    employment and 199
    gender 67, 201
    see also class, consciousness
ideology
    of domesticity 14, 18, 34, 67, 123,
        187, 201
    'separate spheres' 15, 16, 33, 35, 49, 189
    see also division of labour, male
        breadwinner
individualisation, individuation 8–10,
        11, 14, 18, 49, 63, 76, 164, 166, 185,
        199, 202
    and the family 166–8, 169, 201
    entrepreneurship of the self 200, 201
    sufficiency 186
inequality 125, 135, 185, 195
    cultural explanations of 185
    income 91, 212
    see also culture of poverty
International Social Survey Programme
        (ISSP) 23
Irwin, S. 56, 60, 164, 165, 167, 191

job satisfaction 56, 180
    class variation in 180–1

Kanter, R. M. 65
Keynesianism 40
Korpi, W. 125–7, 128, 134, 206
Kvande, E. 144

Labour government 39
    'New Labour' 104, 215, 216
Lee, E. 167
Lewis, Jane 7, 16, 85, 124
Lewis, Suzan 107, 113

male breadwinner see division of labour
management
    'high commitment' 63, 67, 70, 82, 87,
        97, 106, 110, 124, 192
marketised reproductive work see domestic
        employees
marriage bar 39, 41
Marshall, B. 118
Marx, K. 18
McDowell, L. 66, 181
McRae, S. 51, 204
men
    and domestic work 74, 122, 142,
        146, 209
    hours of work 74, 210
    paternity leave 144
Meyers, M. K. 91, 92, 182, 207–8,
        209, 212
Moen, P. 101, 111, 171, 192
motherhood 50
    single mothers 177
    teenage 168
    see also class, mothers' employment and;
        employment, mothers'

neo-liberalism 5, 12–13, 14, 20, 42, 60, 96,
        103, 112, 117, 127, 137, 199, 200,
        211, 213
Nolan, P. 62
Nordic (Scandinavian) countries 123, 126,
        127, 128, 133, 143, 148, 152,
        160, 194
    see also Finland, Norway
norms, normative 147, 164, 205
    theories of domestic labour 140
    see also attitudes; class, attitudinal
        variations in
Norway 129, 132, 134, 144,
        174, 183
    see also Nordic countries
Nussbaum, M. C. 13

O'Connor, J. 14, 120
occupational segregation 6, 36, 123
organisation
    changes in 84
    see also culture, organisational;
        discrimination in organisations

Orloff, A. S. 125
overtime 97, 98, 99

parenting 48
patriarchy 15, 32, 56
Pfau-Effinger, B. 190
Pickvance, C. 183
Polanyi, K. 2, 114, 191, 217
Portugal 95, 130, 143, 144, 145, 153, 176,
    183, 197, 208, 209, 211
postmodernism, postmodernity 8, 14, 191
preference groups 13, 170, 203
privatisation 96
production regimes 116–7
promotion 69–70, 72, 73, 80, 82,
    107, 201
    and managerial women 80
    and routine and manual men 81
    see also class and promotion
Purcell, K. 87

Ragin, C. 24
Rake, K. 92
reflexive modernity 164
retail 67–74
Rubery, J. 97

Savage, M. 64
Seccombe, W. 34–5
Sennett, R. 6, 85, 192
Sevenhuijsen, S. 17
Shaver, S. 14, 120
Sigala, M. 52
Skeggs, B. 55
Soskice, D. 116
state
    and the family 103, 112, 143, 194
    impact of policies 186, 207
    welfare 15, 91, 119
    'woman-friendly' 15, 143
    see also welfare regimes

total social organisation of labour 17–21,
    58, 86, 189
    national variations in 190

United States 91–2, 127, 128, 133, 135,
    144, 176, 215, 216

Wacjman, J. 72, 85
Warren, T. 47
Weber, M. 64
welfare regimes 15–16, 119–20, 125,
    128, 207
    conservative (corporatist) 119, 126, 211
    familialistic see family and caring
    liberal 104, 119, 126, 144, 167, 214
    universalist (social democratic) 120, 144
welfare state see state, welfare
White, M. 110
Williams, J. C. 34, 142, 161
Windebank, J. 151
women
    qualification levels 42
    see also employment, women's; gender
work
    caring 13, 16, 17, 55, 56, 85, 89, 189,
        191–2
    commodification of 191, 194
    culturalisation of 63
    intensification 95–7, 99, 108, 124
    service sector 63, 76, 81, 83, 200
    see also domestic employees
working hours 76, 79, 93–5, 98,
    100, 118, 122, 127, 131, 139,
    201, 218
    household 140, 207
    and work–life conflict 102–3, 134
working time regimes 116, 171
    national variations in 172
work–life articulation 78, 90, 94, 104, 127,
    131, 185, 199, 211
    class variations in 169
work–life 'balance' 7, 78, 91, 217
    careers and 76–84
work–life conflict 78, 80, 130,
    161, 208
    and domestic division of labour 149
    class differences in 79
    national variations in 132
    scale 79
work–life policies
    employer 68, 105–6, 109–10,
        200, 213
    'business case' 109
    employee use of 107–8
    statutory 112